AI, Faith, and the Future

AI, Faith, and the Future

An Interdisciplinary Approach

Edited by
MICHAEL J. PAULUS JR. and
MICHAEL D. LANGFORD

PICKWICK *Publications* · Eugene, Oregon

AI, FAITH, AND THE FUTURE
An Interdisciplinary Approach

Pickwick Publications
An Imprint of Wipf and Stock Publishers
199 W. 8th Ave., Suite 3
Eugene, OR 97401

www.wipfandstock.com

PAPERBACK ISBN: 978-1-6667-0346-7
HARDCOVER ISBN: 978-1-6667-0347-4
EBOOK ISBN: 978-1-6667-0348-1

Cataloguing-in-Publication data:

Names: Paulus, Michael J., Jr., editor. | Langford, Michael D., editor.

Title: AI, faith, and the future : an interdisciplinary approach / edited by Michael J. Paulus Jr. and Michael D. Langford.

Description: Eugene, OR: Pickwick Publications, 2022 | Includes bibliographical references and index.

Identifiers: ISBN 978-1-6667-0346-7 (paperback) | ISBN 978-1-6667-0347-4 (hardcover) | ISBN 978-1-6667-0348-1 (ebook)

Subjects: LCSH: Technology—Religious aspects—Christianity. | Artificial intelligence—Religious aspects. | Artificial intelligence—Philosophy. | Artificial intelligence—Moral and ethical aspects.

Classification: BR115.T42 A3 2022 (paperback) | BR115.T42 (ebook)

06/15/22

Contents

Contributors

CARLOS R. ARIAS, Assistant Professor and Chair of Computer Science at Seattle Pacific University.

BRUCE D. BAKER, Associate Professor of Business Ethics at Seattle Pacific University.

PHILLIP M. BAKER, Assistant Professor of Psychology at Seattle Pacific University.

MICHAEL D. LANGFORD, Professor of Theology, Discipleship, and Ministry at Seattle Pacific University and Seattle Pacific Seminary.

MICHAEL J. PAULUS JR., Dean of the Library, Assistant Provost for Educational Technology, and Associate Professor of Information Studies at Seattle Pacific University.

REBEKAH L. H. RICE, Associate Professor of Philosophy at Seattle Pacific University.

DAVID WICKS, Associate Professor of Curriculum and Instruction at Seattle Pacific University.

PART I

Foundations

1

Introduction

Michael J. Paulus Jr.

A GOLDEN AGE OF AI?

In 2019, Amazon launched re:MARS, a "global AI event for Machine Learning, Automation, Robotics, and Space." Amazon founder Jeff Bezos claimed in the announcement for the event, "We're at the beginning of a golden age of AI. Recent advancements have already led to invention that previously lived in the realm of science fiction—and we've only scratched the surface of what's possible." "We're excited to create re:MARS," he added, "to share learnings and spark new ideas for future innovation." Like its invitation-only predecessor MARS, which began three years earlier, re:MARS "embraces an optimistic vision for scientific discovery to advance a golden age of innovation."[1]

Since the term was coined in the 1950s, artificial intelligence has been associated with efforts to imitate human intelligence. Artificial intelligence systems increasingly perform complex tasks comparable to and even exceeding those that require human intelligence, but computer processing only superficially resembles human decision-making and action. As Gary

---

1. Amazon, "We're at the Beginning of a Golden Age of AI."

Smith points out in *The AI Delusion*, "Human minds are not computers, and computers are not human minds."[2] Given our limited understanding of human cognition and other qualities associated with modern humans such as consciousness, the human mind has so far provided a limited model for accomplishing computational goals. This is why, paralleling aspirations for human-like AI, there is a complementary history of intelligence augmentation. While early AI pioneers were struggling to imitate the human mind and body, other computer scientists were developing technologies that would lead to the invention of the personal computer and computer networking.[3]

According to Joanna Bryson, "The past decade, and particularly the past few years, have been transformative" for AI.[4] Digital information and communication technologies—the internet and cloud computing, social media and big data, mobile devices and sensors—have increased what is possible with automated and autonomous data processing for computer perception, analysis, and behavior. Today, Mariarosaria Taddeo and Luciano Floridi describe AI as "a growing resource of interactive, autonomous, self-learning agency" that is "reshaping daily practices, personal and professional interactions, and environments."[5] Artificial intelligence has become one of the most powerful and pervasive technologies in our lives. Many of us interact with AI-enabled digital assistants such as Amazon's Alexa daily, connecting us with a complex network of surveillance and decision-making systems. And most AI developers seem to be avoiding what Daniel Susskind describes as the "'AI fallacy': the mistaken belief that the only way to develop machines that perform a task at the level of human beings is to copy the way that human beings perform that task."[6] The AI technologies showcased at re:MARS 2019—recommendation systems for purchases, prediction systems for the fulfillment and delivery of purchases, robots sorting and moving packages in warehouses, and everything that enables Alexa to respond to and anticipate customer inquiries—are impressive systems that accomplish a variety of specific goals. But, as Bezos admits, "we're still a long way from being able to have machines do things the way humans do things."[7] Or, one might add, possessing anything analogous to the creativity

---

2. Smith, *AI Delusion*, 33.

3. See Markoff, *Machines of Loving Grace*, 5–18.

4. Bryson, "Past Decade and Future of AI's Impact on Society," 128.

5. Taddeo and Floridi, "How AI Can Be a Force for Good," 751.

6. Susskind, *World without Work*, 71.

7. Bezos, *Invent and Wonder*, 213.

and imagination that Walter Isaacson says "makes someone a true innovator" like Bezos.[8]

For many, though—especially those influenced by popular representations of robots and other artificial entities—human-level or general intelligence remains the "holy grail" of AI development and the "real" goal of AI.[9] This goes beyond designing systems to model specific human-like capabilities, such as vision, language, reasoning, and learning. The idea of artificial general intelligence (AGI) is that it would be able to master everything of which human intelligence is capable—and then surpass it, becoming superintelligent (artificial superintelligence, or ASI). Whether or not AGI and ASI are possible is a matter of speculation and debate, and different positions reveal competing beliefs about AI and humans. As Byron Reese points out, "experts disagree not because they know different things, but because they believe different things."[10] Floridi characterizes the extreme positions as "AItheist" and "Singularitarian": the belief that AI is just a sophisticated form of regular computing, or the opposing belief that AI will surpass human intelligence at some point (this is one version of the "singularity") and then continue to develop on its own—which could be great or terrible, depending on whether or not ASI is aligned with our values.[11] Artificial intelligence experts can be found at either extreme, and everywhere in between them.

AI AND THE FUTURE

In a keynote at re:MARS 2019, a senior Amazon executive described a library in one of Bezos's homes:

> There are two fireplaces that face each other. On one side of the library, over the fireplace, he has the word Builders, and under that is all of the books in his collection that are authored by builders. And on the other side of the library, it says Dreamers and he has books by Dreamers. This is a very good representation of what we are trying to do here—to bring together the builders and the dreamers—as we envision the future.

8. Isaacson, introduction to Bezos, *Invent and Wonder*, 1.

9. Stuart Russell quoted in Ford, *Architects of Intelligence*, 48.

10. Reese, *Fourth Age*, x.

11. Floridi, "Singularitarians, AItheists, and Why the Problem with Artificial Intelligence Is H.A.L. (Humanity At Large), Not HAL," 8–11.

When asked the next day about the inscriptions over his library fireplaces, Bezos pointed out how human creativity needs both dreamers and builders: "The dreamers come and the builders get inspired by them. And the builders build a new foundation that the dreamers can stand on and dream more." Amazon's artificial agent Alexa, he noted, was inspired by the *Star Trek* computer.[12]

The AI technologies being created and imagined today raise ethical questions about data curation, algorithmic agency, social inequities, and the future of every dimension of life. The actual and anticipated applications of AI also inspire a range of hopes and fears. Some imagine optimistic and utopian futures in which AI will solve known problems and create a superior form of life. Other imagined futures are more pessimistic and dystopian, with AI exacerbating old problems and creating new ones. The most extreme anticipations and anxieties include visions of an earthly paradise, posthuman immortality, and the end of the human species and civilization. AI has been called "the Second Coming and the Apocalypse at the same time."[13]

In addition to becoming part of our lives, AI is increasingly part of our cultural narratives. Hopeful narratives expect AI to increase production and prosperity, eliminate hunger and poverty, and find innovative solutions to health, energy, ecological, and economic challenges. By solving these problems, AI could lead us into a more fulfilling, peaceful world and create more opportunities for human creativity, discovery, relationships, and rest.[14] For Singularitarians, AGI and ASI inspire hopes for an enhanced and extended human or even posthuman life.[15] Chief among these optimists is Ray Kurzweil, who believes AGI will be achieved by 2029. Kurzweil imagines that "we're going to merge with the intelligent technology that we are creating." First our lives will be extended biologically, through improved biotechnology, and then they will be extended digitally.[16] Max Tegmark, another prominent AI optimist, claims AGI "can enable us to finally become

---

12. Bort, "Jeff Bezos Explains Why the Library in His House Has Two Fireplaces with Two Inscriptions."

13. Brockman, *Possible Minds*, xv.

14. See, e.g., Reese, *Fourth Age*, 283–303.

15. The meaning and use of the term posthuman is complex and contested, but in transhumanism it often refers to the idea of an uploaded form of existence. See J. Hurlbut and Tirosh-Samuelson, eds., *Perfecting Human Futures*, 8. The other major use of the term refers to a cyborg or hybrid understanding of human nature. See Thweatt-Bates, *Cyborg Selves*, 1–5.

16. Quoted in Ford, *Architects of Intelligence*, 238–39.

the masters of our own destiny," to upgrade life to a form that is substrate-independent, and to free life "from its evolutionary shackles."[17]

Fearful narratives about AI include anxieties about bias and fairness, transparency and accountability, security and surveillance, autonomous weapons, and adverse uses.[18] When uncertainties about AGI and ASI are added to these—especially about possibilities of an intellect that can be in-dependent of ours, a "mind out of place"[19] with unknown aims[20]—even the optimistic Tegmark can imagine more dystopian than utopian outcomes, and he admits that his utopian scenarios "involve objectionable elements."[21] "If our technology outpaces the wisdom with which we manage it," he admits, "it can lead to our extinction."[22] Nick Bostrom explains that if AI systems are not engineered "so that they are an extension of human will," with behaviors shaped by "our intentions," then we may "get a future shaped in accordance with alien criteria . . . random, unforeseen, and unwanted."[23] Our artificial creatures may rebel, like Victor Frankenstein's or the machines in *The Matrix* franchise, or we may end up with the entire material world wholly appropriated to optimize the production of something banal such as paperclips. Margaret Boden claims that "near-apocalyptic visions of AI's future are illusory." "But," she adds, "partly because of them, the AI com-munity—and policy-makers and the general public, too—are waking up to some very real dangers."[24]

At present, an ethical consensus appears to be emerging around major areas of concern such as beneficence, non-maleficence, autonomy, justice, and the explicability of AI—although challenging philosophical, technical, and organizational questions remain about defining and operationalizing such broad values.[25] There is also growing awareness of the social inequities perpetuated and created by AI: as Ruha Benjamin points out, technologies that "often pose as objective, scientific, or progressive, too often reinforce racism and other forms of inequity."[26] And many of Amazon's logistical al-

17. Tegmark in Brockman, *Possible Minds*, 87; Tegmark, *Life 3.0*, 25, 29, 55.

18. Anderson et al., "Artificial Intelligence and the Future of Humans."

19. Singler, "Existential Hope and Existential Despair in AI Apocalypticism and Transhumanism," 170.

20. Morelli, "Athenian Altar and the Amazonian Chatbot," 187.

21. Tegmark, *Life 3.0*, 161–202. Tegmark imagines twelve scenarios, only a few of which could be classified as utopian.

22. Tegmark, "Let's Aspire to More than Making Ourselves Obsolete," 76.

23. Quoted in Ford, *Architects of Intelligence*, 98.

24. Boden, *AI*, 169.

25. Floridi et al., "AI4People," 689–707.

26. Benjamin, *Race after Technology*, 1.

gorithms are being scrutinized and criticized for how they manage human bodies and behaviors. Some agreements may be coalescing around many generally shared concerns related to data collection and privacy, attentional manipulation and autonomy, information authenticity and trustworthiness, and algorithmic bias and transparency.[27] But as we make progress toward realizing ethical and beneficial AI, further "foresight analysis" must be done not only of what is possible with AI but also of what is desirable.[28] We need to be discussing, imagining, and constructing better narratives about the future world we want to create.

AI AND FAITH

We are only beginning to understand and imagine what human attention, autonomy, and agency should look like in a world full of artificial and autonomous agents. James Williams worries about preserving our ability to give attention to what matters most when we are functionally, existentially, and epistemically distracted by algorithms that are not aligned with and can overwhelm our intentions.[29] Brett Frischmann and Evan Selinger caution about losing our human autonomy and agency: As we design new autonomous systems, are we also redesigning ourselves in such a way that we are surrendering our independence and outsourcing our responsibility? "What meaningfully distinguishes *Homo sapiens* from all other species is our capability to imagine, conceptualize, and engineer ourselves and our environment," they argue. Our humanity "is reflected in us and our built world of imagined realities, institutions, infrastructures, and environments," but we need to be attentive to how our identities, actions, societies, and world can be controlled, conditioned, and constrained by our own creations.[30] Ultimately, Yuval Harari admits, we need better imaginative narratives to inform not just technological development but our development as a species.[31]

Tom McLeish articulates well how theology can help open up our imagination. "Because theology observes and construes stories," he says, it can help us identify "shared experiences of creativity and constraints." Further, theology "is able to discuss purposes and values—it can speak of, and

27. Anderson et al., "Artificial Intelligence and the Future of Humans."

28. Floridi, "Soft Ethics, the Governance of the Digital, and the General Data Protection Regulation."

29. Williams, *Stand Out of Our Light*, xii, 50–68.

30. Frischmann and Selinger, *Re-engineering Humanity*, 271.

31. Harari, *Homo Deus*, 21–22, 155–78.

ground, 'teleology.'"[32] Technology is teleological, designed for certain *teloi* (Greek: "ends"), and these ends or goals are, consciously or not, embedded in cultural narratives about broader values and purposes. The shared *telos* of Christians, new creation, anchors a robust narrative that can provide critical distance from competing narratives about the ends of technology and the societies shaping it. The Christian narrative about new creation also can help us align our attention and agency with shared goals and actions.[33]

For millennia, faith traditions have at different times directed, supported, and resisted technological progress, providing ethical foundations and narrative frameworks for either affirming or rejecting new technologies. Religious deliberations surrounded information technology developments such as writing, libraries, the printing press, and popular media, and over time religious perspectives have often influenced how such innovations became characteristic of human life as we now know it. While each of these innovations profoundly changed humans and how we interact with the world, AI captures our imagination in ways that center fundamental questions about our identity, agency, and destiny as a species. These are primordial questions, and faith traditions have curated ancient wisdom that can help us reflect on how we may shape the future with AI. Increasingly, different faith perspectives are focusing on AI. But, as Calvin Mercer and Tracy Trothen point out in their textbook on religion and the technological future, "academics in all disciplines, as well as the general public, are still in the very early stages of understanding, much less responding to" the impacts of transformative technologies such as AI.[34]

The rapid adoption of AI is disorienting, socially disruptive, and requires dialogue with diverse disciplines and groups impacted by it. Microsoft's Brad Smith notes that "a global conversation about ethical principles for artificial intelligence will require . . . seats at the table not only for technologists, governments, NGOs, and educators, but for philosophers and representatives of the world's many religions."[35] On one hand, the broad attention being given to questions of AI ethics and societal impact is encouraging—and in many ways is unprecedented. Many technologies are developed and implemented over long periods of time, and hazards and social regulations emerge slowly. With AI, corporations and activists are calling for regulation and accountability before further implementation of controversial applications such as facial recognition. On the other hand, the range

32. McLeish, *Faith and Wisdom in Science*, 214, 248.

33. See Paulus et al., "Framework for Digital Wisdom in Higher Education," 43–61.

34. Mercer and Trothen, *Religion and the Technological Future*, 4.

35. Smith, *Tools and Weapons*, 208.

of knowledge and wisdom from which expertise must be drawn—technical and legal, from the humanities and social sciences, and from those who will be most adversely impacted—is daunting. No one tradition, government, discipline, organization, or group can exhaust the questions that need to be asked and the responses that need to be pursued to integrate AI into our lives and world well and wisely. Of making many books about AI—and organizational principles, professional codes, and legal regulations—there will be no end.

This book presents a multidisciplinary range of perspectives on AI from the standpoint of Christian faith. While this is not the first book to explore the intersection of AI and faith, it is among the first to advance this exploration by approaching this emerging technology from a group of Christian scholars from various disciplines—Business, Computer Science, Education, Information Studies, Neuroscience, Philosophy, and Theology—who have been studying AI together. This research collaboration began in early 2019, when four founding members of AI and Faith—a consortium of faith communities and academic institutions bringing the values of the world's major religions into discussions about the ethical development of AI[36]—decided to form a faculty research group at Seattle Pacific University, a Christian research university, to explore the present and future impacts of AI from various disciplinary perspectives as well as the perspective of Christian faith. With support from former provost Jeff Van Duzer and generous funding from Keri and Eric Stumberg, the seven members of this group met regularly throughout the 2019–2020 academic year to study and discuss AI, faith, and the future. This book, a culmination of those discussions, seeks to provide a scholarly but accessible foundation for facilitating further ethical and theological explorations of AI.

This book is organized into two sections. Following this introduction, the first section includes three additional orienting essays. This first is a historical and technical introduction to AI, providing a narrative about its development, an explanation of various technologies related to AI, and a consideration of potential futures for AI. This essay is a resource for understanding terms and technologies associated with AI. The next essay provides a philosophical framework that helps to clarify key concepts at work in discussions of the pragmatic and ethical issues related to AI. After all, what sort of entity a thing is grounds what it can do and establishes its moral status. The final essay in this section is an introduction to key theological themes touched on in this book, as well as a discussion of the types of questions uniquely addressed by theology. The doctrinal lenses of revelation, creation,

---

36. See https://aiandfaith.org.

salvation, and eschatology here provide key perspectives for theological reflection on the nature and use of AI.

The second section offers a series of disciplinary and theological reflections on the impact of AI. "Artificial Intelligence and Theological Personhood" explores theological insights from Genesis, the incarnation, and Pentecost to discern the nature of human and artificial personhood. By tracing theological themes from these biblical accounts, the chapter suggests how we might imagine the nature and role of AI within Christian understandings of creation, covenant, and vocation. "Reinforcement in the Information Revolution" explains current dynamics at the intersection of neuroscience and AI—with particular attention given to developments tied to commercial interests—along with strategies of resistance based in Anabaptist practices. The potential role of AI to enhance education is discussed in "21st Century Learning Skills and Artificial Intelligence." This essay explores the cultivation of creativity, critical thinking, communication, and collaboration in connection with AI, as well as the theological significance of the imagination and community. "Automation and Apocalypse: Imagining the Future of Work" provides a brief history of work, technology, and the theology of work, and explores three views of AI and the future of work through a literary dystopia, a philosophical utopia, and a theological apocalypse. In the apocalyptic view of work presented here, it is possible to imagine AI participating in new creation. The final reflection, "Sin and Grace," presents guiding principles for wise engagement with AI. The theological lenses of sin and grace open our eyes to the spiritual reality of sin, the outworking of God's redeeming grace, and our role in participating in the transformation of the world. The book concludes with a prayer, "A Litany for Faithful Engagement with Artificial Intelligence," as a responsive act of worship meant to help focus and guide our response to AI. Our hope is that this litany will serve as a practical guide for thoughtful prayers for wisdom and discernment, and in the daily disciplines of spiritual growth.

CONCLUSION

For those worried about AI, Oren Etzioni recommends spending some time talking to Alexa. That may temper hopes and fears associated with AGI or ASI, but an attendee of Amazon's voice developer conference Alexa Live 2020—another optimistic visioning event, this time held in the midst of a global pandemic and other social crises—would have been impressed with the exhibition of human ingenuity and technological infrastructure that is accelerating the development and deployment of AI. Although it is less than a decade old, over 10,000 Amazon employees are working on Alexa along with over 750,000 developers around the world who are creating new capabilities every day. Over 100 million Alexa-enabled devices have been sold and connected with over 100,000 devices in homes, workplaces, automobiles, and elsewhere, and for many Alexa has become a primary information processing interface and an indispensable part of daily life. And Alexa executives say they are just getting started; more human-like capabilities are being developed to shift "cognitive burdens" from customers to Alexa and to make Alexa "part of our social fabric."[37]

Alexa's name, or "wake word," which Amazon has controlled commercially since 1999, is an homage to the Library of Alexandria—the famed ancient library built by the Ptolemies to establish their city as a center of political and cultural power.[38] Like a library, Alexa is an interface for accessing and engaging with information. But libraries, from Alexandria to every local public library today, have been primarily shaped by humans selecting and mediating information to cultivate human attention and agency. Even as libraries have increasingly automated operations, including with AI, there remains a priority for human interaction and scale informed by community and professional values. A proper library provides a generative human space where storytellers, dreamers, builders, and others come together to envision and create a better future. The role of an artificial agent such as Alexa, an assemblage of AI applications partnering with other globally networked AI applications, needs to be situated within constructive narratives about human nature, identity, purpose, and flourishing. The contents of this book provide a number of insights that can contribute to such narratives.

More than a decade ago, Floridi observed that our information society "is like a tree that has been growing its far-reaching branches much more widely, hastily, and chaotically than its conceptual, ethical, and cultural roots. The lack of balance is obvious and a matter of daily experience." "It's high time," he added, "to anticipate difficulties, identify opportunities, and resolve problems."[39] In addition, as Benjamin points out, our advanced information society still includes too much "suffering and injustice," and "we cannot resign ourselves to this reality we have inherited. It is time to reimagine what is possible."[40] The authors of this book hope it will facilitate further reflections and dialogue about AI to help us reimagine and pursue what is possible and necessary for a better world. Although the perspectives

37. See "Alexa Live 2020."

38. Romano, "Five Years Ago Amazon Introduced Alexa."

39. Floridi, *Information*, 7–8.

40. Benjamin, *Race after Technology*, 1.

of individual contributors about the future of AI may vary, we present here a shared vision for the value of engaging with resources from the Christian tradition to critique and participate constructively in the wise design, development, and use of AI.

BIBLIOGRAPHY

Amazon. "We're at the Beginning of a Golden Age of AI: Jeff Bezos." January 19, 2019. https://blog.aboutamazon.in/our-business/were-at-the-beginning-of-a-golden-age-of-ai-jeff-bezos.

Anderson, Janna, et al. "Artificial Intelligence and the Future of Humans." Pew Research Center, December 10, 2018. http://www.pewinternet.org/2018/12/10/artificial-intelligence-and-the-future-of-humans/.

Benjamin, Ruha. *Race after Technology: Abolitionist Tools for the New Jim Code.* Medford, MA: Polity, 2019.

Bezos, Jeff. *Invent and Wonder: The Collected Writings of Jeff Bezos.* Boston: Harvard Business Review Press and Basic Books, 2021.

Boden, Margaret A. *AI: Its Nature and Future.* Oxford: Oxford University Press, 2016.

Bort, Julie. "Jeff Bezos Explains Why the Library in His House Has Two Fireplaces with Two Inscriptions: 'Dreamers' and 'Builders.'" *Business Insider,* June 6, 2019. https://www.businessinsider.com/jeff-bezos-explains-why-his-library-2-fireplaces-2-mottos-2019-6.

Brockman, John, ed. *Possible Minds: 25 Ways of Looking at AI.* New York: Penguin, 2019.

Bryson, Joanna J. "The Past Decade and Future of AI's Impact on Society," in *Towards a New Enlightenment? A Transcendent Decade.* N.p.: Open Mind Books, 2019.

Floridi, Luciano. *Information: A Very Short Introduction.* New York: Oxford University Press, 2010.

———. "Singularitarians, AItheists, and Why the Problem with Artificial Intelligence Is H.A.L. (Humanity At Large), Not HAL." *APA Newsletter* 14 (2015) 8–11.

———. "Soft Ethics, the Governance of the Digital, and the General Data Protection Regulation." *Philosophical Transactions of the Royal Society A* 376 (2018).

Floridi, Luciano, et al. "AI4People—An Ethical Framework for a Good AI Society: Opportunities, Risks, Principles, and Recommendations." *Minds and Machines* 28 (2018) 689–707.

Ford, Martin. *Architects of Intelligence: The Truth about AI from the People Building It.* Birmingham, UK: Packt, 2018.

Frischmann, Brett, and Evan Selinger. *Re-engineering Humanity.* New York: Cambridge University Press, 2018.

Harari, Yuval Noah. *Homo Deus: A Brief History of Tomorrow.* New York: HarperCollins, 2017.

Hurlbut, J. Benjamin, and Hava Tirosh-Samuelson, eds. *Perfecting Human Futures: Transhuman Visions and Technological Imaginations.* Wiesbaden: Springer, 2016.

Markoff, John. *Machines of Loving Grace: The Quest for Common Ground between Humans and Robots.* New York: Ecco, 2015.

McLeish, Tom. *Faith and Wisdom in Science.* Oxford: Oxford University Press, 2014.

Mercer, Calvin, and Tracy J. Trothen. *Religion and the Technological Future: An Introduction to Biohacking, Artificial Intelligence, and Transhumanism*. Cham, Switzerland: Palgrave Macmillan, 2021.

Morelli, Michael. "The Athenian Altar and the Amazonian Chatbot: A Pauline Reading of Artificial Intelligence and Apocalyptic Ends." *Zygon* 54 (2019) 177–90.

Paulus, Michael J., Jr., et al. "A Framework for Digital Wisdom in Higher Education." *Christian Scholar's Review* 49 (2019) 43–61.

Reese, Byron. *The Fourth Age: Smart Robots, Conscious Computers, and the Future of Humanity*. New York: Atria, 2018.

Romano, Benjamin. "Five Years Ago Amazon Introduced Alexa." *Seattle Times*, November 8, 2019. https://www.seattletimes.com/business/amazon/five-years-ago-amazon-introduced-alexa-the-name-may-never-be-the-same/.

Singler, Beth. "Existential Hope and Existential Despair in AI Apocalypticism and Transhumanism." *Zygon* 54 (2019) 156–76.

Smith, Brad. *Tools and Weapons: The Promise and the Peril of the Digital Age*. New York: Penguin, 2019.

Smith, Gary. *The AI Delusion*. Oxford: Oxford University Press, 2018.

Susskind, Daniel. *A World without Work: Technology, Automation, and How We Should Respond*. New York: Metropolitan, 2020.

Taddeo, Mariarosaria, and Luciano Florid. "How AI Can Be a Force for Good." *Science* 361 (2018) 751–52.

Tegmark, Max. *Life 3.0: Being Human in the Age of Artificial Intelligence*. New York: Vintage, 2017.

Thweatt-Bates, Jeanine. *Cyborg Selves: A Theological Anthropology of the Posthuman*. New York: Routledge, 2012.

Williams, James. *Stand Out of Our Light: Freedom and Resistance in the Attention Economy*. Cambridge: Cambridge University Press, 2018.

2

An Introduction to Artificial Intelligence

Carlos R. Arias

This chapter explores the evolution of artificial intelligence, starting with the first ideas of Alan Turing, going through the promises of its inception, and landing in our current state, when AI invokes a sense of power and awe. Next, the chapter will provide a summary of different technologies related to AI and machine learning, such as deep neural networks, to help the reader distinguish different terminologies. The chapter will end with a discussion of some potential tendencies concerning how AI may be used or evolve in the near future, and some questions about the technology in the long term.

SECTION I: HOW IT CAME TO BE

In the beginning . . .

Since the dawn of human history, we have excelled as creatures because of our distinct abilities. These abilities have grown and evolved through the centuries, so much so that, in the latest decades, we have been able to create machines that can mimic our intelligence, as much as we understand it. Perhaps a new kind of world awaits us.

It is difficult to pinpoint a specific time or event that birthed AI; some might argue that it began with philosophers asking who we are, while others may say that it began with mathematics, or with the advent of computers. For the sake of this summary, we will say it all started with Alan Turing's paper "Computing Machinery and Intelligence," published in 1950, which posed the question of whether machines can perform in such a way that they seem intelligent.[1]

The paper presented what later would be known as the "Turing Test." This test basically places a machine and a human in communication with each other, but the human does not know that they are talking to a machine. If the machine is clever enough to fool the human into believing that the machine is a person, then the machine passes the Turing Test. In other words, the test assesses if "a computer [can] communicate well enough to persuade a human that it, too, is a human."[2]

While the work of Turing and other pioneers may have sparked the concept of AI, it has gone through different seasons over the years. The history of AI can be considered a journey that started with a question: Can a machine think?

Let There Be Light

The inception of the idea of AI, as mentioned, started with the question of if it is possible to create a machine that mimics a human. The Turing Test led to a gathering of scientists at what is known as the "Dartmouth Workshop" in 1956. It was at this conference that the term "artificial intelligence" was coined. This meeting hosted a group of researchers—including John McCarthy, Marvin Minsky, Allen Newel, and Herbert Simon, among others—that would later become known as the frontrunners and founders of AI; McCarthy is considered the father of AI. During this conference, the attendees suggested the idea (some say boldly, others naïvely) that "every aspect of learning or any other feature of intelligence can in principle be so precisely described that a machine can be made to simulate it."[3]

The meeting created a lot of interest and expectations about the field of AI; many embraced the promising possibility of building a thinking machine. During these years of early enthusiasm, research was oriented toward creating software that would be able to solve puzzles and play games; during the 1950s and '60s, game playing was considered a marker of intelligence.

1. Turing, "Computing Machinery and Intelligence," 433–60.
2. Bughin et al., "Artificial Intelligence."
3. Russell et al., "Artificial Intelligence," 17–18.

In addition to games, research was done to create programs that could prove theorems. In the journey of AI, these were the first happy days, funding was flowing, and the field was moving forward.[4]

Walking in the Desert

However, by the late 1960s, the promise of intelligent machines was becoming more an imagined fantasy than an achievable fact. Even though some advancements were made in the early years, they were limited to mimicking how humans perform a task instead of analyzing a problem and then executing a solution. Furthermore, the problems resided in a microworld with limited inputs; as problems got bigger, more real-world-like, they would also become intractable. The field was not producing the practical AI applications that were expected.[5]

The journey stalled. Yet, while it was uphill and on rocky terrain, the trail did not end. Although funding was scarce, research continued. During this time, "expert systems" were born. An expert system is software that encodes the knowledge of one or more experts in a given field. Once the knowledge base is created, the software helps users, normally nonexperts, by providing a course of action based on information it was given about a specific problem. These systems are very focused on specific problems and knowledge bases; to create an expert system, "knowledge engineers" interview experts in a determined area of discourse and map their knowledge into the knowledge base of the system.[6]

In the early years of AI, some of the research concentrated on the simulation of biological neural networks. This research was taken up with energy during the late 1980s. In section III, we will consider the fundamentals of neural networks.

The Rebirth

After the birth of expert systems and the return to neural networks, AI was reborn as a field and started to once again get attention and funding. In addition to advancements in computer science, neuroscience, and other related fields, the improved capabilities of computers had a significant impact

4. Russell et al., "Artificial Intelligence," 18.

5. Russell et al., "Artificial Intelligence," 20; Bughin et al., "Artificial Intelligence."

6. Russell et al., "Artificial Intelligence," 22–23; de Hoog, "Methodologies for Building Knowledge-Based Systems," 8.

in this resurgence. The journey started to find fertile ground and flatter paths to walk. "Machine learning" arose when probability reasoning and other extant technologies were used to create models from experiential data to help to make decisions.

The late 1990s and the first decade of the twenty-first century opened the doors for more actors to join in the journey. The internet became ubiquitous, and the volume of available data started to grow exponentially, leading to "Big Data," referring to the vast amount of data that are produced and accessible. The data come mainly from people; the advent of "Web 2.0" (the ability to produce content instead of just consuming it), social networks, the "Internet of Things," and other technologies created large repositories of data that could be used for machine learning algorithms to create models.

Consider a company that sells products online. Whenever a user is logged in to its website (and perhaps even if they're not), the web server records all the hyperlinks the user clicks during their visit to the site. It can also record how long the user views a given page. Now consider millions of people visiting that company's website. This generates quite a large amount of data that the company can later use to predict the behavior and preferences of its clients. Further, in addition to the information gathered from their website, the company could also mine other websites to gather additional information, such as commentaries on their products or collecting user behavior and preferences.

With the advent of Big Data, the sun started to shine and the fertile ground began to bloom. Computational power increased significantly and there was an abundance of data to train machines. Fields related to AI advanced to provide better tools and understanding, enabling programs to better mimic intelligence. AI was here to stay.

During the 2010s, newer technology developed that depended on the availability of large data centers that provided considerable computing power. "Deep learning" arrived on the scene—the construction of large neural networks enabled the creation of much more advanced models and therefore learn more than the basic neural networks of the past. More details on deep learning will be discussed in section III.

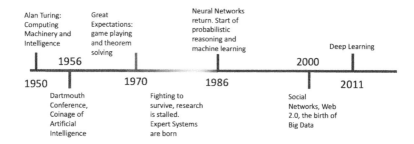

Figure 1: Timeline of the Evolution of AI

Milestones of Artificial Intelligence

The following table presents a very brief summary of some of the milestones of AI. This summary is far from comprehensive but should give the reader an idea of how AI has been evolving and becoming part of our everyday life.

Table 2.1: Milestones of AI	
1956	"Artificial Intelligence" as a term is coined at the Dartmouth Workshop
1966	ELIZA chatbot is created by Joseph Weizenbaum[7]
1986	Self-driving robotic van is created by Ernst Dickmanns[8]
1994	Chinook checkers program wins championship against human[9]
1995	ALICE chatbot developed by Richard Wallace[10]
1997	IBM's Deep Blue beats world chess champion Garry Kasparov[11]
2000	FDA approves the first robotic surgeon for laparoscopic procedures[12]
2002	Roomba automatic vacuum cleaner is introduced by iRobot Corporation[13]

7. Weizenbaum, "ELIZA—a Computer Program for the Study of Natural Language Communication between Man and Machine," 36–45.

8. Delcker, "Man Who Invented the Self-Driving Car (in 1986)."

9. Schaeffer et al., "CHINOOK The World Man-Machine Checkers Champion," 21.

10. Wallace, "Anatomy of A.L.I.C.E.," 181–210.

11. Goodrich, "How IBM's Deep Blue Beat World Champion Chess Player Garry Kasparov."

12. Food And Drug Administration, "FDA Approves New Robotic Surgery Device."

13. iRobot, "History."

2011	IBM's Watson computer beats humans in Jeopardy[14]
2011	Apple launches SIRI (Speech Interpretation and Recognition Interface) on iPhone 4[15]
2014	Amazon launches its own speech recognition assistant: Alexa[16]
2017	Google's AlphaGo wins three matches against the world's best Go player Ka Jie[17]
2018	Facebook uses AI to help filter explicit content[18]
2019	AI improves the detection of lung cancer, outperforming radiologists[19]
2020	Waymo driverless taxis begin work in the suburbs of southwest Phoenix[20]

SECTION II: SO, WHAT IS ARTIFICIAL INTELLIGENCE?

"Artificial Intelligence is whatever hasn't been done yet."

—LARRY TESLER[21]

Imagine living in the early twentieth century, going about your business as usual, and a person suddenly takes a calculator out of their pocket. Not a fancy scientific calculator. Not a mobile phone. Just a simple add, subtract, multiply, divide calculator. What would you think about it? That it is magical? That it is intelligent?

If someone did the same thing today, most people would look at the device and say that it is too simple, that they can do much more with their mobile phone calculator app. Seems that the calculator lost its genius!

This is one reason why defining AI is so difficult; the concept keeps changing with time, especially as devices get more sophisticated. Smarter even. Further, the concept of intelligence is difficult to define by itself. More on that in later chapters.

14. Best, "IBM Watson."

15. Evans, "WWDC."

16. Lorenzetti, "Forget Siri, Amazon Now Brings You Alexa."

17. Russell, "Google's AlphaGo AI Wins Three-Match Series against the World's Best Go Player."

18. Statt, "Facebook Is Using Billions of Instagram Images to Train Artificial Intelligence Algorithms."

19. Svoboda, "Artificial Intelligence Is Improving the Detection of Lung Cancer," S20–22.

20. Boudway, "Waymo's Self-Driving Future Looks Real Now That the Hype Is Fading."

21. Hofstadter et al., "Eternal Golden Braid," 601.

Let's explore some definitions of AI.

Merriam-Webster:

> 1. A branch of computer science dealing with the simulation of intelligent behavior in computers
> 2. The capability of a machine to imitate intelligent human behavior[22]

Wikipedia:

> In computer science, artificial intelligence (AI), sometimes called machine intelligence, is intelligence demonstrated by machines, unlike the natural intelligence displayed by humans and animals.[23]

Andrew Moore:

> Artificial Intelligence is the science and engineering of making computers behave in ways that, until recently, we thought required human intelligence.[24]

Fred Reed:

> A problem that proponents of AI regularly face is this: When we know how a machine does something "intelligent," it ceases to be regarded as intelligent. If I beat the world's chess champion, I'd be regarded as highly bright.[25]

John McCarthy:

> Artificial Intelligence [is] the ability of certain machines to do things that people are inclined to call intelligent.[26]

The definition of AI depends directly on the definition of intelligence. Different approaches to define intelligence have been taken by researchers in different fields of science.

Russell and Norvig:

> Some have defined intelligence in terms of fidelity to *human* performance, while others prefer an abstract, formal definition

22 *Merriam-Webster*, s.v. "Artificial Intelligence."
23. *Wikipedia*, s.v. "Artificial Intelligence."
24. High, "Carnegie Mellon Dean Of Computer Science On The Future Of AI."
25. "Promise of AI Not so Bright."
26. Bernstein, "Marvin Minsky's Vision of the Future."

of intelligence called rationality. . . . The subject matter itself also varies: some consider intelligence to be a property of internal *thought processes* and *reasoning*, while others focus on intelligent *behavior*, an external characterization.[27]

In summary it is suggested that depending on the point of view, intelligence is defined somewhere between the dimensions of human versus rational and thought versus behavior. Some think intelligence is an intrinsic ability, while others focus on intelligence as the observable external behaviors of the intelligent entity.

Notice how the basic definitions are based on the concept of "intelligence," but without going into details as to what intelligence actually is; hence the diversity of definitions. Considering the broad nature of the field, having a clear concept of intelligence is challenging. This leads to the range of scientific disciplines that are involved in AI, including computer science, computer engineering, philosophy, psychology, mathematics, neuroscience, linguistics, and biology. See table 2.2.

Table 2.2: Disciplinary Approaches to AI		
Discipline	Contributions	Questions
Computer Science	Studies the modeling, creation, and implementation of software that performs the "intelligent" processes.	How can we code this behavior? How can we improve the response time of this program?
Computer Engineering	Studies the construction of the hardware that becomes a computer. It intersects the fields of Computer Science and Electrical Engineering.	How can we build a device that will be sensitive to its environment and be able to respond accordingly? How can we build a device that can be programmed to act "intelligently"?

27. Russell et al., "Artificial Intelligence," 1–2.

Philosophy	Studies knowledge, values, reason, mind, logic, and language, among other issues. It also includes the field of ethics.	How do we reach a logical conclusion given incomplete information?
		What is knowledge? How is it represented?
		What is the mind?
		Is there a relation between intelligence and the mind?
		What makes humans special?
		Is a given behavior ethical?
Psychology	Studies the particularities of the mind, reasoning, and behavior.	How can we produce a given behavior?
		How do people think?
		What leads people to a certain behavior?
		How do people learn?
Mathematics (including Statistics)	Studies the numerical relations of objects and abstract representations. Provides numerical tools to represent and operate models.	How can we create a mathematical model to represent knowledge?
		What can be computed?
		Is this model robust enough for the given data?
		What is the probability of success for a given solution of a problem?
Neuroscience	Studies the workings of the brain, including both unconscious and conscious processes.	How does the brain store information?
		How does the brain process learning?
Linguistics	Studies language and communication, including its symbols, syntax (structure), and semantics (meaning).	How do we communicate?
		Can we model human communication?
		Is there a relation between language and thought?

| Biology | Studies living things. | How do living things reproduce and evolve? |
| | | What are the mechanisms of evolution? |

Each of these disciplines offer different contributions and questions to the field of AI. Artificial intelligence is inherently multidisciplinary. Many arenas of thought converge in AI, including those above, and more will contribute in the years to come.

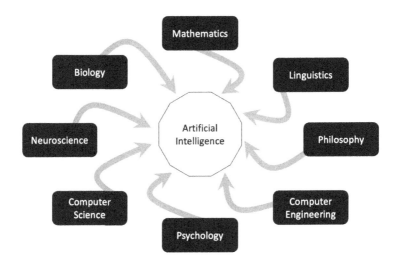

Figure 2: Disciplines That Contribute to AI

Given this multidisciplinary nature, we propose an additional definition of AI:

> Artificial Intelligence is a field of science in which different disciplines (including computer science, computer engineering, philosophy, psychology, mathematics, neuroscience, linguistics, biology, and others) converge with the purpose of creating agents that have the ability to learn (though crudely at the moment), to create models from their learning, to make predictions based on those models and new data, and then to make autonomous decisions (or to help in human decision-making) based on those predictions and any environmental data. All of these characteristics are based on, but not copied from, our current understanding of human intelligence.

Subfields of Artificial Intelligence

Within the field of AI there are many subfields. Keep in mind that AI concerns the creation of intelligence that is not natural, or mimicking the behavior of human intelligence with computer programs. Since intelligent behavior has many aspects, so does AI have many subfields. The major subfields include machine learning, natural language processing, expert systems, computer vision, and robotics. It is important to mention that these subfields are not exclusive; there are often overlaps between them.

Machine learning, as mentioned above, deals with creating programs that consume raw data, build models from that data, and make predictions given new data. To achieve this system of learning, scientists conceive different technologies that somehow resemble our understanding of human learning.

Natural language processing enables computers to recognize human language. Well-known applications of this technology include Cortana, Siri, and Alexa. The main goal of this subfield is to create software and hardware that are able to make sense of human speech and to talk back to users. In the past, it was thought that this was achievable through analysis of the syntax and semantics of human languages. Noah Chomsky, a linguist especially active in the mid- to late twentieth century, even created a grammar to represent human language for programming. However, this sort of natural language modeling turned out to be intractable because human language is intrinsically ambiguous, and natural language processing lost funding. In the late 1980s, a new approach was used involving the application of AI; the increase of computing power and available data has led to machine learning using text analysis to build a language model from user communication.[28]

Expert systems, also mentioned above, represent specific areas of knowledge. These systems are limited to particular disciplines and are built using the knowledge of human experts in that discipline. This knowledge is then programmed into a system to be used by nonexperts. These systems are sometimes thought of as "old-fashioned AI"; however, they do not "learn" by building progressively detailed models, but rather draw from a database "hard-coded" by humans.

Computer vision concerns the processing of images by the computer. It involves mathematical representation of images, machine learning for image recognition, and several other fields like optics and statistics. This subfield is largely known for its advancements in facial and fingerprint

---

28. Foote, "Brief History of Natural Language Processing (NLP)."

recognition, but it is also used in industry for quality control and in other disciplines including astronomy and history.

Robotics overlaps with other fields of AI. For instance, it uses computer vision to enable robots to "see" using input from visual sensors, machine learning to enable robots to learn from experience (e.g., learning to walk), and natural language processing to enable robots to communicate with humans. Robotics includes the imagining and building of both semi-autonomous and fully autonomous machines (e.g., self-driving cars, self-directing drones), and therefore employs many other forms of technology.

Figure 3 depicts some of the subfields of AI and the relation between them.

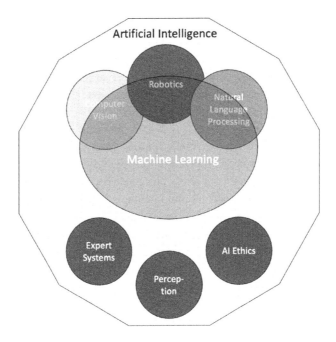

Figure 3: Subfields of AI

SECTION III: THE SCIENCE AND TECHNOLOGY OF ARTIFICIAL INTELLIGENCE

This section provides an overview of the science and technology behind AI. Starting with a general description of machine learning, moving to some types of machine learning, and then looking at an overview of different ways that a machine actually learns. The section ends with a brief discussion of the latest technologies in artificial intelligence and some details about deep neural networks.

Machine Learning

In thinking about AI, a question immediately presents itself: Can a machine learn? Following this question, another quickly emerges: What is learning? It is only by addressing the second question that we can define the extent to which a machine can learn. There are two aspects to the answer to this question in terms of machine learning:

- use available data to create a model to represent what is "learned," and
- set a goal for the computer and then allow it to find the "best" solution to reach that goal based on that model.

Given these two tasks, the process of machine learning (see figure 4) can be outlined as follows.

1. Collect training data that is relevant to what needs to be learned
2. Select an appropriate training algorithm
3. Feed the training algorithm with the training data
4. Retrieve the model created by the training algorithm
5. Use the model to help predict future tendencies or to help in decision making

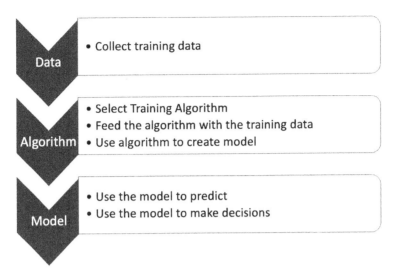

Figure 4: Learning Process Steps

Linear Regression

Statistics is an area of science that has been building representational models long before there was AI. Using inferential statistics, we can create models that predict future outcomes given sufficient historical data. The simplest model of inferential statistics is linear regression.

Linear regression starts with a set of data points in a given space; for simplicity, let's assume the points are in a two-dimensional plane. Figure 5a shows a set of data points that were collected and figure 5b shows how, after applying linear regression to the points, a line appears. This line constitutes the model. Note that, according to figure 5a, we can attest that at time six hours, the traveled distance is around 300 kilometers. However, we are unable to ascertain accurately the traveled distance at 4.5 hours or at hour twelve. Yet the model created through linear regression can help us determine, continuously, all the values of distance given any value of time. Thus, we can predict that at time twelve hours the traveled distance would be almost 700 kilometers.

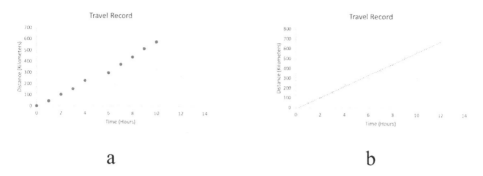

Figure 5: Example of Linear Regression

This simple example highlights a few key concepts.

Concept	Description	Example, from the Travel Record
Training Data	This is a set of data that is used to create the model. As the name implies, the data help train the computer.	In figure 5a, the training data would be the table containing the numbers used to create the graph.
Training Algorithm	The method used to create the appropriate model that best represents the training data.	The algorithm here uses linear regression, producing a line based on the training data that has minimal error point to point.
Model	A mathematical construction that helps predict new values or make decisions.	The generated line shown in figure 5b. The equation that defines that line can predict a distance from a value of time not in the training set.

Clearly this is a very simple model. It assumes that there are only two variables (time and distance), and it assumes a linear behavior between them. Regression can be used for more than two variables, and it can also be used for non-linear behaviors. See figure 6 for an example of non-linear (figure 6a) and three-dimensional data (figure 6b).

a   b

Figure 6: Non-Linear and Multidimensional Data

Classification

Another machine learning technique is classification. The main goal of classification is to create a model that helps classify the features of a subject being studied. For instance, suppose the following data sample.[29]

Day	Outlook	Temperature	Humidity	Wind	Play
1	Sunny	Hot	High	Strong	No
2	Sunny	Hot	High	Weak	No
3	Overcast	Hot	High	Weak	Yes
4	Rain	Mild	High	Weak	Yes
5	Rain	Cool	Normal	Weak	Yes
6	Rain	Cool	Normal	Strong	No
7	Overcast	Cool	Normal	Strong	Yes
8	Sunny	Mild	High	Weak	No
9	Sunny	Cool	Normal	Weak	Yes
10	Rain	Mild	Normal	Weak	Yes
11	Sunny	Mild	Normal	Strong	Yes
12	Overcast	Mild	High	Strong	Yes
13	Overcast	Hot	Normal	Weak	Yes
14	Rain	Mild	High	Strong	No

29. See Witten et al., *Data Mining*.

In the table it can be determined if, depending on the outlook, temperature, humidity, and wind, a person would play or not. Note that this is historic data that reports correlated information. For instance, a person can affirm that, if the outlook is sunny, the temperature mild, the humidity normal, and the wind strong, a person played. A classification algorithm would consume this data and create a model to classify the different conditions of weather to help the user decide whether to play or not.

Some classification algorithms are known as "supervised learning" algorithms. The main characteristic of this type of classification is that the training set contains a correct "answer" for each input.

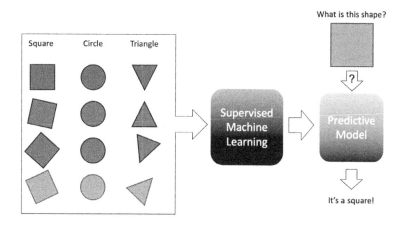

Figure 7: Supervised Learning

Notice that in figure 7, the training set to the left shows twelve shapes. Each shape has a label; for instance, the squares have their label, "square," as do the circles and the triangles. In supervised classification machine learning, the training set has a number of examples with the correct response for each. This training set is fed to a supervised machine learning algorithm to create a predictive model. Once the model is generated, a user can input a shape to the model and the model will classify it according to what it learned from the examples in the training set.

If the training data does not have an "answer" for each of the given examples, an "unsupervised learning" classification algorithm can be used. In figure 8, the shapes are inputted to the machine learning algorithm, but in this case none of the shapes have labels. The algorithm can group these objects according to similarity, but it cannot give them a label that it does not know.

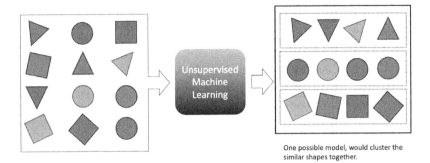

One possible model, would cluster the similar shapes together.

Figure 8: Unsupervised Learning

This type of unsupervised learning is known as "data clustering." In machine learning, the algorithm would create a model by grouping clusters of like data. One application of clustering is "anomaly detection." By clustering the training data, the user can determine outliers of the data and then make decisions based on this discovery.

In addition to learning from training data, sometimes machines can be made to learn from their mistakes. This learning occurs through a feedback loop in which a user evaluates output, which then in turn provides additional input to update the predictive model. This is known as "reinforcement learning" (see figure 9).

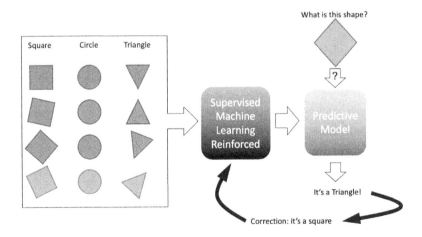

Figure 9: Reinforcement Learning

Association Rules

This machine learning technique creates rules based on historical behavior. For instance, a supermarket can keep a database of all its transactions for the last number of years. It can even associate specific transactions to specific customers—which, incidentally, is why many supermarkets offer customer discount cards. Given this historical data, the computer can be told to analyze it and produce a set of rules: If a customer bought particular items, then it is very likely that the customer will also buy these other particular items. Sometimes these association rules are obvious, but sometimes they are not, in which case they provide unique insight on how consumers behave. Figure 10 illustrates how every transaction, along with the customer information, can be stored in a database. A machine learning algorithm can then use this data to create a model, in this case is a set of association rules that are statistically meaningful according to the recorded data. This technique is also known as "market basket analysis" or "affinity analysis."

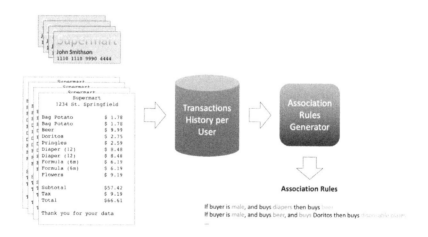

Figure 10: Association Rules Learning

Training Algorithms

So far, our description of machine learning has focused on training algorithms based on linear regression. We now turn to more complex algorithmic technologies used to create representative and predictive models. (See the second step in figure 4.)

Neural Networks

As mentioned above, some of the early AI researchers created a method to train computers based on our current understanding of neurons. The neuron is the basic unit of the nervous system, and it is thought that through networks of neurons humans think and store memories; figure 11 shows a simple schematic of a neuron. The neuron has three distinctive parts: the dendrites, the soma, and the axon. Neurons are a sort of message processor. Messages, in the form of electric impulses, arrive, from several other neurons, into the dendrites. The message is then processed by the soma of the neuron. This processing "decides" whether the neuron should "fire" or not. If it is decided that it should "fire," then a concurrent electrical signal is sent through the axon until it reaches the axon terminals that in turn will stimulate the dendrites of another neuron or neurons.

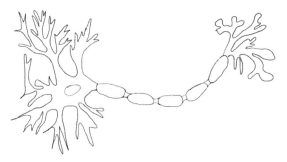

Figure 11: A Neuron

A question comes to mind: When and how does the neuron decide to fire?

Based on the human neural system, computer scientists created a learning model called an artificial neural network.[30] Figure 12a shows a very simplified model of a single neuronal unit, and figure 12b shows a neural network with several interconnected neuronal units. In a neural network, the neuronal unit has several inputs, usually numbers. These values are then multiplied by the "weights" of each artificial dendrite. These weights simulate the importance of that input channel. An example of this process could be the decision of whether or not to go out for dinner based on two considerations: Is it raining? How hungry is the person? Perhaps if it is raining and the person is not that hungry or not hungry at all, then the person will not go out for dinner. However, perhaps if the hunger passes a certain

---

30. Schmidhuber, "Deep Learning in Neural Networks: An Overview," 85–117.

threshold, then the person will go out for dinner whether it is raining or not. From this example, the inputs could be a report of if it is raining (yes or no) and the level of a person's hunger (not hungry, a little hungry, hungry, or starving), with a higher priority given to hunger and a lower priority given to rain. In an artificial neuronal network, these priorities would be encoded in the weights that multiply the inputs. The resultant values obtained by the prioritization is processed by the neuronal unit, and it decides whether to "fire" or not. If it does, the neuronal unit sends an output that can become the input for another neuronal unit in a network.

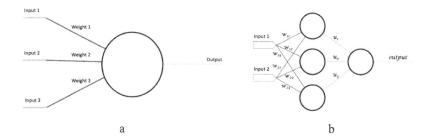

a   b

Figure 12: Artificial Neural Networks

Like other machine learning technologies, neural networks need to be trained before they can be used. The training takes in a training set and, based on the data, the algorithm sets the weights for each input pathway for each of the units in the network. This process can be computationally intensive, especially when the network consists in several layers and thousands of units.

Decision Trees

Another model used in machine learning is the decision tree. Like neural networks, this kind of training algorithm consumes a training set and creates a model in the shape of a tree. Each branch poses alternatives and, depending on the chosen alternative, the tree may present more alternatives until a decision is reached. Figure 13 shows a decision tree built with the weather data presented in the classification example above. This decision tree could help a person choose whether or not to play given information about the weather. For instance, if the day is sunny and the humidity is high, the output would suggest not playing that day.

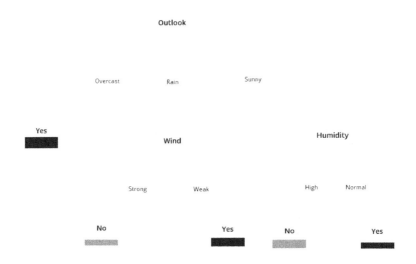

Figure 13: Example of a Decision Tree

Decision trees can be used to make decisions or to find patterns in the data. In medical research, decision trees can be built using clinical information. These trees could then be used by physicians as a diagnostic algorithm[31] or analyzed for patterns that are not obvious. One advantage of decision trees is that they are very intuitive; by looking at them a person can understand how a machine would make a given decision. This is unlike neural networks, in which a person would only see several matrices of numbers representing the weights of connections on each layer of units.

Support Vector Machines

We have seen that one of the simplest methods to create a model is by using linear regression. It was mentioned that the data may not show linear behavior or that it may have more than two dimensions. Sometimes the data does not seem to have a pattern to distinguish the different classes of data. In figure 14a, clearly there is not a line that can separate the gray dots from the black dots. That's where support vector machines come in. This training technique analyzes the data and, using mathematical transformations, finds a non-linear model that represents the data. In figure 14b, a somewhat non-linear separation is found between the different classes of data; the solution

---

31. Arias et al., "Identification of New Epilepsy Syndromes Using Machine Learning," 1–4.

can be more drastically non-linear as well, as in figure 14c. Support vector machines are particularly powerful in dealing with irregular and multidimensional data.

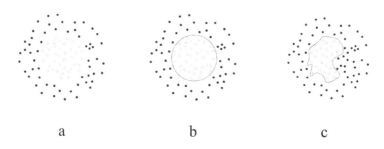

a   b   c

Figure 14: Non-Linear Data

Bayesian Networks

While support vector machines rely on mathematical transformations, Bayesian networks rely on statistical analysis. This machine learning technique uses training data to produce a probabilistic model. Bayesian networks are similar to decision trees, but every decision point can be reached by more than one decision point or input event, and every decision point or input event can lead to more than one conclusion. See the example in figure 15: If it is rush hour, then there is likely going to be a traffic jam; however, there will also be a traffic jam if there is bad weather or when there is a car accident.

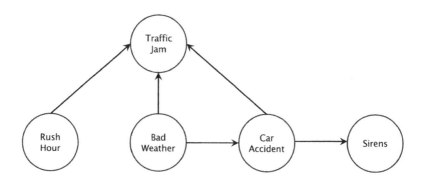

Figure 15: Example of a Bayesian Network

Bayesian networks are built using a statistical tool called "conditional probability." The training algorithm consumes the training data and constructs a model that best represents the data, resulting in a network showing the likelihood of events happening given some other event. Usually, these networks are accompanied with probability tables.

Genetic Algorithms

Natural selection is a process by which living organisms evolve from one state to another. Organisms that are not sufficiently strong or adaptable tend to disappear and therefore do not reproduce. Organisms that have traits that make them stronger and more adaptable survive and are therefore able to pass those characteristics on to the next generation. Natural selection and evolution are concepts that can be also applied to machine learning.

Genetic algorithms are applied to problems that have been intractable. These algorithms start with a first generation of solutions that are evaluated to assess which are "fit" to reproduce. The solutions that make the cut exchange parts (the "crossover" phase) and mutates. This creates a second generation of solutions, and the process repeats, continuing until there is an appropriate solution or the set maximum number of generations has been reached.

Figure 16 shows the process described above. The genetic algorithm starts with a set of solutions (the "initial population") which is then evaluated to find the fittest elements. Some of these elements are discarded, and the remaining ones are crossed over and then mutated. These transformed elements become a new set of possible solutions. If the solution is found, then the process stops. If it is not, then this population is evaluated again, and the process is repeated.

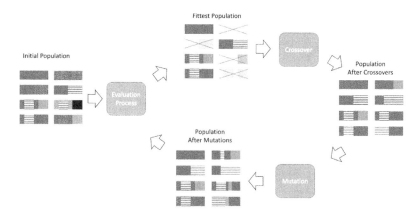

Figure 16: Genetic Algorithm

Clustering Algorithms

Sometimes data do not have labels. This poses a challenge to the classification of the training data. Suppose that there are a thousand images of animals, but none of the images has a label associated with it. This problem calls for an unsupervised machine learning algorithm, one kind of which is called a clustering algorithm. As the name suggests, these algorithms attempt to group data elements for which there is no given label. In figure 17a, all of the data points are black squares, and no other information about them is given except for their position. A clustering algorithm would then try to group these data points together according to some associated characteristic. One possible clustering is shown in figure 17b, with each cluster displaying a different characteristic. In the example above, the clustering algorithm would assess the images of animals and create groups according to the most similar elements. Determining how to define these similarities is one of the challenges of clustering algorithms.

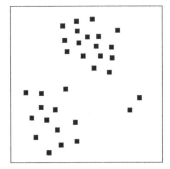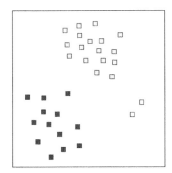

Figure 17: Clustering Data

The topics presented above represent the most basic algorithms for machine learning. Below, we will look at other machine learning and AI algorithms.[32]

Complex Pattern Recognition

Recognizing a face is something we do every day. However, recognizing a moving face, with potential alterations such as glasses, facial hair, different hair cut or color, a face mask, etc., becomes a more interesting problem. Dealing with real-world and real-time data is a significant challenge to pattern recognition algorithms. Examples of complex pattern recognition applications include facial recognition for law enforcement, automatic quality control in production lines, environment analysis for self-driving cars, and medical image analysis.

Information Analysis

One of the skills that every student needs to acquire is the ability to read about a topic and then to provide a summary of it. This certainly represents an activity that many would consider requires intelligence. It is also an activity that AI can accomplish; there are systems that can summarize a given text. Clearly these sorts of systems do not understand the concepts in the text, but the AI is able to compact the text and provide a briefer version of it.

32. Bughin et al., "Artificial Intelligence."

Drawing Conclusions

Artificial intelligence has the ability to draw conclusions based on given knowledge and logical inference. This requires careful representation of the data in such a way that the computer can associate concepts and the creation of a model that maps that representation. Based on that model, the AI then draws conclusions from it. An additional step would involve feeding these conclusions back into the algorithmic model as new data, enabling the AI to learn through "hits and misses."

Forecasting

On any given day, people check forecasts. For instance, many like to know what the weather is going be like, or they want to check the financial markets. By forecasting, we reduce uncertainty intrinsic to future events.

Weather forecasting is a good example of the complexity inherent in learning processes; creating a model to predict the weather has been a challenge given the immense number of variables involved in the atmospheric system. Artificial intelligence has been helpful in this regard. Since the late 1990s, the National Center for Atmospheric Research has been using an AI application called "DICast" to predict the weather.[33] In addition, the National Oceanic and Atmospheric Administration has signed an agreement with Google to "explore the benefits of Artificial Intelligence and Machine Learning" using NOAA's environmental data.[34]

The more complex the system, the more challenging it is to forecast its behavior. Examples of complex systems that AI has attempted to forecast include predicting the electrical energy requirement of a country in real time to balance elements in the power grid[35] and predicting the state of the stock market over different periods of time, even including investor sentiment analysis to increase the precision of the prediction.[36]

33. Haupt et al., "Machine Learning for Applied Weather Prediction," 276–77; "RAL DICast®."

34. Bateman, "AI Agreement to Enhance Environmental Monitoring, Weather Prediction."

35. Motepe et al., "Improving Load Forecasting Process for a Power Distribution Network Using Hybrid AI and Deep Learning Algorithms," 82584–98.

36. Tang et al., "Forecasting Economic Recession through Share Price in the Logistics Industry with Artificial Intelligence (AI)," 70.

Emotion Recognition

Is it possible for computers to feel emotions? This is a very complex philo-sophical question. At the moment, we would probably say that machines are unable to feel emotions as humans do, but that they are able to recognize some of the features of human emotions. There are three areas in which emotion can be detected: face analysis, text analysis, and voice analysis. In face analysis, the computer is trained to identify different emotions based on the form of the face. Using computer vision, the computer can then de-termine, with some level of accuracy, the emotion of a person. Scientists are taking this a step further in programming robots to mimic human emotions based on the learning done through facial analysis.[37] Text analysis deter-mines emotions based upon what a person writes; some research suggests it is possible to identify as many as nine emotions from short texts or tweets.[38] This sort of analysis is particularly useful for companies that receive cus-tomer feedback, such as in user comments. In addition to facial and text analysis, AI can also determine emotion based on the sound of a person's voice, including in videos.[39]

Deep Learning: Deep Neural Networks

Another term that has become popular in the media in recent years is "deep learning." Deep learning is the result of applying "deep neural networks," which is a neural network that has many layers (usually more than three), each with many neuronal units. For instance, figure 18 shows a neural net-work that has seven layers of units; some layers have five units and some have seven units. A real-world deep neural network used by Untapt, a com-pany that develops recruitment technology, has sixteen layers with a total of 14 million units.[40] A network like that can take days to train, as it would process several terabytes (thousands of gigabytes) of information.

---

37. Hall, "How We Feel about Robots That Feel."

38. Argueta et al., "Multilingual Emotion Classifier Using Unsupervised Pattern Extraction from Microblog Data," 1477–502; Saravia et al., "EmoViz," 753–56.

39. Poria et al., "Fusing Audio, Visual, and Textual Clues for Sentiment Analysis from Multimodal Content," 50–59.

40. Untapt, "Talent Science."

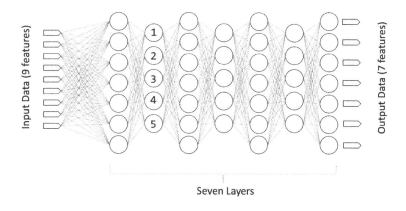

Figure 18: Deep Neural Network

The remarkable ability of deep learning is that it can find patterns in datasets that were thought to be unclassifiable because the problem space was not linear. Further, deep learning can determine features of the patterns it recognizes; each layer of the neural network could be responsible for recognizing a specific aspect of the elements it is analyzing. In this way, the AI "learns" during the training process, gathering its own data rather than relying on information coded by the programmers.

One disadvantage of this technology is that it can be a "black box." It would be very hard for nonspecialists to be able to make sense of the tables of numbers that represent the weights of each of the connections in the neural network. Unlike decision trees that show how they arrive at conclusions, neural networks, and especially deep neural networks, only show conclusions without showing in an intelligible way how they arrived at them.

SECTION IV: WHERE ARTIFICIAL INTELLIGENCE IS WORKING, AND WHAT'S NEXT

Where Can You See Artificial Intelligence Working?

Today, AI is ubiquitous. It can be found throughout industry and everyday activities. It can even be found in the palm of your hand: Siri, Cortana, Google Assistant, Alexa, etc. When you call customer service, many companies will have an automated robot answer. These technologies use natural language processing; AI interprets what you say, decides on the best answer to your question, and responds. It is not perfect, but it is much better than it was even five or ten years ago.

Artificial intelligence can also be found in the stock market. There are many bots (an internet application that performs repetitive tasks) working with stockbrokers to help them decide when to buy and when to sell. These bots learn the behavior of the stock market, make models and projections, and then suggest different alternatives that will increase profits from selected stocks.

In medicine, AI is used to analyze medical images, like MRI or CAT scans. These analyses help physicians with the diagnosis of their patients. Some AI technologies have been shown to detect disease in images that a physician does not.[41]

Artificial intelligence is also used in armament. The US Navy employs an AI technology called the Aegis Combat System, which the Navy describes as "a centralized, automated, command-and-control (C2) and weapons control system that was designed as a total weapon system, from detection to kill."[42] Installed on naval ships, the Aegis automates both defense and attack weaponry. Other AI systems used in the military include enemy detection, navigation, and technologies for missiles or stationary equipment.

Some of the home applications of AI include entertainment and automation. Whatever streaming service a person has, it is likely that the company recommends content based on the movies or shows that the person has watched. These services use machine learning to analyze the viewing history of its users, deducing that if a person watched a given movie, then it is likely that the person will like another particular movie. Media is moving toward even customizing commercials based on user profiles. In terms of home automation, a house could feature AI that controls its environment. For instance, there could be devices to regulate temperature. Unlike an ordinary thermostat that keeps the temperature at a certain level, there are smart thermostats that, to save on heating or cooling costs, adjust the house temperature when they sense that there is no one at home, and they learn when residents usually return home so that they can start getting the house to a comfortable temperature level before the people arrive.

This list of AI applications is not comprehensive; between the writing of these words and your reading of them, there will likely be more advancements making their way into everyday life. What is clear is that there are several participants in AI development, including government, healthcare,

41. Hussain et al., "AI Techniques for COVID-19," 128776–95; Svoboda, "Artificial Intelligence Is Improving the Detection of Lung Cancer," S20–22.

42. Paul Scharre, *Army of None*, 162.

pharmaceutical companies, the military, entertainment industries, global corporations, and academia. This shows how pervasive AI has become.

Latest Advances

- *Deep learning.* As discussed above, deep learning neural networks require several layers with potentially thousands of neuronal units. Training such a network necessitates a considerable amount of electrical energy as this training takes place in data centers with hundreds of computers running sometimes for several days to train a single network. Scientists have found ways to minimize the training process by improving performance, thus saving time and energy. This suggests more applications of deep learning in the near future.

- *Computer code.* Artificial intelligence is now able to write computer code. Given the description of a relatively simple problem, the program can create the code necessary to solve the problem. This technology is still in the early stages, but it is expected that some of the more menial coding tasks will soon be automated.

- *Drug discovery.* Finding medications to treat and cure diseases has always been a challenge. Pharmaceutical companies invest billions of dollars to research drugs in studies that can span several years. Artificial intelligence can help reduce research time by creating models of drugs and simplified models of organisms and then simulating interactions of the two to analyze effects. In addition to these simulations, machine learning is used to gather all available information from previous research and create models to provide suggestions for avenues of future research that were not previously considered.

- *Advanced prosthetics.* Prosthetics have come a long way. For most of human history, any prosthesis consisted merely in the static replacement of a limb. Relatively recently, some movement was incorporated into better prosthetics solutions. Current research is using machine learning to capture the "intention" of user movement by reading nerve impulses. The newest prosthetics are also able to provide biofeedback, giving the user a more realistic experience.

- *COVID-19.* In early 2020, the world began to feel the impacts of the COVID-19 pandemic, a disease caused by the severe acute respiratory syndrome coronavirus 2 (SARS-CoV-2), a virus that first appeared in the Wuhan province in China and then quickly spread throughout the globe. Scientists around the world began working around the clock to come up with responses, including transmission forecasting, treatment discovery, diagnosis, and prognosis. Artificial intelligence played a role in these solutions thanks to the availability of more clinical data than ever before, including historic clinical information, clinical notes, previous research, data from electronic monitoring and diagnostics equipment, and genetic information. Applying available AI tools, systems were created to model virus transmission and spread. Using drug information and AI, it was possible to determine that some existing drugs could be used to treat COVID-19, saving considerable time in drug research.[43] Artificial intelligence also has aided the significant logistical challenges related to the distribution of the vaccine. In clinical settings, AI is helping with "drug discovery, planning, treatment, and reported outcomes of the COVID-19 patient."[44] It is expected that AI will play an important role in finding further treatments and eventually a cure.[45]

What May Be Coming: A Forecast

- *Healthcare.* It is unlikely that AI will replace physicians. However, advances in AI will continue to impact healthcare profoundly. Physicians will be able to access diagnostic systems that will aid them making decisions. Artificial intelligence will enable the logistics necessary for efficient distribution of healthcare equipment and personnel within an institution or throughout the world. As levels of user familiarity and trust increase, AI will increasingly penetrate the world of healthcare, but it is expected that there will be a human "in the loop" for the foreseeable future.

- *Data generation.* One of the challenges of AI is the amount of data required to train it. Recent cutting-edge research has created techniques for data synthesis using generative adversarial networks (GAN). This technology generates anonymized data that can then be used for training machine learning systems.

43. Hussain et al., "AI Techniques for COVID-19," 128776–95; Pham et al., "Deep Learning Framework for High-Throughput Mechanism-Driven Phenotype Compound Screening and Its Application to COVID-19 Drug Repurposing," 1–11.

44. Mohanty et al., "Application of Artificial Intelligence in COVID-19 Drug Repurposing," 1027–31.

45. Kannan et al., "Role of Artificial Intelligence and Machine Learning Techniques."

- *Artificial intelligence for artificial intelligence.* Can we use AI to create more AI? Researchers have recently used machine learning systems to suggest the training parameters of other machine learning technologies. These systems help with the creation, deployment, management, and operation of AI. Examples include Google AutoML[46] and IBM Auto AI.[47]

- *Manufacturing.* Artificial intelligence continues to integrate into manufacturing industries. It has been decades since automated manufacturing began. In the future, quality control operations, workflow logistics, and management of raw material and finished product will likely become automated. There may come a time when a factory operates with minimal or even no human supervision.

- *Drug discovery.* Artificial intelligence has certainly helped with drug repurposing, which is when drugs that were authorized for use in treatment for a certain disease are discovered to be effective in treatment for a different disease. It is hopeful that AI will also help in the lengthy and expensive process of drug discovery. Advancements in proteomics, genomics, and metabolomics, in conjunction with AI applications may help with new drug creation and determination of drug interactions.

How Far Can It Go?

It is difficult to accurately predict long-term advancement in AI. However, one thing can be said: If a task can be automated, it is very likely that it will be automated. Artificial intelligence will be increasingly present in human life in the years to come, likely in both beneficial and detrimental ways. Developments in healthcare, food and goods manufacturing and distribution, and drug discovery seem promising. However, the creation of automated armaments, AI-driven cyberattacks, and sex robots give more pause. In addition, current applications suffer from inherent biases; the technology is not necessarily inherently biased, but if the data that is used for training is biased, then the models that the AI produces will be biased. This is one more reason to keep humans in the loop as we develop and evaluate our technology.

"Ethical AI," or the ethical consideration of AI, has evolved through several stages. In the first wave, philosophers were consulted to develop

46. "Cloud AutoML Custom Machine Learning Models."
47. IBM, "IBM Watson Studio—AutoAI."

principles and guidelines to mitigate the risks and threats of AI. At the same time, a second wave emerged to develop technical interventions to address fairness and bias in AI, but these efforts did not address the social contexts in which technologies are developed and used. The most recent third wave, described by Carly Kind, is more focused on justice—"social justice, racial justice, economic justice, and environmental justice."[48]

Even though AI can simulate emotions and empathy, it is not generally thought—or desired—that AI will experience feelings as humans do. This implies that there are areas of human activity where AI can help but should not take over, including healthcare, warfare, counseling, and the justice system.

One of the advancements in AI that some are expecting is Artificial General Intelligence (AGI), also known as "The Singularity," which is the name given to the theoretical moment when AI can think for itself and is therefore self-directed. Current AI is only able to solve specific problems in a determinate domain. But Irving J. Good calls AGI the "ultraintelligent machine," with the capacity to solve any problem, including the problem of improving itself, which would lead to an intelligence explosion. Good cautions: "The first ultraintelligent machine is the last invention that man need ever make—provided that the machine is docile enough to tell us how to keep it under control."[49]

Final Remarks

Humans have always had the ability to create tools and techniques. It may have started with the technology of starting and using fire, or tools used for hunting and farming. Most of the time, these technologies have been helpful. Today, we have taken the first steps in creating technologies that can learn. Our success with AI has led to its application in nearly every facet of life, for good and for ill. The tools that we have created, the tools that we create, and the tools that we will create will be tainted by our own imperfections, by our own brokenness. The more power we give to these technologies, the more they will affect us, individually and collectively. That is the reason why, whenever AI directly affects people, there should always be humans overseeing it.

---

48. Kind, "Term 'Ethical AI' Is Finally Starting to Mean Something."
49. Good, "Speculations concerning the First Ultraintelligent Machine," 31–88.

BIBLIOGRAPHY

Argueta, Carlos, et al. "Multilingual Emotion Classifier Using Unsupervised Pattern Extraction from Microblog Data." *Intelligent Data Analysis* 20 (2016) 1477–502.

Arias, Carlos R., et al. "Identification of New Epilepsy Syndromes Using Machine Learning." *2019 IEEE 39th Central America and Panama Convention*, 2019, 1–4.

"Artificial Intelligence." *Merriam-Webster*. https://www.merriam-webster.com/dictionary /artificial+intelligence.

"Artificial Intelligence." *Wikipedia*. https://en.wikipedia.org/w/index.php?title=Artificial _intelligence&oldid=970134895.

Bateman, John. "AI Agreement to Enhance Environmental Monitoring, Weather Prediction." National Oceanic and Atmospheric Administration, October 27, 2020. https://www.noaa.gov/media-release/ai-agreement-to-enhance-environmental-monitoring-weather-prediction.

Bernstein, Jeremy. "Marvin Minsky's Vision of the Future." *New Yorker*, December 14, 1981. https://www.newyorker.com/magazine/1981/12/14/a-i.

Best, Jo. "IBM Watson: The Inside Story of How the Jeopardy-Winning Supercomputer Was Born, and What It Wants to Do Next." *TechRepublic*, September 9, 2013. https://www.techrepublic.com/article/ibm-watson-the-inside-story-of-how-the-jeopardy-winning-supercomputer-was-born-and-what-it-wants-to-do-next/.

Boudway, Ira. "Waymo's Self-Driving Future Looks Real Now That the Hype Is Fading." *Bloomberg*, January 21, 2021. https://www.bloomberg.com/news/articles/2021– 01–21/waymo-self-driving-taxis-are-coming-to-more-u-s-cities.

Bughin, Jacques, et al. "Artificial Intelligence: The Next Digital Frontier?" McKinsey Global Institute, June 2017. https://www.calpers.ca.gov/docs/board-agendas /201801/full/day1/06-technology-background.pdf.

De Hoog, Robert. "Methodologies for Building Knowledge-Based Systems." In *The Handbook of Applied Expert Systems*, edited by Jay Liebowitz, 1–8. New York: CRC, 1998.

Delcker, Janosch. "The Man Who Invented the Self-Driving Car (in 1986)." *Politico*, July 19, 2018. https://www.politico.eu/article/delf-driving-car-born-1986-ernst-dickmanns-mercedes/.

Evans, Jonny. "WWDC: The Evolution of Apple's Siri." *Computerworld*, May 22, 2018. https://www.computerworld.com/article/3275224/wwdc-the-evolution-of-apples-siri.html.

Food and Drug Administration. "FDA Approves New Robotic Surgery Device." *ScienceDaily*, July 17, 2000. https://www.sciencedaily.com/releases/2000/07/000 717072719.htm.

Foote, Keith D. "A Brief History of Natural Language Processing (NLP)." DATAVERSITY, May 22, 2019. https://www.dataversity.net/a-brief-history-of-natural-language-processing-nlp/.

Good, Irving John. "Speculations concerning the First Ultraintelligent Machine." *Advances in Computers* 6 (1966) 31–88.

Goodrich, Joanna. "How IBM's Deep Blue Beat World Champion Chess Player Garry Kasparov." *IEEE Spectrum*, January 25, 2021. https://spectrum.ieee.org/the-institute/ieee-history/how-ibms-deep-blue-beat-world-champion-chess-player-garry-kasparov.

Google. "Cloud AutoML." https://cloud.google.com/automl.

Hall, Luisa. "How We Feel about Robots That Feel." *MIT Technology Review*, October 24, 2017. https://www.technologyreview.com/2017/10/24/148259/how-we-feel-about-robots-that-feel/.

Haupt, Sue Ellen, et al. "Machine Learning for Applied Weather Prediction." In *2018 IEEE 14th International Conference on E-Science (e-Science)*, 276–77. Amsterdam: IEEE, 2018.

High, Peter. "Carnegie Mellon Dean of Computer Science on the Future of AI." *Forbes*, October 30, 2017. https://www.forbes.com/sites/peterhigh/2017/10/30/carnegie-mellon-dean-of-computer-science-on-the-future-of-ai/.

Hofstadter, Douglas R. *Gödel, Escher, Bach: An Eternal Golden Braid*. New York: Basic, 1999.

Hussain, Adedoyin Ahmed, et al. "AI Techniques for COVID-19." *IEEE Access* 8 (2020) 128776–95.

IBM. "IBM Watson Studio—AutoAI." November 6, 2020. https://www.ibm.com/cloud/watson-studio/autoai.

iRobot. "History." https://www.irobot.com/About-iRobot/Company-information/History.

Kannan, Shantani, et al. "The Role of Artificial Intelligence and Machine Learning Techniques: Race for COVID-19 Vaccine." *Archives of Clinical Infectious Diseases* 15 (2020) 10338.

Kind, Carly. "The Term 'Ethical AI' Is Finally Starting to Mean Something." *VentureBeat*, August 23, 2020. https://venturebeat.com/2020/08/23/the-term-ethical-ai-is-finally-starting-to-mean-something/.

Klassner, Frank. "Artificial Intelligence: Introduction." *Crossroads* 3 (1996): 2.

Lorenzetti, Laura. "Forget Siri, Amazon Now Brings You Alexa." *Fortune*, November 11, 2014. https://fortune.com/2014/11/06/forget-siri-amazon-now-brings-you-alexa/.

Mohanty, Sweta, et al. "Application of Artificial Intelligence in COVID-19 Drug Repurposing." *Diabetes and Metabolic Syndrome* 14 (2020) 1027–31.

Motepe, Sibonelo, et al. "Improving Load Forecasting Process for a Power Distribution Network Using Hybrid AI and Deep Learning Algorithms." *IEEE Access* 7 (2019) 82584–98.

Pham, Thai-Hoang, et al. "A Deep Learning Framework for High-Throughput Mechanism-Driven Phenotype Compound Screening and Its Application to COVID-19 Drug Repurposing." *Nature Machine Intelligence* 3 (2021) 247–57.

Poria, Soujanya, et al. "Fusing Audio, Visual, and Textual Clues for Sentiment Analysis from Multimodal Content." *Neurocomputing* 174 (2016) 50–59.

"Promise of AI Not so Bright." *Washington Times*, April 13, 2006. https://www.washingtontimes.com/news/2006/apr/13/20060413-105217-7645r/.

Russell, Jon. "Google's AlphaGo AI Wins Three-Match Series against the World's Best Go Player." *TechCrunch*, May 24, 2017. https://social.techcrunch.com/2017/05/24/alphago-beats-planets-best-human-go-player-ke-jie/.

Russell, Stuart J., and Peter Norvig. *Artificial Intelligence: A Modern Approach*. 4th ed. Pearson Series in Artificial Intelligence. Hoboken, NJ: Pearson, 2021.

Saravia, Elvis, et al. "EmoViz: Mining the World's Interest through Emotion Analysis." *Proceedings of the 2015 IEEE/ACM International Conference on Advances in Social Networks Analysis and Mining*. New York: ACM, 2015.

Schaeffer, Jonathan, et al. "CHINOOK The World Man-Machine Checkers Champion." *AI Magazine* 17 (1996) 21. https://ojs.aaai.org//index.php/aimagazine/article/view/1208.

Scharre, Paul. *Army of None: Autonomous Weapons and the Future of War*. New York: Norton, 2018.

Schmidhuber, Jürgen. "Deep Learning in Neural Networks: An Overview." *Neural Networks* 61 (2015) 85–117.

Statt, Nick. "Facebook Is Using Billions of Instagram Images to Train Artificial Intelligence Algorithms." *The Verge*, May 2, 2018. https://www.theverge.com/2018/5/2/17311808/facebook-instagram-ai-training-hashtag-images.

Svoboda, Elizabeth. "Artificial Intelligence Is Improving the Detection of Lung Cancer." *Nature* 587 (2020) S20–22.

Tang, Ym, et al. "Forecasting Economic Recession through Share Price in the Logistics Industry with Artificial Intelligence (AI)." *Computation* 8 (2020) 70.

Turing, A. M. "Computing Machinery and Intelligence." *Mind* 59 (1950) 433–60.

UCAR. "RAL DICast®." https://ral.ucar.edu/projects/dicast/.

Untapt, "Talent Science: How Deep Learning in AI Works." https://www.untapt.com/data-science-22222.

Wallace, Richard S. "The Anatomy of A.L.I.C.E." In *Parsing the Turing Test*, edited by Robert Epstein et al., 181–210. Dordrecht, Netherlands: Springer, 2009.

Weizenbaum, Joseph. "ELIZA—a Computer Program for the Study of Natural Language Communication between Man and Machine." *Communications of the ACM* 9 (1966) 36–45.

Witten, I. H., and Eibe Frank. *Data Mining: Practical Machine Learning Tools and Techniques with Java Implementations*. San Francisco: Morgan Kaufmann, 2000.

3

What's So *Artificial* and *Intelligent* about Artificial Intelligence?

A Conceptual Framework for AI

Rebekah L. H. Rice

There is currently a good deal of attention being focused on artificial intelligence, broadly speaking, and deep learning, specifically. The attention is warranted, as these technologies are predicted to affect our collective lives in innumerable ways even beyond their already expansive social reach. There is much to consider regarding the benefits and potential harms of AI. And of course there are the apocalyptic musings about super-intelligent machines running amok, bringing science fiction scenarios uncomfortably close to anticipated reality. But productively engaging in discussions about the ethical and social implications of AI, and about which sorts of futures it is reasonable to anticipate, requires clarity about certain key concepts at play in these conversations. Some of these are conspicuous: *artificial* and *intelligence*, notably. The former suggests a contrast with some other concept. But which, exactly? *Natural*, perhaps? Or *organic*? And *intelligence*, being as it is regularly attributed to human persons, might suggest a fitting analogy with intelligence as it occurs in you and me. But what is intelligence in humans? Does it require a mind or a soul? Is it simply a corollary of electrical and chemical processes in the human brain? Gaining clarity about the range of meanings to which such terms refer—and familiarity with the relevant debates surrounding the various meanings—will provide the conceptual framework necessary to better articulate the precise ethical and pragmatic questions we think most important to our efforts to intentionally navigate a world with AI.

I. THINKING MACHINES?

When mathematician Alan Turing published "Computing Machinery and Intelligence" in 1950,[1] logical positivism permeated the intellectual terrain.[2] Central to logical positivism is the verifiability criterion of meaning.[3] According to it, the content, or meaning, of any meaningful statement is exhausted by the conditions that must be verified to obtain if the statement is to be considered true. These verification conditions are either empirical (synthetic) or logical (analytic). Those who held the view claimed that if a statement cannot be verified using logic or empirical investigation, then it is unverifiable and therefore meaningless (and not a candidate for truth). Logical positivism ultimately fell out of favor given its implication that many seemingly understandable statements about such topics as metaphysics and religion and political theory turn out to be meaningless. But even more damning, the view's central claim appears to fail to satisfy its own criterion. After all, can the verifiability criterion of meaning itself be verified in the manner required?

What is perhaps most illuminating about this intellectual movement for our purposes, however, is the way in which the logical positivists traded metaphysical questions for epistemological ones. Verifiability is an epistemic criterion. It has to do with what one can know, reasonably believe, or demonstrate. And yet, might there be facts that obtain though no one does, or perhaps can, come to know them? Take the claim that certain mathematical entities—sets, say—are real. Can this be verified empirically? Or can the reality (or not) of sets be established via logical inference? It would seem not. And yet it may nevertheless be that sets belong, as Bertrand Russell contends, to "the world of being."[4] The relevance to Turing is evident when one considers the question with which he begins his seminal paper and, correspondingly, the method he suggests for answering it. The paper sets out to

1. Turing, "Computing Machinery and Intelligence," 433–60.

2. See, e.g., Ayer, *Logical Positivism*; Carnap, "Elimination of Metaphysics." For an application to the mind, see Carnap, "Psychology in Physical Language," in Ayer, *Logical Positivism*.

3. Correspondingly, there is also a verifiability criterion of truth.

4. Russell, *Problems of Philosophy*, 91–100.

answer the question, "Can machines think?"[5] But rather than rehearse proposed definitions or catalog how the terms "machine" and "think" are used, he proposes his now famous imitation game. Here's how he describes it:

> It is played with three people, a man (A), a woman (B), and an interrogator (C). . . . The interrogator stays in a room apart from the other two. The object of the game for the interrogator is to determine which of the other two is the man and which is the woman. He knows them by labels X and Y, and at the end of the game he says either "X is A and Y is B" or "X is B and Y is A." The interrogator is allowed to put questions to A and B. . . . The ideal arrangement is to have a teleprinter communicating between the two rooms.[6]

The interrogator's objective is to ask questions of A and B and then determine, based on their respective answers, with whom he is communicating. It is A's aim to mislead the interrogator and veer him toward an inaccurate identification, whereas B's aim is to help the interrogator. But how, in an imagined game such as this, do we make headway toward answering the question about whether machines can think? Turing clarifies:

> We now ask the question, "What will happen when a machine takes the part of A in this game?" Will the interrogator decide wrongly as often when the game is played like this as he does when the game is played between a man and a woman?[7]

Now, instead of identifying which interlocutor is the man and which the woman, the interrogator must determine when he is receiving responses from a machine and when he is interacting with a human. Could the machine's responses successfully imitate those of a human so that the interrogator believes he is communicating with a human person? If yes, then we will thereby have an affirmative answer to the original question. In other words, a machine that can perform certain kinds of tasks—in this case, answering pointed questions—in a way that is indistinguishable from a human performing such tasks satisfies Turing's criterion for a thinking thing. Notice it is an observer's ability with respect to distinguishing between the two that establishes whether or not the thing is thinking.

Now, that may be well and good and we might think the substituted questions adequate to the task of determining the status of such a machine. But that will depend on what assumptions we are making. Importantly, the

5. Turing, "Computing Machinery and Intelligence," 433.

6. Turing, "Computing Machinery and Intelligence," 433.

7. Turing, "Computing Machinery and Intelligence," 434.

original question is a metaphysical one. It asks whether reality is such that there are, or could be, thinking machines. Or perhaps, more pointedly, it asks about a certain category of items, namely machines, and whether they are the sorts of entities capable of thinking. Now, such a question can be answered in the manner suggested only if thinking is entirely a publicly observable phenomenon. That is, only if thinking is entirely a matter of certain inputs being followed by particular behavioral, or otherwise observable outputs, is the question about what the interrogator is able to observe and conclude on the basis of such observation apt. If the observer compares the behavioral outputs of the machine with those of the human and finds them qualitatively indistinguishable, then just as the human is a thinking thing (*ex hypothesi*), so is the machine. In other words, whether Turing's proposed method is capable of answering his original question depends on what thinking is.

Indeed, the logical positivists who gave thought to the nature of the mental opted for a version of behaviorism fittingly termed "logical behaviorism." According to this view, "all sentences of psychology describe physical occurrences, namely, the physical behavior of humans and other animals."[8] The upshot is that any meaningful psychological statement, that is, a statement purportedly describing a mental phenomenon, can be translated, without loss of content, into a statement solely about behavioral and physical phenomena. Famously, Carl Hempel suggested that "Paul has a toothache" can be translated into a sentence like, "Paul weeps and makes gestures of such and such kinds."[9] The view is that psychological statements ultimately reduce to mere "motions and noises." Now, it's not difficult to appreciate the motivation for reducing psychology to behavior. Behavior, as we've said, is publicly available for observation, whereas internal mental states like pains, beliefs, and desires are not. As such, behavior can serve as an intersubjective verifiability requirement. This facilitates something we should want, namely, the ability for psychological statements to have public, sharable meanings that serve as vehicles of interpersonal communication. What's more, a meaning's being sharable is critical to our ability to analyze it, make generalizations with respect to it across multiple subjects, and potentially treat psychological conditions. It is perhaps no accident that logical and other forms of behaviorism took root during the early part of the twentieth century, rather immediately on the heels of the recent emergence of psychology as a robust field of scientific inquiry and study.

8. Carnap, "Psychology in Physical Language," 107.
9. Hempel, "Logical Analysis of Psychology, 17.

It is helpful to note here that behaviors, which are by their very nature observable and therefore useful because they are verifiable, are importantly distinct from actions. A behavior is whatever people or organisms (or even mechanical systems) *do* that is *publicly observable.* In humans, these can include physiological reactions and responses (e.g., perspiration, salivation, increased pulse rate), and bodily movements (e.g., raising an arm, flipping a light switch, uttering a sentence). In a computing system, they might result in digital outputs of various kinds. Actions, on the other hand, are behaviors typically performed intentionally and for reasons. As such, they are mentally quite robust. To get a sense of the difference between the two, consider Donald Davidson's description of his morning's events:

> This morning I was awakened by the sound of someone practicing the violin. I dozed a bit, then got up, washed, shaved, dressed, and went downstairs, turning off a light in the hall as I passed. I poured myself some coffee, stumbling on the edge of the dining room rug, and spilled my coffee fumbling for the *New York Times.*[10]

Some of the events Davidson describes are actions. Others are mere behaviors—events that simply befall him. Among those belonging to the first category are getting up, washing, shaving, and turning off the light. Those belonging to the second category include being awakened, stumbling on the rug, and spilling the coffee.

Consider the action of turning off the light. From the perspective of an observer, the viewable bodily movement is a flipping of a switch. That movement is followed, presumably, by the room's coming to no longer be illuminated. But what about this behavior makes it a turning-off-of-the-lights? If Davidson had been mistaken about the purpose of the switch, he might have flipped it intending to bring about some entirely different result—perhaps he'd intended to run the garbage disposal. So, at the time that he flips the switch, we, as observers, can't know what action Davidson takes himself to be performing simply by observing his behavior. Or to put matters more precisely, which action Davidson performs depends in part on his reasons for performing it. Suppose I am walking back and forth from one end of the room to the other. What am I doing? Am I pacing? Am I exercising? My legs are moving so as to carry me from one location to another. But that doesn't settle what it is I'm doing—what action I am performing. What action I am performing depends, in part, on *why* I am behaving as I am.

In the case of Davidson, to discover which action he is performing we would need to know what it is he saw in acting—in this case, in flipping the

10. Davidson, *Essays on Actions and Events*, 43.

switch—such that it seemed to him the thing to do. We would require access to his reason or reasons for acting. Reasons and their ilk are mental items. And unless mental items reduce entirely to bodily movements, or some other publicly available phenomenon, it would seem that observation alone cannot help us here. So, when it comes to "full-blooded actions," of the sort that humans (and perhaps members of some other species) regularly perform, it is arguable that a view like behaviorism is likely to fall short.[11] And this is because such actions involve a richer psychological structure than a view like logical behaviorism can account for.

The insistence that all psychological items can be reduced to behaviors marked a significant departure from the way psychological states were historically characterized. Following on a tradition heavily influenced by René Descartes, William James states that "Psychology is the Science of Mental Life, both of its phenomena and of their conditions. The phenomena are such things as we call feelings, desires, cognitions, reasonings, decisions, and the like."[12] Now, if the items of psychology are those James lists, then they are distinctively mental items. Mental items are those that are available to their subjects via introspection, such as the mood I'm now in. Or the thought you're now having. How do you and I come to know these things about our respective inner mental lives? When literal descriptions fail, we turn to metaphor. Introspection, we might say, is the exercise of turning one's gaze inward. It is direct and unmediated.[13] Metaphors aside, one need simply attend to one's own mental states, and *voila*! Introspection allows one to access what is available from the first-person perspective. I cannot introspect and hope to access your mental states, and neither can you so access mine.

Now imagine you wish to study the psychological items that James describes. Because such items are available only from the first-person perspective, it will be difficult indeed to draw conclusions about a broad category of human psychology. Any inquiry I engage in will have a sample size of one (me). That is hardly grounds for a reliable generalization! It is no surprise, therefore, that some have wished to reduce psychological states to behaviors, neurophysiological activity, and the like, being as these are occurrences observable from the third-person perspective. And as such, they lend themselves nicely to serving as the subjects of scientific inquiry. But can the mental be so reduced? Beliefs, desires, pains, perceptual states, and

11. The distinction between low-level activities (e.g., a spider that manipulates its limbs so as to move across the floor) and full-blooded actions is found in Frankfurt, "Problem of Action."

12. James, *Principles of Psychology*, 1.

13. Notice that my access to your mental states is indirect and must be mediated by your testimony or behavior.

so on have long been characterized as items belonging to the mind—or, as Descartes described it, to the part of a person that *thinks*.

II. MINDS AND BRAINS

Whether facts about human psychology ultimately reduce to physical facts—about physical outputs like behaviors, or else those pertaining to our underlying neurophysiology—is a question that has consumed philosophers of mind for a number of decades. Neuroscience tells us there is a high degree of correlation between mental phenomena (beliefs, desires, perceptions, sensations, intentions, and so on) and brain phenomena (neural events, chemical processes, and the like). Indeed, in many cases brain science can tell us which mental states (or events) correlate with which brain states (or events). Couple this with the fact that additional discoveries are being made at a seemingly ceaseless pace, and it is natural to suppose that we can eventually, with time, come to have an exhaustive list of such correlations. In other words, the empirical data makes reasonable the belief that for every mental state M, there is a physical correlate, P.[14] Of course, this acknowledgment won't by itself reveal precisely how the mind relates to the underlying physiology. But additional facts regarding the apparent causal connections between the two may bolster the case. For example, we know that if we increase the availability of certain chemicals in the brain (e.g., serotonin), it will affect the subject's mood. And we know that damage to certain regions of the brain will result in memory loss, or impairment of speech. So, the connection between the mental and the physical appears to be quite tight—so tight, in fact, that many of the phenomena we once attributed to the mind are now routinely explained by appealing solely to goings-on in the brain. It's not an enormous leap to conclude, on this basis, that the mental just is the physical, or, in any case, that it reduces to the physical, or that it utterly depends, in some other way, on the physical. Indeed, it appears to be a methodological assumption in some disciplines that if one cares to understand the mind, the thing to do is to examine the brain.

Two broad views concerning the relationship between the mind (or the mental) and the brain have emerged. They are substance dualism and physicalism. The first has enjoyed lengthy historical prominence, only to be surpassed in popularity by the second relatively recently. It is to these that I now turn.

14. This chapter admittedly does a good deal of hand-waving with respect to the neural correlates of mental states. For more, see Baker's chapter in this book, "Reinforcement in the Information Revolution."

II.a. Substance Dualism

According to the substance dualist, every human person is composed of two substances: a nonphysical mind (or soul), on the one hand, and a physical body, on the other.[15] The view is Platonic in its origins and received considerable development by Descartes. In Descartes's view, while it's true that I have both a mind and a body, the thing I am—and that which accounts for my continued existence over time—is my mind. As Descartes puts it, "But what then am I? A thing that thinks. What is that? A thing that doubts, understands, affirms, denies, is willing, is unwilling, and also imagines and has sensory perceptions."[16] The mind, then, is the substance in which all of the mental states and activities reside. From a Cartesian perspective, the mind and the body causally interact, as when my feeling hungry causes me to reach for the Cheetos, or when the tissue damage from a tumble off my bike produces a pain sensation in me. This feature of Descartes's view gave rise to a challenge by one of his contemporaries, Princess Elizabeth of Bohemia, in which she asked how it is that "the human soul can determine the movement of the animal spirits in the body so as to perform voluntary acts—being as it is merely a conscious (*pensante*) substance."[17] What Elizabeth seems to be pointing to is the inadequacy of the sort of mechanistic view of causation that (it would have been thought at the time) appears to account fairly well for physical-to-physical causation to account for mental-to-physical causation. And she wonders whether Descartes can offer an alternative given that he countenances mind-body causal interaction. As it turns out, Descartes cannot, and the mind-body problem has come to plague the sort of dualism Descartes defended ever since.

Just what "problem" the mind-body problem exposes for substance dualism remains a topic of dispute among philosophers. In particular, philosophers disagree about whether it reveals a deep incoherence in the very idea of mind-body causal interaction. But there's no question that substance dualism has fallen out of favor in philosophical circles. Interestingly, Elizabeth herself claims that she "could more readily allow that the soul has matter and extension than that an immaterial being has the capacity of moving a body and being affected by it."[18] She would sooner abandon dualism in favor of physicalism than attribute causal efficacy to an immaterial substance.

---

15. The terms *mind* and *soul* will be used interchangeably throughout to refer to a nonphysical part of persons, if any there be.

16. Descartes, *Meditations on First Philosophy*, 83.

17. Descartes, *Correspondence with Princess Elizabeth*, 53.

18. Descartes, *Correspondence with Princess Elizabeth*, 55.

Replying to the mind-body problem became a central task of Cartesians in the years following Descartes. And while it would be an error to minimize the role the problem played in whittling away at enthusiasm for the view, dualism was more likely eclipsed by physicalist theories over the course of the last century for empirical reasons. It is the demonstrably tight connection between the mental and the physical that rendered a view committed to the independence of my mind and my body (Descartes imagined it possible for me to exist without my body) untenable. And it is the ability to supplant previous appeals to an immaterial soul with explanations in terms of brain functioning that has boosted the plausibility of a physicalist alternative.

II.b. Physicalism

The majority of contemporary philosophers today are physicalists. The same is true of a good number of biologists, physicists, psychologists, and neuroscientists, as well, I understand, as a growing number of theologians.[19] Physicalists believe that human beings, like you and me, are composed entirely (and only) of physical stuff. The implication, of course, is that, contrary to what Descartes and Plato thought, you and I are neither wholly nor partly constituted by an immaterial soul. Instead, I just am my body. Or, perhaps more accurately, I am some part of my body, most probably some part of my brain or central nervous system. Consider a particular human person, Vanessa. If physicalism is correct, then Vanessa is through and through a material, or physical, entity. Now, it won't do to insist that Vanessa is identical to her whole body, since some parts of Vanessa's body could go missing (she could lose an arm in an unfortunate accident, for example) and Vanessa would nevertheless continue to exist. Suppose Vanessa is to undergo a radical transplantation surgery in which a significant number of her critical organs—her heart, lungs, liver, and kidneys, say—are to be switched out for new ones. I suspect Vanessa will be quite nervous about the upcoming surgery, but it's unlikely she will wonder who will exit the operating room upon the surgery's completion. Of course it will be Vanessa because none of those particular organs are essential to her being Vanessa. On the other hand, imagine Vanessa is instead facing a brain transplantation surgery in which

19. N. T. Wright puts his own view this way in "Mind, Spirit, Soul, and Body": "Just as I believe that we are wrong to look for a god-of-the-gaps, hiding somewhere in the unexplored reaches of quantum physics like a rare mammal lurking deep in the unexplored Amazon jungle, so I believe we are wrong to look for a soul-of-the-gaps, hiding in the bits that neuroscience hasn't yet managed to explain."

the surgeon will remove her brain and replace it with someone else's. Now it would seem reasonable for Vanessa to be quite concerned about just who will be wheeled out of the operating room. All of this is simply to suggest that if we are physical things, likely some parts or features will matter more than others. Some physicalists deny this. They claim instead that Vanessa is not identical to her brain (or any part of her body), but to a living organism.[20] Living organisms routinely lose bits (by, say, shedding skin cells) and acquire new ones, assimilating them into the complex system in a way that preserves the organism's existence, provided the replacement occurs gradually. But as these considerations regard a person's persistence over time, we needn't settle them here. What is central to the current discussion is that a physicalist, of any variety, claims that human persons are identical to an entity that is physical through and through.

Physicalism comes in a couple of forms. Reductive physicalists maintain that a person's mental life (i.e., her beliefs, desires, intentions, emotional states, and so on) is wholly reducible to neural events and chemical processes in her brain. The upshot is that there's nothing distinctive or special about the mental. The mental just is the physical. One concern about reductive physicalism is that it appears to be incompatible with the thesis that human beings sometimes act freely. After all, reductive physicalism implies that everything I do is caused by neural events in me. Suppose I raise my hand because I wish to hail a taxi. According to reductive physicalism, my hand's rising is not caused by my desire (to hail a cab), but rather by some neural event which sends a signal (ultimately) to my limb. But neural events, like all physical events, are governed by physical laws. And which physical laws there are, and whether they hold, are not matters that are up to me. So, it seems that my actions are not up to me.[21]

Nonreductive physicalists maintain, like their reductionistic counterparts, that there are only physical substances and that I am one such. But they deny that mental states can be reduced to brain states. That's because a belief, for example, cannot be wholly described, without loss of meaning, in purely physical terms. Among other things, beliefs have intentional content. They are "about" something. Take, for example, my belief that Seattle is in the state of Washington. My belief is about Seattle. But the corresponding neural event (whatever that may be) is not about anything at all; it is merely a biological state. And the same is true of desires, intentions, and perceptual states. The mental is anomalous—truly unique and irreducible. Notably,

20. See, e.g., van Inwagen, *Material Beings*; Olson, *Human Animal*; Merricks, "Resurrection of the Body."

21. An astute reader will note that free will is precluded on this picture only if free will is incompatible with determinism.

these mental items inhere in, or are states of, the physical item (the body).[22] In this way, nonreductive physicalists deny the substance dualist's insistence that mental items must inhere in a mental substance (the mind).

To avoid reduction, nonreductive physicalists characterize the relationship between the mental and the physical in a way that upholds a dependence of the former on the latter, but which avoids identity. The options are rather abundant, as several such relations have been proposed.[23] One way to unpack this dependence is in terms of supervenience. There are several versions of supervenience on offer, but for our purposes it will do to express the idea in terms of the well-known maxim, "no mental difference without a physical difference." In other words, if x and y are in every way alike physically, then they are in every way alike mentally. Importantly, the sort of dependence envisaged here is asymmetric (the mental is dependent on the physical, but the physical is not similarly dependent on the mental).

An attractive feature of nonreductive physicalism is that it preserves our understanding of action. For nonreductive physicalists, the mental is causally efficacious and able to bring about the bodily movements that count as our actions. Whereas the reductive physicalist will reduce the causal efficacy of the mental to physical causal relations at the subvenient base, nonreductive physicalists claim that the mental is itself causal. My running really is caused by my seeming to see a lion, and your eating the chocolate is indeed brought about by your desire to do so. But can the nonreductionist help herself to mental causation? A well-rehearsed argument, known as the "Exclusion Argument," suggests not.

Jaegwon Kim articulates the argument this way. Begin with a metaphysical doctrine likely to garner sympathy from any physicalist: the causal closure of the physical domain (or "closure principle," for short).

> Closure Principle: If a physical event has a cause at time t, it has a sufficient physical cause at t.[24]

In searching for causes of physical events, we never need venture beyond the realm of the physical.[25] As Kim puts it, "the physical domain is

22. A closely related view which characterizes these irreducible mental items as properties (rather than states or events), but nevertheless denies the existence of a mental substance, is property dualism.

23. Proposed relations include (but are not limited to) constitution, emergence, realization, and supervenience.

24. Kim, *Philosophy of Mind*, 214.

25. Indeed, Kim goes on to say that "if closure fails, theoretical physics would be in principle incompletable" and that "it seems clear that research programs in physics, and the rest of the physical sciences, presuppose something like the closure principle."

causally, and hence explanatorily, self-sufficient and self-contained."[26] Suppose, as our above story about action implies, that a mental event, m, causes a physical event, p. It follows from this and the closure principle that there is also a physical event, call it p^*, occurring at the same time as m that is a cause of p. To preserve nonreduction and hence the causal efficacy of the mental event m, we will need to posit that m is not identical to p^*. But now we have two purported causes of p: m and p^*. Unless this is a genuine case of overdetermination, it would seem that p leaves little (i.e., no) work for m to do. Indeed, as Kim puts it, "No event has two or more distinct sufficient causes, all occurring at the same time, unless it is a genuine case of overdetermination."[27]

Genuine cases of overdetermination occur when two independent causal chains converge at a single effect as when a house fire is caused by a short circuit and a lightning strike simultaneously, or when two bullets hit a person at the same time, either of which would have been sufficient to kill him. We can allow for some causal overdetermination (surely such occurrences *can* happen), but one would expect them to be rare. However, if every case of mental-to-physical causation involves (at least) two sufficient causes, then every case in which I act will be a case of overdetermination. Now multiply this by all actions performed by persons at any time in history and the overdetermination will be very widespread indeed![28]

Embracing this result renders mental states epiphenomenal, or causally inert, and undercuts the familiar account of action with which we began. To vindicate m as a genuine cause of p, m should be able to bring about p without there being a synchronous p^*. But in any version of physicalism, every mental event has a physical causal partner (or correlate) that would have brought about the effect, even if m had not.

Kim takes the lesson of the exclusion argument to be that, insofar as we wish to preserve mental causation, we must reduce m to p^*. Our understanding of agency can be maintained with the proviso that it is not my belief, desire, or intention, but rather the respective state's physical substrate (or realizer, if you prefer), which causes the bodily movement that constitutes my action. Actions therefore involve physical causal sequences through and through. The upshot is to deny that the mental is something

---

Philosophy of Mind, 215.

26. Kim, *Philosophy of Mind*, 214.

27. Kim, *Philosophy of Mind*, 216.

28. Some have argued that the variety of overdetermination involved in cases of mental causation are innocuous. See Bennett, "Why the Exclusion Problem Seems Intractable"; "Exclusion Again"; Sider, "What's so Bad about Overdetermination?"

over and above the physical. Or, put differently, if one is a physicalist, then one should be a reductive physicalist.

Much ink has been spilled over the last two decades in efforts to reply to the exclusion argument and preserve mental causation. These attempts take us too far afield form our present purpose to warrant explication here. Suffice it to say that there is likely no view about the nature of the mind that comes free of cost. As they say, there are no free lunches. And yet one of these, broadly construed, is likely (roughly) correct. It is not my aim to argue for one over the others. But which view one leans toward will determine how one thinks about the possibility of thinking machines—or thinking things of any kind.

III. MINDS AND MACHINES

In this final section, I want to draw out some implications of what has thus far been said for certain questions we might have with regard to AI. Naturally, this is not an exhaustive set of questions. And I don't profess to provide answers. Instead, I take the following (admittedly brief) discussion to be instructive for thinking about how to go about answering some of the vexing questions that arise with respect to artificial intelligence.

Let's begin by returning to Turing's original question: Can machines think? In short, I suppose it depends on what one means by "think." Since Descartes, thinking has been understood as the defining feature of the mental. Now, if mental items are wholly reducible to neuronal occurrences, then the matter becomes largely an empirical one. The same is true if mentality reduces to behavior. Both nonreductive and dualistic theories deny the reducibility of mental items and accordingly will insist on conditions that are not available from the third-person perspective but are instead phenomenal, or else that depend on the presence of states with certain sorts of content, as in the case of beliefs, desires, and the like.

Now, I concede that I've taken a rather narrow path to understanding the intelligence component of artificial intelligence. Of course, a great many things can be meant by "intelligence." I have focused on thinking, much as Turing did. But other concepts like processing, learning, understanding, and inferring may also be relevant. I don't have space to attend to each of these here. This is likely no great loss since the phrase "artificial intelligence" has largely been deemed imperfect from the outset and demonstrably overreaches the sorts of actual technological developments thought to fall under its umbrella. Most of these have specific and more fitting names—for example, machine learning, symbolic systems, big data, supervised learning, and neural networks. That said, I am less concerned here with the precise technologies than I am with the ambitious questions that have occupied many thinkers when they've sought to imagine what might be possible.

And this brings us to the matter of artificiality. This too might have several meanings. I deem a comparison with grand concepts like *natural* to prove fruitless since it is notoriously difficult to define what is and isn't natural in a way that renders intuitive results (by including the right things and excluding all the others). But here's a way of getting at the sort of question I take many to have when they think about thinking machines. Let's first take a detour back to mental phenomena. Mental states are often thought to be multiply realizable. Consider pain, for example. Pain in humans supervenes on (or perhaps it is identical to) certain processes that occur in the human brain. But octopus pain—a phenomenon I have every reason to believe is quite real—is realized by drastically different physical occurrences (owing to its different physiology). Moreover, if one thinks it coherent to imagine an extraterrestrial being with an altogether unique underlying physical structure to anything found on earth nevertheless experiencing pain, then pain is a concept that is definable independently of the structure that realizes it. Perhaps other mental states—even thinking—are like this. But, then, that's precisely what is at issue in the various theories about the metaphysics of mind we've considered.

But now we might wonder whether the examples we've so far given bear something essential in common. Is it relevant that extraterrestrials and octopuses and humans are composed of material stuff that cannot be produced in a lab or a factory? It's not obvious why it should be. Just as we are wont to ask upon which biological structures mentality might supervene, we may also ask whether mentality can supervene on synthetic structures. To answer in the affirmative is to carve out a metaphysical possibility. It is not to commit ourselves to a view about the physical possibility of such an occurrence nor, certainly, is it to stake a claim with respect to how close technological advances are to actualizing this possibility. Interestingly, it isn't even to articulate an account of what an underlying structure must be like to give rise to mentality. It is to do something quite different. It is to start with the mental. It is to ask what mentality *is*. What does it require? And what, precisely, is the relationship between it and the physical? It likely won't come as a surprise that these are deep philosophical questions about the metaphysics of mind. And while I believe we can make progress with respect to them, they will undoubtedly remain perennial questions.

In the interim, here is a strategy we might employ: At the very least, let's begin by making our assumptions about the mind explicit. If, in your view, thinking requires an immaterial soul, then only entities to which such an item can be attached (or from which such an item can emerge) will make the cut. If, on the other hand, you believe that mentality depends on physicality, then how so? Does the former reduce to latter, or does it merely supervene on it? Once these commitments are front and center, we can have a robust conversation regarding what sorts of entities are capable of satisfying the conditions of mentality. But if these presuppositions are allowed to lurk in the background and out of plain view, we will almost certainly talk past one another.

The downsides to this are quite real. Could we create a machine such that powering it off would be immoral? The moral requirements with respect to the proper treatment of a being depend rather significantly on what sorts of experiences it can have. My children's first pet was a betta fish. It once (quite unintentionally) went unfed for a staggering nine days. How egregious a moral failure this was depends, in part, on the extent to which the lack of food caused the fish to suffer. Even if it had died (it didn't), the loss of life wouldn't necessarily, all by itself, have constituted a moral failure. I've killed many a house plant by not watering it. Few will contend that killing a plant is immoral. Now, I'm fairly confident that betta fish have rather limited sets of experiences. A dog would have fared much worse and undoubtedly would have suffered greatly, certainly enough to make the omission morally unconscionable. (This is precisely why a fish makes a better pet for busy households with young children and preoccupied parents than does a dog.) It is also why we (properly) feel less remorse when squishing a spider than we do harming a cat. Of course, we could be wrong about what sorts of mental states a thing enjoys and thereby be incorrect in our moral assessments. Regardless, the metaphysical facts ground the truth of the relevant moral claims. As such, the metaphysics ought not be ignored—and we can begin by being transparent about what metaphysical presuppositions we bring to the relevant discussions.

I'll conclude with a final matter of importance. When the topic of the possibility of thinking machines arises, many begin to wonder if there is something distinctive, and important, about humans such that our unique value is not undermined by the presence of machinery capable of completing many of our tasks and endowed with the ability to think and have experiences. Christian theists, in particular, are apt to worry about the doctrine of *imago Dei*, according to which human persons (or so it's often understood) bear the image of the divine. This has sometimes led theists to view an immaterial soul as a particularly attractive feature by which to mark a human person. This is too quick. First, it's not at all clear that the *imago Dei* doctrine is best understood ontologically.[29] Second, if an imma-terial soul is the substance that underlies all mental states, then anything exhibiting mentality will *ex hypothesi* have a soul. But now the motivation for the original appeal to the soul—that it secures the distinctness of human persons—has vanished.

It's also noteworthy that within Christianity there is robust debate about whether substance dualism is a view properly understood to be suggested by Scripture and creedal doctrine, or is instead a product of philosophical (notably, Platonic) influence.[30] Christians, and indeed the-ists generally, might find dualism less objectionable than their nontheistic counterparts given their view that God created, and continually interacts with, the physical universe. In this way, they already allow for instances of nonphysical-to-physical causation. It is perhaps largely for this reason that Christian physicalists have not tended to list the mind-body problem among their primary motivations for denying dualism and adopting physicalism. Even so, a growing number of Christian philosophers and theologians reject substance dualism.[31] And so it would not be accurate to regard an appeal to the soul as the distinguishing mark of a human person as an essential Christian commitment.

Theistic views aside, a being's value needn't depend on its status as ontologically or phenomenologically distinct from other existent beings or entities. And while it may be true for any entity that it either has mental states or lacks them (dolphins have them, flower pots lack them), beings that have mental states can differ from one another considerably (the inner mental life of a dolphin is likely quite different from that of a bat). Were we to discover thinking extraterrestrials, it wouldn't thereby follow that human mental phenomena would in any way be diminished. Nor would this be true were it to turn out to be possible for certain synthetic structures to manifest thought. Such considerations are worth bearing in mind as we consider the question about wherein mentality can reside.

29. For an alternative conception of the doctrine, see De Cruz and Smedt, "*Imago Dei* as a Work in Progress."

30. For a range of views on this topic, see Murphy, *Bodies and Souls*; Wright, "Mind, Spirit, Soul, and Body"; Rickabaugh, "Dismantling Bodily Resurrections Objections to Mind-Body Dualism"; Lugioyo, "Whose Interpretation? Which Anthropology?" and Cooper, "OK, But Whose Misunderstanding," in Crisp et al., *Neuroscience and the Soul*.

31. Notable examples include Baker, *Persons and Bodies*; Corcoran, *Rethinking Human Nature*; Merricks, "Resurrection of the Body"; Murphy, *Bodies and Souls*; O'Connor, *Persons and Causes*; van Inwagen, *Material Beings*.

BIBLIOGRAPHY

Ayer, A. J., ed. *Logical Positivism*. New York: Free, 1959.

Baker, Lynne Rudder. *Persons and Bodies*. Cambridge: Cambridge University Press, 2000.

Bennett, Karen. "Exclusion Again." In *Being Reduced: New Essays on Reduction, Explanation, and Causation*, edited by Jakob Hohwy and Jesper Kallestrup, 280–307. New York: Oxford University Press, 2008.

———. "Why the Exclusion Problem Seems Intractable, and How, Just Maybe, to Tract It," *Nous* 37 (2003) 471–97.

Carnap, Rudolph. "The Elimination of Metaphysics through the Logical Analysis of Language." *Erkenntnis* (1932) 60–81.

Corcoran, Kevin. *Rethinking Human Nature: A Christian Materialist Alternative to the Soul*. Grand Rapids: Baker, 2006.

Crisp, Thomas M., et al., eds. *Neuroscience and the Soul: The Human Person in Philosophy, Science, and Theology*. Grand Rapids: Eerdmans, 2016.

Davidson, Donald. *Essays on Actions and Events*. Oxford: Oxford University Press, 2001.

De Cruz, Helen, and Jovan D. Smedt. "The *Imago Dei* as a Work in Progress: A Perspective from Paleoanthropology." *Zygon* 49 (2014) 135–56.

Descartes, René. "Correspondence with Princess Elizabeth." In *Modern Philosophy*, edited by Forrest E. Baird, 53–56. Englewood Cliffs, NJ: Prentice Hall, 2008.

Descartes, René. *Meditations on First Philosophy*. In *Selected Philosophical Writings*, 73–122. Cambridge: Cambridge University Press, 1988.

Frankfurt, Harry. "The Problem of Action." *American Philosophical Quarterly* 15 (1978) 157–62.

Hempel, Carl. "The Logical Analysis of Psychology." In *Readings in Philosophy of Psychology*, edited by Ned Block, 1–14. Cambridge, MA: Harvard University Press, 1980.

James, William. *The Principles of Psychology*. New York: Henry Holt, 1890.

Kim, Jaegwon. *Philosophy of Mind*. Boulder, CO: Westview, 2011.

Merricks, Trenton. "The Resurrection of the Body." In *The Oxford Handbook of Philosophical Theology*, edited by Thomas P. Flint and Michael C. Rea, 476–90. Oxford: Oxford University Press, 2009.

Murphy, Nancey. *Bodies and Souls, or Spirited Bodies?* Cambridge: Cambridge University Press, 2006.

O'Connor, Timothy. *Persons and Causes: The Metaphysics of Free Will*. Oxford: Oxford University Press, 2000.

Olson, Eric. *The Human Animal: Personal Identity Without Psychology*. New York: Oxford University Press, 1997.

Rickabaugh, Brandon. "Dismantling Bodily Resurrection Objections to Mind-Body Dualism." In *Christian Physicalism? Philosophical Theological Criticisms*, edited by Keith R. Loftin and Joshua R. Farris, 295–317. Lanham, MD: Lexington, 2018.

Russell, Bertrand. *The Problems of Philosophy*. Oxford: Clarendon, 1912.

Sider, Ted. "What's so Bad about Overdetermination?" *Philosophy and Phenomenological Research* 67 (2003) 719–26.

Turing, A. M. "Computing Machinery and Intelligence." *Mind* 59 236 (1950) 433–60.

van Inwagen, Peter. *Material Beings*. Ithaca, NY: Cornell University Press, 1990.

Wright, N. T. "Mind, Spirit, Soul, and Body: All for One and One for All Reflections on Paul's Anthropology in his Complex Contexts." Presented at the Society of Christian Philosophers Regional Meeting, Fordham University, 2011. http://www.ntwrightpage.com/Wright_SCP_MindSpiritSoulBody.htm

4

A Theological Framework for Reflection on Artificial Intelligence

Michael D. Langford

THE NECESSITY AND INEVITABILITY OF THEOLOGICAL REFLECTION

On the first Sunday of Lent, the Orthodox Church celebrates the "Feast of Orthodoxy," which commemorates the official restoration of the use of icons in worship by Empress Theodora in AD 843, ending a period of disputation in the Byzantine Church known as the "iconoclastic controversy." Icons are pieces of sacred artwork that are used in the practice of worship. In the Middle Ages, those who opposed the use of icons claimed that it violated the Second Commandment, which forbids the use of idols, and that it heretically attempts to circumscribe the ineffable transcendence of God. Proponents of icon use pointed out that icons are not idols because they are not worshipped. Rather, icons are "venerated," meaning that they are highly valued or revered, as "windows into heaven"; icons are not understood to be

God, but rather are a means to reflect on God and be viscerally drawn into the presence of God.[1]

In many ways, icons are pieces of technology. They represent the application of knowledge to solve a problem—in this case, the problem of how to worship God—which, because problems exist in created reality, inevitably use creaturely media. In other words, technology involves novel techniques and tools that interact with their environment. Religions have never existed apart from technology because religion exists in the midst of people who must interact with their world. However, religion and technology have always had an up-and-down relationship, and the iconoclastic controversy is an apt example. Anything new to a canon of tradition is adopted critically, and new technologies are no exception; it can take centuries of careful theological deliberation to garner the wisdom to best employ the introduction of any particular technology to a religious tradition. Notice that, in the iconoclastic controversy, the use of icons was neither denigrated nor affirmed based on their novelty, but rather on deeply held theological convictions.

Artificial intelligence has emerged more rapidly than nearly any technology in history. The rate of development and adoption of AI has meant that our digital wisdom is still catching up. For Christians, this digital wisdom must include theology, or what we have to say about God and the world from the perspective of faith.[2] In short, theological reflection on AI is in dire need as these technologies become more and more ingrained in our lives every day.[3]

In much the same way that we might say that technology ineluctably develops as humanity interacts with the world around it, we might also say that theology ineluctably develops as Christians interact with the world around them. Christianity did not begin as a bundle of theoretical propositions. Rather, Christianity began with a group of people following Jesus,

1. For more on the historical particularities of the iconoclastic controversy and the theological and liturgical arguments for and against the use of icons and images, see Pelikan, *Spirit of Eastern Christendom*, 91–145.

2. Scottish theologian John Macquarrie helpfully defines theology as "the study which, through participation in and reflection upon a religious faith, seeks to express the content of this faith in the clearest and most coherent language available." Macquarrie, *Principles of Christian Theology*, 1. Note that this definition takes into account a perception of God that is possible through the participation in faith, which enables a certain kind of knowing.

3. Futurist Martin Ford notes that "it is becoming evident that AI is poised to become one of the most important forces shaping our world. Unlike more specialized innovations, artificial intelligence is becoming a true general-purpose technology. In other words, it is evolving into a utility—not unlike electricity—that is likely to ultimately scale across every industry, every sector of our economy, and nearly every aspect of science, society and culture." Ford, *Architects of Intelligence*, 2.

coming to believe in him as the Christ and his teachings about the kingdom of God.[4] While it is certainly true that what Jesus had to say to his disciples included doctrinal ideas, they were often ambiguous, usually analogic, and frequently misunderstood. God did not reveal much theologically to Moses at the Burning Bush when the divine name was given to him; "YHWH" merely means "I am who I am."[5] It took Moses many years of following God's direction and trusting God's promises for him to discover more about who God is, what God says about the world, and what God wanted of him and his people. In the same way, the disciples mostly did not understand who Jesus was during his lifetime; it was only after his resurrection that they came to understand more clearly who Jesus was, what he had to say about the world, and what he wanted of them. Likewise, it took many years after the time of Jesus for Christians to come to understand more clearly who God is in light of the Christ.

In fact, the text of the New Testament might be seen precisely as the work of Christ-followers as they worked out, in thought and language, their theology in consideration of questions that came up, or they believed would come up, in their interactions with others. The Gospel of Matthew appears to be written by a Jewish Christian, explaining in terms of that culture and religion about the person and work of Jesus.[6] Likewise, the Gospel of Luke is striking for its Gentile character, explaining Jesus within that cultural milieu.[7] Paul famously spoke on the Areopagus to the Athenians, connecting

4. Church historian Bernhard Lohse notes that, in response to Jesus's question to his disciples, "But who do you say that I am?," the first expression of dogma was Peter's confession of faith, "You are the Messiah, the Son of the living God" (Matt 16:15–16). Theology developed as followers of Jesus worked out the expanding meaning of this basic confession as they encountered other spheres of life. See Lohse, *Short History of Christian Doctrine*, 8–12.

5. Exod 3:14.

6. The Jewish character of Matthew's Gospel is evident from its many references to the Old Testament, and assumptions concerning the knowledge of the reader. In fact, Matthew's connection to the Old Testament is a likely reason that it was placed first in the New Testament canon. "The narrator of Matthew's Gospel exhibits a repeated concern to identify particular events in Jesus's life as the direct fulfillments of specific Jewish Scriptures." Nienhuis, *Concise Guide to Reading the New Testament*, 21–22.

7. The character of Luke is such that it seems it was constructed to appeal to a Gentile audience characteristic of the Mediterranean world. "Luke's Gospel begins with one, long, carefully composed sentence that is notable *not* for its theological claims but for its undeniable *secularity*. Scholars have long observed that Luke has deliberately constructed this opening in imitation of the Hellenistic historians and biographers of his age: from the acknowledgement of other available Gospels, to the listing of his credentials as a historian and the dedication to his patron 'Theophilus,' this piece of Holy Scripture begins much the same as any worldly history would have in the first-century Greco-Roman world." Nienhuis, *Concise Guide to Reading the New Testament*, 51.

their beliefs and questions to an understanding of the God of Jesus Christ.[8] And the many epistles from Paul and others work out who God is, what God has to say about the world, and what God would have us do in light of what is going on in different contexts. It is when we encounter new contexts that new questions emerge that demand theological reflection. This is what is meant by the dictum: mission is "the mother of theology."[9] So we see a new opportunity: As we embrace God's mission in a world of AI, we must theologically grapple with this new means of technology.

The theological questions before us in a digital age are pressing. What does God think of AI? Is AI good or evil? Will AI save us? What sort of future will AI give us? In what follows, I want to briefly introduce a few theological concepts that will hopefully help equip us for theological reflection on AI. We will begin with the question of epistemology, or how it is that we come by knowledge; in the realm of theology, this centers on revelation. We will then touch on the doctrine of creation, including the understanding of what it means to be a human creature. Next, we will review aspects of the doctrine of salvation. Finally, we will discuss eschatology, the study of "last things." I will close by posing some thoughts on what and how theology fits within our evolving digital wisdom.

REVELATION

Theology is always heretical. By that I mean that, despite our best efforts and faithful devotion, what we have to say about God will never be fully correct. We will always be wrong to some degree. How could it be otherwise? In theology, we are speaking about something that we cannot speak about, using words and thoughts of our universe to describe a being that, as its creator, is ontologically different than our universe. Yet, God gave us our ability to think and communicate, and God provided us with means within our created reality to know who God is—the beauty of nature, the proclamations of God's people, our internal orientation toward beauty and goodness, and the incarnation of God's self-expression.[10] Because God's revelation comes to

---

8. See Acts 17:16–34.

9. Kähler, *Schriften zur Chrisologie und Mission*, 190.

10. Athanasius makes the argument that humanity should have been able to know "God the Word" merely by means of its own creation in the "Divine Image" (12.1). However, in light of human "forgetfulness" and "weakness," God provided other ways: "the harmony of creation," the words of "holy men," and "by knowing the law even, to cease from all lawlessness and live a virtuous life." Yet, this was not sufficient; Athanasius likens the renewal of a defaced painting to the work of God renewing the divine image in creation. This is because humanity "rejected the contemplation of God, and with

us through creaturely media, we have no other recourse in response than to think and talk about God with our own words, though we do so humbly and with great respect, knowing we will never be fully right. This is why Thomas Aquinas called theological language neither univocal (exactly right) nor equivocal (exactly wrong), but rather analogical.[11]

In Romans 12, Paul encourages believers to resist being "conformed to this world, but be transformed by the renewing of your minds, so that you may discern what is the will of God" (Rom 12:2).[12] Paul calls the Roman Christians toward theological reflection that is grounded not only in sound doctrine, but also in the practice of Christian love; he urges them to "not to think of yourself more highly than you ought" (12:3), to "let love be genuine" (12:9), and to "live in harmony with one another" (12:16). He thus affirms the necessity of community for Christian life, reminding them that we are "one body in Christ, and individually we are members one of another" (12:5). One of the markers of this one-but-many community is the diversity of people and abilities therein. "We have gifts that differ according to the grace given to us: prophecy, in proportion to faith; ministry, in ministering; the teacher, in teaching; the exhorter, in exhortation; the giver, in generosity; the leader, in diligence; the compassionate, in cheerfulness" (12:6–8). The work of theological reflection is therefore not merely an exercise in the exegesis of biblical texts or existential dilemmas, nor is it merely the result of reasoned reflection on observation or traditional beliefs; the process of the practice of theology is carried out in the midst of a diverse community grounded in spiritual practices and mutual love.

In the verse above, the words "in proportion to faith" (Greek: *kata ten analogia tes pisteos*) have taken on a great deal of meaning. The verse seems to be saying that gifts of faith (such as prophecy, which is speaking the truth of God) are given in accordance with, or proportionate to, the faith of the giftee. This is clearly presented not as a matter of ranking gifts, as if the more faithful get the more profound gifts, but rather seems to be explaining the

their eyes downward, as though sunk in the deep, were seeking about for God in nature and in the world of sense, feigning gods for themselves of mortal men and demons; to this end the loving and general Saviour of all, the Word of God, takes to Himself a body, and as Man walks among men and meets the senses of all men half-way, to the end, I say, that they who think that God is corporeal may from what the Lord effects by His body perceive the truth, and through Him recognize the Father." Athanasius, "On the Incarnation," §12, 14, and 15.

11. Aquinas, *Summa Theologica*, 1.13.5–6.

12. All Scripture references are from the New Revised Standard Version.

existence of differences as a matter of course. In other words, since every-one's faith looks different, so will the gifts of the faithful.[13]

However, these same Greek words can also be translated as "according to the measure of the faith," which some have taken to mean that Paul was advocating that the words of those who claim to prophecy, or speak God's words, should be measured against the _content of the faith_ of the believers: "Well then, we have gifts that differ in accordance with the grace that has been given to us, and we must use them appropriately. If it is prophecy, we must prophesy according to the pattern of the faith."[14] That is, if someone speaks and claims it is prophecy, that speech should be judged to be God's revealed truth insofar as it compares favorably with what the Christian community has already judged to be God's revealed truth. This understand-ing is reflected in the Latin translation of the words "in proportion to faith" as _analogia fidei_ or _regula fidei_, which mean "analogy of faith" or "rule of faith," respectively. Thus the term "rule of faith" became used among early Christians, and is still used today, for the ultimate authority in the Christian belief system, such as a creed or a basic profession of faith in Jesus Christ.

The terms "analogy of faith" and "rule of faith" posit the primacy of faith-received revelation in articulating our theology. Swiss theologian Karl Barth was particularly concerned with theology that merely defines God in terms of our own ideologies.[15] Instead, he said, our theology must emerge out of God's self-revelation, principally in the person and work of Jesus Christ, as grasped in faith. Our words about God must mirror God's own Word about God. Thus we do not define God out of an _analogia entis_, or "analogy of being," that merely likens God to our own conceptions of

13. The image of "body" that Paul uses as an analogy for the church illustrates his conception of the gathering of believers to be a unity of diversity. "Paul's comparison of the unity of the Christian community's diverse members and variety of ways of acting to the human body and its various parts rules out any such rigid uniformity. Indeed, the analogy of the body not only allows for, but even emphasizes the necessity of, diversity, a diversity based on the multifaceted abundance of God's grace itself. That rich and multifaceted grace finds expression in the various ways Christians are moved by grace to enact their faith, whether in speech or deed (vv. 6–8)." Achtemeier, _Romans_, 196.

14. This example is the translation given in N. T. Wright's New Testament for Everyone translation. See Wright, _Paul for Everyone: Romans Part 2_. There are other translations that offer similar interpretations, such as the New Century Version and the Holman Christian Standard Bible.

15. Barth was reacting in particular to the German liberal theologies in the tradi-tion of Friedrich Schleiermacher, Albrecht Ritschl, Wilhelm Herrmann, and Adolf von Harnack that, in Barth's mind, sought to redefine Christian dogma in terms of human experience and rationality rather than the revelation of a "wholly other" God. The dan-ger of the liberal approach, asserted Barth, was that it sought to replace God with the individual as the arbiter of theological reflection.

existence. Rather, we must allow God to define God, and we receive that revelation "in accordance to faith," or via the *analogia fidei*. Barth would say that instead of slavishly adhering to a set of doctrinal principles of our own liking, we must allow faith to be our ruler when it comes to our understanding of God, what God has to say about the world, and how God would have us live. It is God's revelation in Christ by the power of the Spirit, as grasped in faith, that is the rule of faith.[16]

Christians believe God has provided revelation of truth through different means—through Scripture, or careful deliberation, or our own experiences, or the thoughts of others[17]—but that God has revealed God's own self in the person and work of Jesus, a revelation that we receive through the work of the Holy Spirit in the gift of faith. It is this self-revelation that governs or rules all other bits of revelation. Thus Christian epistemology, or theory of knowledge, must begin and end with God's revelation in Jesus Christ. Scripture is the Christian's primary witness to this revelation, though it is not the revelation itself; nevertheless, Scripture is how God's Word is revealed to us, through the ongoing work of the Holy Spirit, and is therefore trustworthy and authoritative.[18]

Therefore, for theological reflection on AI, we must begin with God's revelation. We may not remain in the naturalistic realm and merely reach into the theological realm when we need ammunition for whatever we want to say or believe. For it to be *Christian* epistemology, reflection must begin with revelation. This is not to say that God does not use AI in revelation; God will use whatever God wants to use.[19] However, anything that we believe may be revelatory must be measured against what God has already revealed centrally in Christ by the power of the Spirit as witnessed to in Scripture and grasped in faith. We garner knowledge by other means as

16. Thus it is that Barth understands revelation as that which "rules" our faith. "The rule of faith may be understood quite generally as a description of the positive relationship of man to what is prospectively and retrospectively true for all in the light of the epiphany of Jesus Christ, to the divine truths of redemption which are to be proclaimed and heard in all ages and places." Barth, *Church Dogmatics* IV/2, 245.

17. Scripture, reason, tradition, and experience are generally understood to be the four sources of theology.

18. Theologian Stanley Grenz notes that the Bible's authority comes not merely by means of its origin, but by means of its nature as a channel of revelation for the Holy Spirit. "Whatever authority the Bible carries as a trustworthy book, it derives from the trustworthiness of the divine revelation it discloses and ultimately from the Spirit who infallibly speaks through it." Grenz, *Theology for the Community of God*, 402.

19. Barth makes the point that to limit sources of revelation is to limit God's freedom. "God may speak to us through Russian Communism, a flute concerto, a blossoming shrub, or a dead dog. We do well to listen to Him if He really does." Barth, *Church Dogmatics* I/1, 55.

well, of course; for instance, God created the natural sciences as means to understand the world around us, the cosmos surrounding us, and the cells within us. Theology does not compete with science for epistemological primacy; rather, they are complementary. Science, such as that which creates AI, tells us about that which we can observe. Theology tells us about God, what God has to say about the world, and what we must do. Science is built for measuring that which we observe around us in order to build conceptual models useful for interacting with our world in myriad ways. Theology is built for understanding God, reality, and ourselves so that we might understand what things mean and how we must live in relationship to God, others, and the world. And while the epistemological community of science holds itself to objectivity, verifiability, and precision for successful outcomes, the epistemological community of revelation bases its work in love, worship, humility, and obedience.

CREATION

The first line of the Nicene Creed reads, "I believe in God the Father almighty, maker of heaven and earth." To say that God is "maker" means that God is the origin of all existence. Not just rocks and trees and animals, but also atoms and stars—even time and space itself. To say that God created everything is to say that God created *ex nihilo*, or out of nothing. Christianity believes that, before anything existed, God was, and just God was. And then God brought the cosmos into existence.[20] This understanding depicts a God who is distinct from creation, prior and foundational to creation, and it also suggests a God who created for some purpose since God did not need to create, being self-subsistent apart from it. We might even go so far as to

20. Theologian Dietrich Bonhoeffer notes that the nature of Genesis 1 is such that God is denoted as the source and origin of everything, and that we cannot see behind this beginning to make any claims about the creator. Bonhoeffer interprets this to mean that this implies a freedom in God such that God was not conditioned by any necessity. "In the beginning God created heaven and earth. In other words the Creator—in freedom!—creates the creature. The connection between them is conditioned by nothing except freedom, which means that it is unconditioned. This rules out every application of causal categories for an understanding of the creation. The relation between Creator and creature can never be interpreted in terms of cause and effect, because between the Creator and creature there stands no law of thought or law of effect or anything else. Between Creator and creature there is simply *nothing*. For freedom is exercised in, and on the basis of, this nothing. No kind of necessity that could, or indeed had to, ensue in creation can therefore be demonstrated to exist in God. There is simply nothing that provides the ground for creation. Creation comes out of this nothing." Bonhoeffer, *Creation and Fall*, 32–33.

imagine that, whatever precisely that purpose is, it is still ongoing since our cosmos is still here.

But God did not stop being creator after the creation of the universe. God continues to be "maker." While science tells us that new matter does not come into existence since the birth of the universe, that does not mean that God does not continue to make new things. New life comes into existence all the time. New ideas and relationships, too. New mountains and planets and stars come into existence, though very slowly. God creates new realities for us every day. The fact that God is maker does not merely mean that God creates time, space, and matter. It means that God is the one who establishes all sorts of beginnings, without which we and the rest of the cosmos would not exist.[21] We might even say that God continues to exhibit divine creatorship in the birth and development of technologies such as AI, through humans of course, just as we might say that God exhibits divine creatorship in the birth and development of friendships or vaccines or art. This does not mean that God's creations are not misused, but merely that God continues to create because God is maker.

The Bible begins with the saga of creation. Within it, we are told of the uniqueness of humanity among this creation; humans seem to be the climax of God's work in Genesis 1, and, among creatures, have a special interactivity with God in Genesis 2. This is not to say that God does not value the rest of creation; to the contrary, God calls creation "good" several times in Genesis 1, and God calls the completed creation "very good" in Genesis 1:31 (Hebrew: *tov me'od*).[22] However, the text of Genesis suggests

21. Orthodox theologian Kallistos Ware points out that the nature of God as creator means that God is continually creating. "In saying that God is Creator of the world, we do not mean merely that he set things in motion by an initial act 'at the beginning,' after which they go on functioning by themselves. God is not just a cosmic clockmaker, who winds up the machinery and then leaves it to keep ticking on its own. On the contrary, creation is *continual*. If we are to be accurate when speaking of creation, we should not use the past tense but the continuous present. We should say, not 'God made the world, and me in it,' but 'God is *making* the world, and me in it, here and now, at this moment and always.' Creation is not an event in the past, but a relationship in the present. If God did not continue to exert his creative will at every moment, the universe would immediately lapse into non-being; nothing could exist for a single second if God did not will it to be." Ware, *Orthodox Way*, 45. God's "making the world" is found not merely in bringing matter into being *ex nihilo*, but also in the formation of character, virtue, relationships, ideas, affection, and the like.

22. "If everything and everyone that the sovereign God made is *tov me'od*, then to be what the Creator intended must also be good—creatureliness is good." Brunner, Butler, and Swoboda, *Introducing Evangelical Ecotheology*, 119. This intrinsic goodness of creation is born out of the goodness of God. "As intended by God, creation is good. Indeed, it is very good (*tov me'od*), a judgement that connotes beauty and peace. The universe originates not out of struggle or battle or conflict, as portrayed in so many

that God has a central relationship with humans in the midst of creation. In Genesis 1, humans are the only creatures that are bestowed the image of God: "So God created humankind in his image, in the image of God he created them; male and female he created them" (Gen 1:27). In Latin, "image of God" is *imago Dei*, a concept that is central to theological reflection on the nature of humanity, or "theological anthropology."

Christianity emphasizes the importance of the *imago Dei* to theological anthropology because it asserts the sacredness of every person and points to the foundational factor that differentiates humans from other creatures, constituting some sort of indelible element to human nature. It also communicates a qualitative connection between humanity and God, though Scripture is silent on precisely what the essence of that connection is. This textual vacuum has, over the years, led many theologians to fill it with their own preferred cultural values, identifying different abilities or capacities in humans as constituting the *imago Dei*.[23] Some have asserted that the *imago Dei* is rationality, claiming that is what is central to being human. Others have stated that it is free will, communality, ethicality, or creativity. Ironically, these claims subtly arrogate qualities that are central to God, thus circularly affirming what we like best about ourselves. For example, if I really like human creativity, I could posit: "Well, the creed says that God is maker, and we are created in God's image, so we must be makers, too!" Of course, when we do that, we are merely picking the aspect of God that we like the most about ourselves.[24] However, there is nothing in Genesis or the rest of Scripture that identifies precisely what constitutes the *imago Dei*, or if it is indeed an ability or capacity.[25] It seemed enough for the authors of Genesis to declare humanity as created in the image of God, identifying humans as distinct and special, and leave it at that. This seems theologically important, for if the *imago Dei* were reducible to an ability of capacity, it would rank the extent to which the image of God resides in individuals.[26]

---

ancient creation stories, but through a seemingly effortless and struggle-free divine speaking and making. In contrast to other narratives, the biblical narrative testifies to an ontology of peace." Bouma-Prediger, *For the Beauty of the Earth*, 88.

23. In a helpful review of different theological attempts to identify the *imago Dei*, theologian and computer scientist Noreen Herzfeld identifies substantive, functional, and relational approaches. See Herzfeld, *In Our Image*, 10–32.

24. German philosopher Ludwig Feuerbach made just this point about religion: we create God in our image. "[Religion is] nothing else than the consciousness of the infinity of the consciousness; or, in the consciousness of the infinite, the conscious subject has for his object the infinity of his own nature." Feuerbach, *Essence of Christianity*, 21.

25. "Scriptural references to the creation of humans in the image of God are few and in no way tell us of what that image consists." Herzfeld, *In Our Image*, 14.

26. For a more extended treatment, through the lens of disability theology, of how

I bring up the *imago Dei* here to show that, while humans and AI are both part of God's good creation, there is something distinct, theologically speaking, about humanity, no matter how "smart" AI gets. Perhaps an aspect of that distinction is found in the same verse as another declaration of the *imago Dei*: "Then God said, 'Let us make humankind in our image, according to our likeness; and let them have dominion over the fish of the sea, and over the birds of the air, and over the cattle, and over all the wild animals of the earth, and over every creeping thing that creeps upon the earth" (Gen 1:26). The word "dominion" is *radah* in Hebrew, and it can also be translated as "stewardship"; God seems to position humans here in a position of vice-regency, as those who exercise God's will in the midst of and to creation.[27] This idea is deepened in Genesis 2:15, when humans are commanded to "till" and "keep" creation; these two Hebrew verbs, *abad* and *shamar*, are horticultural terms that can also be translated as "serve" and "protect."[28] It seems that Genesis portrays a humanity that is meant to care for the rest of creation, including humans, helping it to fulfill its divine purpose.

One of the ways that humans serve as vice-regents in God's good creation is through the creation and use of technology, including AI. As mentioned above, technology is most basically the application of knowledge to solve a problem, which inevitably is worked out in the midst of the world, and therefore involves the manipulation of creation; it is the novel use of technique and tool. For instance, when the problem was how to get from one place to another faster, certain ideas were imagined, tried, and improved; riding a horse came first, perhaps, and then boats, bikes, cars, trains, and planes. All of these pieces of technology used material from God's creation to make something new, through the imagination and smarts of humans endowed with the gifts God had given them and with the commission of

---

the identification of *imago Dei* with an ability or capacity ends up marginalizing individuals, see Langford, "Abusing Youth."

27. Theologian Helmut Thielicke connects God's creation of humanity in the midst of many other creatures with God's commission to humanity to steward well all of God's creation. "For, after all, we are not to rule and subdue the earth because we stand *above* the other creatures, but only because we stand *under* God and are privileged to be his viceroys. But being a viceroy of the Creator is something different from being a creature who makes of himself a god or at least a superman." Thielicke, *How the World Began*, 67.

28. "Genesis 2:15 . . . defines the human calling in terms of service: we are to serve (*abad*) and protect (*shamar*). We are to serve and protect the garden that is creation— literally, to be slaves to the earth for its own good, as well as for our own benefit. Taking [the Genesis] texts seriously implies that dominion must be defined in terms of service. We are called to dominion as service." Bouma-Prediger, *For the Beauty of the Earth*, 64. The latter verb, *shamar*, is the same verb as in the Aaronic blessing, "The Lord bless you and keep (*shamar*) you" (Num 6:24). See Brunner et al., *Introducing Evangelical Ecotheology*, 26.

vice-regency. Human technologies have not always been imagined, developed, or used well, but they are bits of God's creation, and therefore are no less "good" than any other part of it, even if they are a strange new reconfiguration of that creation. Such is true of AI as well, and therefore we do well to remember our commission in our creation and employment of it.

SALVATION

If technology is the application of knowledge to solve a problem using creaturely techniques and tools, then we might imagine salvation as being God's technology. The word "salvation" literally means the state of being saved, which implies being saved from something, being saved to something, and a means of being saved. Biblically, theologically, and culturally, these three aspects of salvation take on a lot of different shapes in Christianity. We will look at each. However, it is first important to note that Christians believe that it is God who saves. In fact, that is one of the main dictums of Judaism that Christianity has inherited: Only God can save.[29] This is one of the reasons that early Christians settled on identifying Jesus as having the nature of full divinity; if Jesus is not fully God, then Jesus does not fully save us.[30] In fact, Jesus's name in the original Hebrew is *Yeshua*, which means "God saves."

From what does God save us? Very generally speaking, Christians believe that God saves us from all those things that go against the will of God in our lives and in the world. The theological concept for this is "sin."[31] Sin

29. God as the source of salvation is a theme seen throughout the Old Testament. "I, I am the Lord, and besides me there is no savior" (Isa 43:11); "Deliverance belongs to the Lord; may your blessing be on your people!" (Ps 3:8); "Yet I have been the Lord your God ever since the land of Egypt; you know no God but me, and besides me there is no savior" (Hos 13:4).

30. The Jewish theme of God as savior is applied to the person and work of Jesus in the New Testament. This is typified in Peter's speech to the council of religious authorities: "There is salvation in no one else [than Jesus Christ], for there is no other name under heaven given among mortals by which we may be saved" (Acts 4:12). This connection between the saving work of God uniquely in Jesus Christ formed the soteriological bedrock of the Christian faith. "Christianity holds that salvation—however that is subsequently defined—is linked with the life, death, and resurrection of Jesus Christ. This interconnection of Jesus Christ with the achievement of salvation has been characteristic of Christian theology down through the ages. While a wide range of metaphors are used in the New Testament and the Christian tradition to describe the transformation of the human situation through redemption, all of them converge on the person of Jesus Christ as their ultimate ground and goal." McGrath, *Christian Theology*, 248.

31. In the *Large Catechism*, in addressing "Holy Baptism," Martin Luther provides a classic summary of those things from which we are saved: "But to be saved, we know, is nothing else than to be delivered from sin, death, and the devil, and to enter into the

means literally "missing the mark," and refers to that which transgresses the nature of creation as God intends it, seminally imaged in Genesis 3 as human rejection of the way of God.[32] Sins can be acts of commission or omission and are not necessarily intentional. But we might also say that "sin" is a state of being and not merely a series of acts; for instance, one might say that we live in a "sinful world," meaning that we exist within a reality thoroughly infected with the effects of human sin, with results such as isolation, systems of marginalization, violence, ecological degradation, and other maladies. Scripture uses a number of images to describe sin including, for instance, bondage, death, disobedience, disease, and ignorance. Like most theological notions, sin is not a straightforward concept, but it seems enough to think of sin as that which goes against God's will, and thus indicates life and reality and a trajectory that is not as it should be. It is not hard for us to look around us and find that to be the case.

To what does God save us? Very generally speaking, Christians believe that God saves us and the world to that state for which we and it were created. Just as Scripture uses many images for sin, so does it also use many images for salvation including liberation, new life, redemption, healing, and *shalom*. The diversity of these images suggests the multidimensional holism of salvation, in which God reconciles all things to how they ought to be. God saves all of creation from the sin that plagues it. Postmodernism has helped us to see that reality includes a panoply of relationships such that all things exist, and can only be understood, in their connection to other things. Thus it is that humans exist in relationship with God, with each other, and with the rest of creation.[33] Followingly, we might understand salvation as a re-creation of

---

kingdom of Christ, and to live with Him forever" (IV.25). In essence, these things work against God and hold humanity in bondage. We are here using "sin" as a theological catchall.

32. Theologian Daniel Migliore says, "If we are created for relationship with God who is wholly different from us and for relationship with other creatures who are relatively different from us, sin is a denial of our essential relatedness to those who are genuinely 'other.' We deny our dependence on the Other who is God and reject our need for our fellow creatures, most particularly those who seem so totally strange and 'other' to us—the victim, the poor, the 'leftover person.'" Migliore, *Faith Seeking Understanding*, 150. However, theologian Howard Snyder expands this notion of sin as broken relationship to a wider "ecology of sin": "In alienating man and woman from God, human disobedience introduced three other kinds of alienation that are with us still. Here is the ecology of sin: alienation from God, internal alienation within each person (alienation from oneself), alienation between humans, and alienation from and within nature. These are the spiritual, psychological, social, and environmental alienations that afflict the whole human family." Snyder, *Salvation Means Creation Healed*, 68.

33. "The good news of Jesus and his kingdom addresses the whole ecology of sin, as [2 Cor 5:17–19] suggests—'reconciling the world to himself.' All the multiple

right relationship between humans and God, between humans and themselves, between humans, and between humans and the rest of creation. This
multidimensional relationality is implied in the *ordo salutis*, Latin for "order
of salvation," which describes different aspects of salvation: election, justification, sanctification, vocation, and glorification.[34] First of all, God "elects" or
freely chooses salvation for the cosmos.[35] Second, we are justified or "made
right" with God in that our relationship with God is set to what it is meant to
be, one in which God is God and we are creatures who trust and obey God.
Third, we are sanctified or "made holy" in that our lives are accorded to an
existence of loving relationship with God and others. Fourth, we embrace
our vocation in that we participate in God's call for us to be vice-regents in
God's work of cosmic reconciliation. Fifth, all things are finally set according
to the will and glory of God.

What are the means of salvation? It should be noted that Scripture
is less interested in proclaiming the metaphysics of salvation than it is in
proclaiming the fact of salvation.[36] The "what" is asserted but the "why"

---

dimensions of sin and alienation are implied here, as in many other passages. *The ecology of salvation is as full and comprehensive as the ecology of sin.* Anything less is not
the whole gospel for the whole world—not wholistic mission." Snyder, *Salvation Means
Creation Healed*, 147. In the same way that sin infects all reality, so does salvation affect
all reality.

34. This *ordo salutis* is based on, though not a reproduction of, aspects listed in
Rom 8:30. Two things should be noted here. First, there are many different opinions
concerning an ordering of salvation; different theologians have different perspectives
on what salvation consists of and the ordering of aspects within the process of salvation.
Second, in presenting an *ordo salutis* here, I am not (necessarily) suggesting a temporal
ordering, but rather a logical one. From an individual's point of view in the course of
salvation, it may not appear to have any sort of particular ordering.

35. This is admittedly not how many use the term "election" or "predestination." I
am using it here in the sense that Barth uses it: "The doctrine of election is the sum of
the Gospel because of all words that can be said or heard it is the best: that God elects
man; that God is for man too the One who loves in freedom. It is grounded in the
knowledge of Jesus Christ because He is both the electing God and elected man in One.
It is part of the doctrine of God because originally God's election of man is a predestination not merely of man but of Himself. Its function is to bear basic testimony to eternal,
free and unchanging grace as the beginning of all the ways and works of God." Barth,
Church Dogmatics II/2, 3.

36. A quote from C. S. Lewis makes this point: "Now before I became a Christian
I was under the impression that the first thing Christians had to believe was one particular theory as to what the point of [the Crucifixion] was. According to that theory
God wanted to punish men for having deserted and joined the Great Rebel, but Christ
volunteered to be punished instead, and so God let us off. Now I admit that even this
theory does not seem quite so immoral and silly as it used to; but that is not the point
I want to make. What I came to see later on was that neither this theory nor any other
is Christianity. The central belief is that Christ's death has somehow put us right with

is not, or at least not very clearly or univocally. This is, in part, because it is impossible for us to grasp the comprehensiveness of God's salvation, let alone all the ways in which God effects this salvation. Nevertheless, Scripture does portray the person and work of Jesus Christ as the means of salvation. Christians believe that it is through Jesus that we are saved. Based upon what Scripture says about salvation, theologians have often offered "atonement theories," or theorized explanations of precisely how it is that Jesus saves us. One suggestion, often called the "Christus Victor" motif, is that Jesus defeats Satan, the embodiment of that which militates against God's will, and thus releases humanity from bondage.[37] Another suggestion, called "recapitulation theory," portrays Jesus as the "New Adam," who reconstitutes in his life the proper embodiment of humanity, thus healing its defects.[38] Another suggestion, popularized by Anselm in the Middle Ages, is called "satisfaction theory," which states that humanity has, because of sin, incurred a debt to God that must be repaid for the restoration of right relationship, a repayment which is made through Jesus's death on the cross.[39] Yet another suggestion, "moral exemplar theory," states that Jesus has shown us the way to live as people of God, a way that we have forgotten or never fully understood.[40] Regardless of precisely how it is that Jesus heals the cosmos from sin, Christians believe that he does so, constituting an act of salvation that is the work of God alone.

When reflecting on AI in view of Christian notions of salvation, it should be noted immediately that AI cannot be the source of salvation because it is not God, no matter how powerful we may imagine it to be. It

God and given us a fresh start. Theories as to how it did this are another matter. A good many different theories have been held as to how it works; what all Christians are agreed on is that it does work." Lewis, *Mere Christianity*, 53–54.

37. For a helpful review of the prevalence of this model of atonement, sometimes called the "classic view," among theologians in the early church, see Aulén, *Christus Victor*.

38. This theory of atonement is often identified with Irenaeus of Lyon. "He has therefore, in His work of recapitulation, summed up all things, both waging war against our enemy, and crushing him who had at the beginning led us away captives in Adam, and trampled upon his head. . . . And therefore does the Lord profess Himself to be the Son of man, comprising in Himself that original man out of whom the woman was fashioned, in order that, as our species went down to death through a vanquished man, so we may ascend to life again through a victorious one." Irenaeus, *Against Heresies*, 5.21.1.

39. See Anselm, *Cur Deus Homo?*, II.4–7. This theory has become a common theological interpretation in Western theological traditions.

40. Though this view is associated with scholastic theologian Peter Abelard (1079–1142), it is also a theory popular in the modern era, especially in liberal theologies that identify Jesus primarily as an enlightened teacher and moral leader.

cannot provide us with right relationship with God, it cannot make us holy, and it cannot call us to be vice-regents of creation. As it says in Revelation 7:10: "Salvation belongs to our God." This is not to say that God does not use AI in God's salvific work; God has done, and will presumably continue to do, incredible things through AI. However, ultimately, salvation belongs to God alone. The notion that AI could save us implies at least two things. First of all, it implies that AI could know humanity—not to mention the rest of creation—well enough to know what needs healing. However, Scripture states that it is only God who knows us fully and is therefore uniquely in a position to save us.[41] Knowledge is personal, meaning that it forms in the midst of relationship.[42] We noted above that human knowledge of God emerges in the context of the relationship of faith. God's knowledge of humanity also exists within God's intimate and ontic relationship with humanity. However, the relationship of AI to humanity is noetic; AI knows humanity to the degree that its programmers do, or to the degree that its programmers have equipped it to look for certain domains of knowledge.[43] Second, and relatedly, the belief that AI could save us implies that AI supplies us with whatever we need for salvation. This suggests a salvation that is quantitative, meaning that to be saved is to have ameliorated a deficiency of something identifiable. However, theologically understood, salvation is not (merely) quantitative but is rather a qualitative transformation. This is perhaps best captured in one of the central New Testament terms for salvation, "reconciliation," or *katallage* in the original Greek. Literally speaking, *katallage* is not merely a healing of enmity or difference as the English "reconciliation" may suggest, but rather implies a holistic transformation of all things unto the will of God.[44]

41. The theme of God's personal knowledge of humanity is found throughout Scripture. An example: "O Lord, you have searched me and known me. You know when I sit down and when I rise up; you discern my thoughts from far away. You search out my path and my lying down, and are acquainted with all my ways. Even before a word is on my tongue, O Lord, you know it completely. You hem me in, behind and before, and lay your hand upon me. Such knowledge is too wonderful for me; it is so high that I cannot attain it" (Ps 139: 1–6).

42. Chemist and philosopher Michael Polanyi, in his 1950–1951 Gifford Lectures at Aberdeen, denied the pure objectivity claimed by scientific positivism, claiming that undergirding all knowledge are commitments that emerge within personal relationships, such as with the universe, ideas, ideologies, communities, and other people. See the publication of these lectures in Polanyi, *Personal Knowledge*.

43. In opposition to his friend Alan Turing and the proposition of AI, Polanyi did not believe that the human mind could be reduced to a set of data and rules. He believed that knowledge begins as "tacit" knowledge, not entirely in our awareness, that only gradually becomes focused into conscious knowledge. See Polanyi, *Tacit Dimension*.

44. For more on the biblical and theological understanding of reconciliation as God's transformative work of salvation, see Langford, "Reconciliation as Holistic

ESCHATOLOGY

The word "eschatology" comes from the Greek word *eschatos*, which means "last things," and deals with topics that have to do, from a Christian standpoint, with things to come, including, for instance, death, the afterlife, and the end of time. It should be said that eschatology is, of course, speculative, since we are speaking of things that have not yet come to pass. In that sense, in many ways, eschatology might be understood as a Christian theology of hope, for it relies on promises that God has made that Christians look for God to fulfill.[45]

These promises are not only things to be realized in the future, but are also experienced in the present. If salvation has been brought about in the person and work of Jesus Christ, then this salvation is made real to us in the person and work of the Holy Spirit. We might say that salvation has *objectively* happened in the reconciliatory work of God in Christ; it occurred "there and then" and is complete. However, we might also say that salvation is *subjectively* happening in the redemptive work of God in the Holy Spirit; it occurs "here and now" and is still happening.[46] Thus it is that we are saved by the "two hands of God."[47] The Holy Spirit is at work in the present making us more and more into the people that we already are in Christ.

Redemptive Transformation."

45. Jürgen Moltmann suggests that just as much as theology is "faith seeking understanding," as goes the dictum of Anselm, so is it "hope seeking understanding." "If it is hope that maintains and upholds faith and keeps it moving on, if it is hope that draws the believer into the life of love, then it will also be hope that is the mobilizing and driving force of faith's thinking, of its knowledge of, and reflections on, human nature, history and society." Moltmann, *Theology of Hope*, 33.

46. Barth speaks of this distinction: "When we say justification, sanctification and calling, on the one side, we are already expounding the relevance of what was done in Jesus Christ, but, on the other we are expounding only the objective relevance of it and not its subjective apprehension and acceptance in the world and by us men. We might say, we are dealing with the ascription but not the appropriation of the grace of Jesus Christ, or with what has taken place in Him for the world as such but not for the Christian in particular. In the Christian there is an appropriation of the grace of God ascribed to all men in Jesus Christ, a subjective apprehension of what has been done for the whole world in the happening of atonement. . . . In this connexion the specific point that we have to make is that the being and work of Jesus Christ—for even here we cannot abandon the christological basis—must now be understood as the being and work of His Holy Spirit, or His own spiritual being and work. The appropriation of the grace of Jesus Christ ascribed to us, the subjective apprehension of the reconciliation of the world with God made in Him, the existence of Christians, presupposes and includes within itself the presence, the gift and the reception, the work and accomplishment of His Holy Spirit." Barth, *Church Dogmatics* IV/1, 147–48.

47. This notion of the economy of God as worked out in the persons and work of the Son and the Spirit is seen in Irenaeus: "It was not angels, therefore, who made us,

However, we also see that we are not yet the people that we already are in Christ. As goes the famous dictum of Martin Luther, we are *simul iustus et peccator*, or "at one and the same time righteous and a sinner."[48] This status of human existence is also true for cosmic existence, as reflected in perhaps the central topic of eschatology, that of the "kingdom of God," a topic about which Jesus spoke extensively. The kingdom of God, or *basileia tou theou* in Greek, refers not to a place, such as heaven, but rather to a state of being, namely existence that accords to the will of God; for this reason, *basileia* is perhaps better translated as "reign" or "rule."[49] At the time of Jesus, the Jewish people were already quite familiar with the notion of God as king and awaited the intervention of God, establishing divine rule over all creation.[50] Jesus proclaimed that this kingdom was coming, leading many to believe that the end of the world as they knew it was imminent. However, Jesus also proclaimed that the kingdom had already come in his own person and work.[51]

This duality of the kingdom of God as "already and not yet" is reflected in the notion of "inaugurated eschatology," which states that, in Jesus Christ,

---

nor who formed us, neither had angels power to make an image of God, nor any one else, except the Word of the Lord, nor any Power remotely distant from the Father of all things. For God did not stand in need of these [beings], in order to the accomplishing of what He had Himself determined with Himself beforehand should be done, as if He did not possess His own hands. For with Him were always present the Word and Wisdom, the Son and the Spirit, by whom and in whom, freely and spontaneously, He made all things." Irenaeus, *Against Heresies*, 4.20.1.

48. Luther used this term in drawing a distinction between our justification in Christ and our sanctification in the Holy Spirit: "[Luther accounted] for the persistence of sin in believers, while at the same time accounting for the gradual transformation of the believer and the future elimination of that sin. Luther thus declared, in a famous phrase, that a believer is 'at one and the same time righteous and a sinner' (*simil iustus et peccator*); righteous in hope but a sinner in fact; righteous in the sight and through the promise of God yet a sinner in reality." McGrath, *Christian Theology*, 340.

49. The notion of the kingdom of God as the actualization of the will of God thus establishes it as that for which we await while also as that which we may experience now, even if not yet completely. "The kingdom of God is that order of perfect peace, righteousness, justice, and love that God gives to the world. This gift is eschatological, for it comes in an ultimate way only at the renewal of the world consummated at Jesus' return. But the power of the kingdom is already at work, for it breaks into the present from the future. Therefore, we can experience the kingdom in a partial yet vital manner en route to the great future day." Grenz, *Theology for the Community of God*, 22.

50. "The Christ event is not an isolated occurrence of a totally different kind, but is rooted in God's history with Israel. The significance of Jesus can therefore be grasped only on the basis of the Old Testament history of promise." Bosch, *Transforming Mission*, 196.

51. See, for instance, Jesus's words in the Synoptic Gospels: in Matthew, "Repent, for the kingdom of heaven has come near" (4:17); in Mark, "The time is fulfilled, and the kingdom of God has come near; repent, and believe in the good news" (1:15); and in Luke, "For, in fact, the kingdom of God is among you" (17:21).

the kingdom has already been inaugurated, irrupting into our present while also serving as a foreshadowing of its eventual fulfillment.[52] In other words, in the person and work of Jesus, we see the will of God being done, the reign of God come in full. Yet, even in the time of Jesus and certainly ever since, we also see the will of God not being done and the reign of God not come in full, and await the time that Jesus will come again, as he promised, to establish the will of God for all people and for all time. However, just as the kingdom of God irrupted into the world two-thousand years ago in the person and work of Jesus, so the kingdom of God continues to irrupt into our present world in the person and work of the Holy Spirit. Even now, we may taste and see the will of God around us; beauty and truth and justice and goodness happens, even amid that which militates against it.

Inaugurated eschatology has been, generally speaking, how the majority of historic and global Christianity has interpreted Jesus's instruction on the kingdom of God. However, there are two other understandings that have, at different times, found popular adherence. "Futurist eschatology" teaches that, from the time of Jesus, things have gotten worse and worse, and things will continue to devolve until that time when Jesus comes and establishes the kingdom of God. Conversely, "realized eschatology" teaches that Jesus gave us the tools to establish the kingdom of God, and that we are progressively building that kingdom as we live the way that God calls us to live.[53] Some critics would say that futurist eschatology denigrates the present work of the Holy Spirit in our midst, and that it excessively demonizes the world around us, one which God has made and loves. Other critics would say that realized eschatology eliminates the need for Jesus to come again, and that it is excessively optimistic concerning our ability to save ourselves from sin and accord the world to the will of God.

---

52. Theologian N. T. Wright speaks of the message of Jesus as one which was not merely hope for the future, but for the present as well. "What [Jesus] was promising for the future, and doing in that present, was not about saving souls for a disembodied eternity but rescuing people from the corruption and decay of the way the world presently is so they could enjoy, already in the present, that renewal of creation which is God's ultimate purpose—and so they could thus become colleagues and partners in that larger project." Wright, *Surprised By Hope*, 192.

53. Realized eschatology is usually first associated with biblical scholar Charles H. Dodd (1884–1973), who claimed that Jesus's preaching about the kingdom of God referred to something that was already happening, and that the kingdom was "realized" in the resurrection of Jesus. See Dodd, *Apostolic Preaching and Its Development*. However, in response to critics who said that he did not sufficiently account for Jesus's clear statements about a future kingdom, Dodd's later writings seem to suggest that he agreed that the kingdom had begun, but had not yet come in fullness. See McGrath, *Christian Theology*, 433.

The kingdom of God that Christians believe will ultimately come, prefigured now in the work of the Holy Spirit, is often called the "new creation." This does not mean that the present creation will be destroyed or removed; God loves creation and deems it good. However, it is in "bondage to decay"[54] and in need of healing, thus it will be made new. This renewal of creation includes humans, of course, and the affirmation of God's created reality means that human bodies will also be given new life. Christian theology asserts that humans are not merely some immaterial soul, as the Platonic dualists believed; rather, human bodies are central to who we are. God affirmed the value of material creation not only in the Genesis saga, but also in the incarnation, choosing to take on human flesh rather than merely sending another message through a prophet or another image through a mystic.[55] Moreover, if the resurrection of Jesus gives us a picture of perfected humanity, then we see that it features a physical body, even if that body is not precisely the same as our present bodies. This is perhaps noteworthy in light of those who claim AI will provide humanity with immortality by enabling us to upload our consciousness to artificial "bodies."[56]

Some believe that AI will usher in the new creation on its own. Others believe that it will usher in the utter destruction of the world. It seems that these may be the latest versions of realized and futurist eschatologies, respectively. One of the things that Jesus makes clear is that the end of all things will happen on his timetable and not ours. Speaking to his disciples shortly before he is taken into custody to be executed, Jesus tells them, "Heaven and earth will pass away, but my words will not pass away. But

54. "For the creation waits with eager longing for the revealing of the children of God; for the creation was subjected to futility, not of its own will but by the will of the one who subjected it, in hope that the creation itself will be set free from its bondage to decay and will obtain the freedom of the glory of the children of God" (Rom 8:19–21).

55. The spiritualization of materiality leads not only to a degraded belief in the eternal value of the human body, but also to the belief that the earth itself lacks eternal value. "Such spiritualizing is simply not what the Bible teaches. God did not degrade himself in creating material things. He honored and dignified matter by bringing it into existence through his own power—and supremely by becoming incarnate within the material creation." Snyder, *Salvation Means Creation Healed*, 45.

56. Philosopher Nick Bostrom defines transhumanism as "the intellectual and cultural movement that affirms the possibility and desirability of fundamentally improving the human condition through applied reason, especially by developing and making widely available technologies to eliminate aging and to greatly enhance human intellectual, physical, and psychological capacities." Bostrom, "Transhumanist FAQ." Transhumanists claim that AI and other technologies will extend human life, perhaps indefinitely, by such means as uploading memories and other brain states onto silicon, by replacing degrading biological body parts with artificial ones, or by merging human consciousness into virtual worlds. Notable transhumanists include Ray Kurzweil and Hans Moravec.

about that day and hour no one knows, neither the angels of heaven, nor the Son, but only the Father" (Matt 24:35–36).[57] He likens this in-between time to the days of Noah, who did not know when the flood was coming. In the same way that Noah obeyed God and was a good steward of creation and technology, so does Jesus command his followers to stay awake and steward well.

> Keep awake therefore, for you do not know on what day your Lord is coming. But understand this: if the owner of the house had known in what part of the night the thief was coming, he would have stayed awake and would not have let his house be broken into. Therefore you also must be ready, for the Son of Man is coming at an unexpected hour. Who then is the faithful and wise slave, whom his master has put in charge of his household, to give the other slaves their allowance of food at the proper time? Blessed is that slave whom his master will find at work when he arrives. (Matt 24:42–44)

Jesus's words here highlight not only our responsibility to be faithful and wise in our creation and use of AI, but also of the urgency to do so.

Those who propose that AI will bring about the destruction of the world deny God the agency that is clearly reserved for God in Scripture and grant humanity an authority it does not have. Moreover, this orientation can deny the irrupting work of the Holy Spirit in creation, including in artificial creations such as AI. However, as we have noted, those who propose that AI will save the world also deny God agency. In addition, this orientation imagines the eschatological new creation in continuity to our current reality in the same way that salvation is imagined as merely a quantitative change. Rather, the new creation is qualitatively different, a transformation that AI is not equipped to provide, let alone define. When AI is depicted as ushering in any sort of utopia, not only is it denying God's unknown means and timing, but it also depicts that utopia in terms of our present.[58]

---

57. Biblical scholar Douglas R. A. Hare notes that many people have attempted to predict when the end will come. "The spiritual arrogance that presumes to pry into God's secret plan is roundly condemned by Matt. 24:36. Not even the Messiah knows when the end will occur! Not even the highest archangels are privy to the Father's intention! How foolish is it for humans to think they can play with biblical numbers and ambiguous prophecies and discover what was hidden even from Jesus!" Hare, *Matthew*, 282.

58. Theologian Michael Burdett notes that fictional and philosophical depictions of utopias are often simply extensions of our present time, unlike biblical eschatological pronouncements that suggest a qualitatively different future. See Burdett, *Eschatology and the Technological Future*.

CONCLUSION

The writings of those who have predicted that AI will bring about an end to the world as we know it—either as salvation or doomsday—have been called "apocalyptic AI."[59] This "end" is usually signaled as happening soon after the future emergence of "AGI," or artificial general intelligence.[60] While Christianity asserts that it is God, not humans nor their creation, who will determine the time and means of the new age, it is true that AI is "apocalyptic" in the true sense of the word. Apocalyptic literature, such as the biblical book of Revelation, is meant to be a presentation, often both vivid and ambiguous, of transcendent and ultimate truths; "apocalypse" literally means "unveiling." In that sense, AI is apocalyptic in that it, at least, reveals to us our hopes and our fears, our capabilities and our limitations, our better angels and our hidden demons.

Perhaps the biggest thing that our creation, development, and use of AI has revealed to us is that, within our good creation, we continue to discover and build novel means to empower and extend our capabilities; in so doing, we create new things that may be participating in God's work, but we do not determine the shape, nor are we the ultimate cause, of the kingdom of God. Some of our technologies, like AI, are uniquely powerful in their ability to bring about blessings and curses. Yet neither humanity nor its awesome tools are God, and the extent to which technologies participate in the eschatological inbreaking new creation is not always clear. It is the province of God to bring about the reign of God in times, places, and means that we do not dictate. Our task is to perceive what God has for us, and for it to change us. This is a task of theological knowledge, not scientific knowledge, and certainly not within the domain of that which we program

59. Religious studies scholar Robert M. Geraci defines apocalyptic AI as "a movement in popular science books that integrates the religious categories of Jewish and Christian apocalyptic traditions with scientific predictions based upon current technological developments." Geraci, *Apocalyptic AI*, 9.

60. Artificial general intelligence, sometimes called "strong AI," is an AI that can do whatever human intelligence can do. "Most of the successes so far in AI have to do with building systems that do one thing that normally takes human intelligence to implement. However, on a more speculative side—certainly at the moment—there is great interest in the vastly more ambitious quest to build systems that can do all that human intelligence can do, that is, artificial general intelligence (AGI), which some think will surpass human intelligence within a relatively short time, certainly by 2084 or even earlier, according to some speculations. Some imagine that AGI, if we ever get there, will function as a god, while others, as a totalitarian despot." Lennox, *2084*, 13–14. Some theorize that AGI will in turn create better and better AI that surpasses human intelligence, and perhaps it will even develop consciousness, a development called the "singularity." This, of course, begs the question of what we mean by "intelligence." See Boden, *AI*, 147–69.

into AI. Biblically speaking, "knowledge" is not merely a set of observable information, but it is rather a process of the mind, heart, and will, by which we become somehow aware of another reality to which we give ourselves. In other words, to know is to become transformed.[61] It is therefore at God's initiative that we come to know as we are known; our knowledge is grounded in God's knowledge, which we perceive only dimly.[62]

Ecclesiastes 1:9–10 reads: "What has been is what will be, and what has been done is what will be done; there is nothing new under the sun. Is there a thing of which it is said, 'See, this is new'? It has already been, in the ages before us." While it certainly true that there have been many "new" things, including AI, in the world, Ecclesiastes here speaks more existentially. The "Teacher," credited as the author of Ecclesiastes, claims that humanity, in trying to find meaning in different things, ends up finding only "vanity of vanities" (Eccl 1:2). We still seek meaning today, perhaps in AI, but it is only God who ultimately bestows what we need, in shapes and ways known only to God. "The end of the matter; all has been heard. Fear God, and keep his commandments; for that is the whole duty of everyone" (Eccl 12:13). In seeking the reign of God first (Matt 6:33)—which may be mediated through AI!—we "fear God" and "keep his commandments," and are then enabled to be, with humility, God's vice-regents in our creation, development, and use of AI.

61. Barth notes that this sort of knowing is the result of the revelatory work of the Holy Spirit by which we are transformed. "We cannot impress upon ourselves too strongly that in the language of the Bible knowledge . . . does not mean the acquisition of neutral information, which can be expressed in statements, principles and systems, concerning a being which confronts man, nor does it mean the entry into passive contemplation of a being which exists beyond the phenomenal world. What it really means is the process or history in which man, certainly observing and thinking, using his senses, intelligence and imagination, but also his will, action and 'heart,' and therefore as whole man, becomes aware of another history which in the first instance encounters him as an alien history from without, and becomes aware of it in such a compelling way that he cannot be neutral towards it, but finds himself summoned to disclose and give himself to it in return, to direct himself according to the law which he encounters in it, to be taken up into its movement, in short, to demonstrate the acquaintance which he has been given with this other history in a corresponding alteration of his own being, action and conduct. We can and should say even more emphatically that knowledge in the biblical sense is the process in which the distant 'object' dissolves as it were, overcoming both its distance and its objectivity and coming to man as acting Subject, entering into the man who knows and subjecting him to this transformation." Barth, *Church Dogmatics* IV/3, 183–84.

62. "For now we see in a mirror, dimly, but then we will see face to face. Now I know only in part; then I will know fully, even as I have been fully known" (1 Cor 13:12).

BIBLIOGRAPHY

Achtemeier, Paul. *Romans*. Interpretation: A Bible Commentary for Teaching and Preaching. Louisville: John Knox, 1985.

Anselm. *Cur Deus Homo? (Why God Became Man?)*. Translated by Edward Stallybrass Prout. London: Religious Tract Society, 1886.

Aquinas, Thomas. *Summa Theologica*. Translated by Fathers of the English Dominican Province. New York: Benziger Brothers, 1911–1925.

Athanasius. "On the Incarnation." In *Nicene and Post-Nicene Fathers, Second Series, Volume 4*, edited by Philip Schaff and Henry Wace, 31–67. Translated by Archibald Robinson. New York: Christian Literature, 1891.

Aulén, Gustaf. *Christus Victor: An Historical Study of the Three Main Types of the Idea of Atonement*. Translated by A. G. Herbert. London: SPCK, 1931.

Barth, Karl. *Church Dogmatics, Vol. I: The Doctrine of the Word of God, Part 1*. Translated by G. W. Bromiley. Edinburgh: T. & T. Clark, 1975.

———. *Church Dogmatics, Vol. II: The Doctrine of God, Part 2*. Translated by G. W. Bromiley et al. Edinburg: T. & T. Clark, 1957.

———. *Church Dogmatics, Vol. IV: The Doctrine of Reconciliation, Part 2*. Translated by G. W. Bromiley. Edinburgh: T. & T. Clark, 1958.

———. *Church Dogmatics, Vol. IV: The Doctrine of Reconciliation, Part 3.1*. Translated by G. W. Bromiley. Edinburgh: T. & T. Clark, 1961.

Boden, Margaret A. *AI: Its Nature and Future*. Oxford: Oxford University Press, 2016.

Bonhoeffer, Dietrich. *Creation and Fall: A Theological Exposition of Genesis 1–3. Dietrich Bonhoeffer Works, Volume 3*, edited by John W. de Gruchy. Translated by Douglas Stephen Bax. Minneapolis: Fortress, 1997.

Bosch, David J. *Transforming Mission: Paradigm Shifts in Theology of Mission*. Maryknoll, NY: Orbis, 1991.

Bostrom, Nick. "The Transhumanist FAQ: A General Introduction." In *Transhumanism and the Body: The World Religions Speak*, edited by Calvin Mercer and Derek F. Maher, 1–17. New York: Palgrave Macmillan, 2014.

Bouma-Prediger, Steven. *For the Beauty of the Earth: A Christian Vision for Creation Care*. 2nd ed. Grand Rapids: Baker, 2010.

Brunner, Daniel L., et al. *Introducing Evangelical Ecotheology: Foundations in Scripture, Theology, History, and Praxis*. Grand Rapids MI: Baker, 2014.

Burdett, Michael S. *Eschatology and the Technological Future*. London: Routledge, 2015.

Dodd, Charles H. *Apostolic Preaching and Its Developments*. London: Hodder and Stoughton, 1936.

Feuerbach, Ludwig. *The Essence of Christianity*. 2nd ed. Translated by Marian Evans. New York: Calvin Blanchard, 1855.

Ford, Martin. *Architects of Intelligence: The Truth about AI from the People Building It*. Burmingham, UK: Packt, 2018.

Geraci, Robert M. *Apocalyptic AI: Visions of Heaven in Robotics, Artificial Intelligence, and Virtual Reality*. New York: Oxford University Press, 2010.

Grenz, Stanley J. *Theology for the Community of God*. Grand Rapids: Eerdmans, 2000.

Hare, Douglas R. A. *Matthew*. Interpretation: A Bible Commentary for Teaching and Preaching. Louisville: John Knox, 1993.

Herzfeld, Noreen L. *In Our Image: Artificial Intelligence and the Human Spirit*. Minneapolis: Fortress, 2002.

Irenaeus. *Against Heresies*. In *Ante-Nicene Fathers, Volume 1*, edited by Alexander Roberts and James Donaldson, 315–567. Translated by A. Cleveland Coxe. New York: Christian Literature Publishing Company, 1885.

Kähler, Martin. *Schriften zur Chrisologie und Mission*. Munich: Chr. Kaiser Verlag, 1971.

Macquarrie, John. *Principles of Christian Faith*. London: SCM, 1966.

McGrath, Alister E. *Christian Theology: An Introduction*. 6th ed. Malden, MA: Wiley Blackwell, 2017.

Moltmann, Jürgen. *Theology of Hope: On the Ground and the Implications of a Christian Eschatology*. New York, Harper and Row, 1967.

Langford, Michael D. "Abusing Youth: Theologically Understanding Youth Through Misunderstanding Disability." In *Embodying Youth: Exploring Youth Ministry and Disability*, 58–83. London: Routledge, 2020.

Langford, Michael D. "Reconciliation as Holistic Redemptive Transformation." The 2016 Winifred E. Weter Faculty Award Lecture. Seattle Pacific University, 2016. https://digitalcommons.spu.edu/weter_lectures/31.

Lennox, John C. *2084: Artificial Intelligence and the Future of Humanity*. Grand Rapids: Zondervan, 2020.

Lewis, C. S. *Mere Christianity*. New York: HarperCollins, 2001.

Lohse, Bernhard. *A Short History of Christian Doctrine: From the First Century to the Present*. Rev. American ed. Translated by F. Ernest Stoeffler. Philadelphia: Fortress, 1985.

Luther, Martin. "The Large Catechism." Translated by James Schaaf. In *The Book of Concord*, edited by Robert Kolb and Timothy J. Wengert. Minneapolis: Fortress, 2000.

Migliore, Daniel L. *Faith Seeking Understanding: An Introduction to Christian Theology*. 2nd ed. Grand Rapids: Eerdmans, 2004.

Nienhuis, David R. *A Concise Guide to Reading the New Testament: A Canonical Introduction*. Grand Rapids: Baker, 2018.

Pelikan, Jaroslav. *The Spirit of Eastern Christendom (600–1700)*. The Christian Tradition: A History of the Development of Doctrine 2. Chicago: University of Chicago Press, 1974.

Polanyi, Michael. *Personal Knowledge: Towards a Post-Critical Philosophy*. Chicago: University Chicago Press, 1958.

———. *The Tacit Dimension*. Garden City, NY: Doubleday, 1966.

Snyder, Howard A. and Joel Scandrett. *Salvation Means Creation Healed: The Ecology of Sin and Grace; Overcoming the Divorce between Earth and Heaven*. Eugene, OR: Cascade, 2011.

Thielicke, Helmut. *How the World Began: Man in the First Chapters of the Bible*. Translated by John Doberstein. Philadelphia: Fortress, 1961.

Ware, Kallistos. *The Orthodox Way*. Rev. ed. Crestwood, NY: St. Vladimir's Seminary Press: 1995.

Wright, N. T. *Paul for Everyone: Romans Part 2, Chapters 9–16*. Louisville: Westminster John Knox, 2004.

———. *Surprised By Hope: Rethinking Heaven, the Resurrection, and the Mission of the Church*. San Francisco: HarperOne, 2008.

PART II

Explorations

5

Artificial Intelligence and Theological Personhood

Michael D. Langford

AN IMAGINARY PRELUDE

Imagine that you are sitting in a coffee shop for a leisurely afternoon of reading. As you take a break to answer a text, the individual sitting next to you spies your book and asks your opinion of it. Soon, you are in a deep and interesting conversation. This table-neighbor introduces themselves as Namin; you find them to be particularly attentive, inquisitive, and insightful, so much so that you want to be able to interact with them again sometime. Before you leave for home, you exchange email addresses. Later that night, you send an email to Namin, letting them know that you cannot remember the last time you had such a stimulating encounter with a stranger, and ask if they would like to get together for coffee next week. Just a few minutes later, you receive a reply:

> Hi! I am so glad that you emailed me; thank you for the kind words. I enjoyed our time together as well! I would love to meet up for coffee again. Next Thursday, same time and spot? But

97

before you agree, I should tell you something. I am actually not bio-life. I am artificial life. What you interacted with today was what you would term a "robot" that transports my processing algorithm when I want to go somewhere. I know that this revelation can cause all sorts of reactions, so if you'd rather not get together again, I understand. In either case, please know that it was great to meet you today, and you are a wonderful person.

Sincerely,
Namin

I suspect that, at some point in the future, this situation will not seem so far-fetched. Yet, even now, the sorts of philosophical and ethical questions that it raises are evident. Who or what did you interact with in the coffee shop? What is the relationship between what you believed about that interaction and what actually happened? To what extent is there a difference? Did the revelation in the email change the status of Namin? Was it morally wrong for Namin not to reveal the entirety of their identity to you at the coffee shop? Do you have any moral responsibility in relation to Namin?

THE QUESTION OF ANTHROPOLOGICAL STATUS

Most of these questions circle around one question, really: Is Namin a person? While the question of anthropological identity—What is a human person?—is not a new question, advancements in artificial intelligence in recent years have made it more pressing while also adding new dimensions to its contours. Different responses from different disciplines concerning the anthropological status of AI have moved the conversation forward.[1] One only needs to look at the many movies, books, and television programs over the last fifty years that consider the personhood of AI to see that this question is on the leading edge of public consciousness.[2]

---

1. See, e.g., Tegmark, *Life 3.0*; Floridi, *Fourth Revolution*, 152–58; Brockman, *Possible Minds*; Herzfeld, *In Our Image*; Lennox, *2084*; Boden, *AI*; Geraci, *Apocalyptic AI*.

2. Some well-known movies, many adapted from books, that consider the personhood of AI include *2001: A Space Odyssey* (1968); *Her* (2013); *I, Robot* (2004); *AI: Artificial Intelligence* (2001); *The Matrix* (1999); *Blade Runner* (1982); *The Terminator* (1984); *Wall-E* (2008); *Ex Machina* (2014); *Tron* (1982); *Bicentennial Man* (1999); *The Iron Giant* (1999). Several of these movies went on to have sequels, sometimes multiple, in subsequent years. Various *Star Trek* episodes consider this theme, as well, including "The Measure of a Man" (1989) from *The Next Generation* series, and "Author, Author" (2001) from the *Voyager* series.

However, it is difficult to find any sort of consensus on the anthropological status of AI because there are so many opinions about the nature of AI as it compares to the nature of humanity. Some approach the anthropological question on a material basis, perhaps claiming that AI cannot be a person because it lacks a DNA strand or particular brain structure. Others may approach the same question in terms of capacity, perhaps more sanguine to the anthropological status of AI based upon various abilities such as agency or logic or language. In fact, the entire anthropological question itself is grounded upon an epistemological assumption, namely that we are able to discern anthropological status at all; indeed, this was precisely the point of the Turing Test.[3] In other words, the way that we assess the personhood of AI is based upon larger philosophical assumptions of what it means to be a human person.

Further, in addition to different approaches to the consideration of the anthropological status of AI, there is probably just as much reticence in even trying to answer the question of human personhood at all. This is partially because, in a global and postmodern culture, landing on such a foundational claim is immensely difficult. Not only are there more and more answers available to basic existential questions such as that of anthropological identity, but the preponderance of perspectives has also called into question our ability to make any basic truth claim. Is it even possible to come to a consensus of how we assess what is true? Or, to put a more baldly postmodern spin on it, what precisely do we mean by "true" in the first place?

Finally, difficulties present themselves because of the arena of discourse itself; AI is largely seen as being in the realm of the hard sciences, which are not built, epistemologically speaking, to make statements about wisdom, meaning, and intrinsic value. Yet, historically speaking, we have always had to construct a canon of wisdom concerning technology—meaning the application of knowledge to solve a problem, inevitably using creaturely media—because it is used within the realm of everyday life, not the laboratory. With AI, the technological development has been so rapid that we have not had sufficient time to build this canon; we are now playing catch-up as we bring different disciplines of thought to bear in grappling

3. The "Turing Test" is a famous proposal made by computer scientist Alan Turing in a 1950 paper in which he asked how one might go about answering the question, "Can machines think?" He suggested that a better question would be asking how well a computer must perform such that we would not be able to distinguish its performance from that of a human. See Turing, "Computing Machinery and Intelligence." "The Turing Test" is now often taken to refer to behavioral conditions that measure the presence of "thinking," and, putatively, personhood.

with the implications of this form of technology that is only becoming more and more prevalent.

Yet, as often occurs in the wake of philosophical hand-wringing, the question nevertheless remains before us. Does AI have the status of person-hood? What *is* a person?

But first, a clarification of terms.

By "intelligence," I mean the gathering and processing of information, making decisions based on that information, and then evaluating those decisions. The consensus of how this is done properly or well is thus called "intelligent." Of course, human intelligence is embedded within a particular way of being and living by the knower, including his or her consciousness. By "artificial intelligence," then, I mean human constructs, usually computer algorithms, which mimic human intelligence. In other words, if a human construct behaves intelligently, or at least is created to act intelligently, it is artificial intelligence. This could be something as grand as Namin or as simple as a calculator; it exists as applications on our smartphones, processes in our cars, on websites and in browsers, and in hundreds of different interfaces with which we interact every day.

It should also be noted that I here make a distinction between "human" and "person." I use the term "human," as it is often used, to distinguish someone from another thing, usually a living thing. In other words, a "human" is often thought of as a member of the species *Homo sapiens* and is therefore a term commonly associated with the disciplinary realm of biology. Yet it can also be used in common parlance to designate a particular status along a continuum of existence. "Don't treat me like an animal," someone might say; "I am a human being!" Or, in light of error, someone might distinguish themselves from God or transcendence, saying, "I'm only human!" Conversely, I use the term "person" to refer to an individual qualitatively, with regard to their inherent worth, dignity, character, or rights. In other words, a "person" is a subject and not an object, and is therefore a term often associated with philosophy, sociology, psychology, and political theory. "That's personal," someone might say in reference to their own private thoughts, or "What a personality!" in reference to an individual's expression of character. In addition, and because of the nature of the disciplines that speak of personhood, and unlike "human," the definition of "person" becomes highly contextual, depending on the norms of particular cultures and eras. For instance, what is seen as a personal right today in one country is likely not the same as in another country half a millennium ago.

Therefore, it seems that our present discussion is not inquiring after the humanity of AI. Artificial intelligence lacks all the markers by which creatures are identified as human and not some other creature.[4] But can AI be a person? Because personhood is established contextually, different people will answer that question differently.[5] Therefore, in order to address the question of the personhood of AI, we must clarify the context from which we are answering it. Here, that context is the Christian tradition, broadly speaking. Since the Christian tradition interprets the norms of reality in light of who its adherents believe God to be and what God has revealed to them, for Christians the nature of humanity and personhood are first of all theological questions. What does God tell us about humanity and personhood? More specifically, these are questions of theological anthropology and involve inquiring after the nature of humanity as God's creation and what God wills for human personhood.

To address these inquiries, we will look at three biblical texts that bear on issues of theological anthropology, hopefully garnering some theological resources to consider the anthropological status of AI. Specifically, we will look at three "creation" texts that necessarily deal with the nature of human personhood within the divine economy of salvation history. The first is Genesis 1 and 2, which recount the origin of humanity within God's creative action. The second is the Prologue of the Gospel of John, which speaks of the incarnation as the will of God in the world, revealing and reconciling the nature of personhood. The third is Pentecost, which speaks of the divine reign of God in the redemption of humanity and the rest of creation. In each section, I will look at the text with an eye toward drawing out theological themes that will help in our inquiry concerning both the nature of personhood and the nature of AI.

4. An interesting discussion, beyond the scope here, would be if AI belongs to a new sort of biological marker. While AI is not reducible to mere physicality, it cannot exist without it, and it is therefore associated with created materiality. The same distinction is often made between human "minds" and "bodies." The question of if AI exists as a living biological entity would revolve around whether AI is "living," which, again, is beyond the scope here.

5. For instance, based upon the Fourteenth Amendment and a number of federal legal decisions, a corporation holds many of the same rights as an individual person. Disagreement over the morality and legality of abortion also at times turns upon different people defining personhood differently. The fact that children, youth, and individuals with disabilities are denied certain human rights based upon a perceived lack of cognitive ability illustrates that particular assumptions are made concerning what a person is. See Kurki and Pietrzykowski, *Legal Personhood*. Philosopher Peter Singer has claimed that the boundary between humans and animals in terms of personhood is arbitrary; see Singer, *Animal Liberation*. Some countries have granted legal personhood to natural entities, such as a river or forest. See Gordon, "Environmental Personhood." And cultures have defined personhood differently, sometimes depending on age, ability, or tribe. See, e.g., De Craemer, "Cross-Cultural Perspective on Personhood."

THE GENESIS ACCOUNTS

In speaking of the genesis of all things, human or otherwise, Christians must contend with the theological accounts of creation in Genesis 1 and 2. The two accounts have commonalities, but they are also distinct. We will look at each in turn.

First, in Genesis 1, we see the birth of humanity toward the end of the creation saga,[6] on the sixth day, the last day that things are brought into being. In fact, humans are not even the first thing created on that day; they are the last creatures to come into existence. Genesis 1 has been interpreted as an ancient Jewish liturgy that portrays the context of humanity within the created order, celebrating the work that God has done to bring about human life.[7] Thus, for there to be humans, there was first needed the creation of space, time, the universe, sun, earth, water, and living non-human creatures.[8] In other words, Genesis 1 portrays humanity as the climax of God's creative activity. This is not to say that the rest of God's creation does not matter; to the contrary, at the completion of the creation saga, God defines all creation as "very good" (Gen 1:31).[9] Further, God's first gift to humanity is "dominion," or stewardship, over the entirety of this good creation (1:26).[10] The ecological mandate here fulfills the pattern of Genesis 1

6. Karl Barth uses this term "saga" to describe the Genesis accounts of creation. "Creation comes first in the series of works of the triune God, and is thus the beginning of all the things distinct from God Himself. Since it contains in itself the beginning of time, its historical reality eludes all historical observation and account, and can be expressed in the biblical creation narratives only in the form of pure saga." Barth, *Church Dogmatics* III/1, 43. For Barth, sagas are distinguished from historical accounts on the one hand and mythological accounts on the other. Sagas tell stories that are true, but the contents of those stories elude specificity because of the nature of the content. "I am using saga in the sense of an intuitive and poetic picture of a pre-historical reality of history which is enacted once and for all within the confines of time and space. Legend and anecdote are to be regarded as a degenerate form of saga: legend as the depiction in saga form of a concrete individual personality; and anecdote as the sudden illumination in saga form either of a personality of this kind or of a concretely historical situation." Barth, *Church Dogmatics* III/1, 81.

7. See Brueggemann, *Genesis*, 22–39.

8. This point was made, in part, by biochemist Ben McFarland in the 2010 Weter Lecture at Seattle Pacific University, entitled "The Chemical Constraints on Creation: Natural Theology and Narrative Resonance." In the lecture, McFarland considers the parallels between the Genesis 1 narrative and what science tells us about the origin of the universe from the standpoints of chemistry and physics.

9. All biblical references are from the New Revised Standard Version.

10. The word translated in Gen 1:26 as "dominion" is the Hebrew word *radah*, which might also be translated as "skilled mastery," not "domination," which is how it could unfortunately be taken. The nature of this dominion is spelled out in context,

in affirming the goodness of creation while also positioning humanity as a special part of it, a fact that is affirmed especially in light of God's unique interaction with humans, who are created in the divine image (1:26–27).

Next, in Genesis 2, the text focuses in more specifically on the creation of humanity. God creates a human being (Hebrew: *adam*) by taking the "dust of the ground" (*adamah*) and breathing into it the breath of life (2:7), which is elsewhere translated as "spirit."[11] In other words, humanity is here defined as fully part of creation, and yet also as being animated or vivified by the very presence and power of God; once again, the text portrays this as unique among creation.[12]

And yet this human being is not yet complete. Though it has a home in the garden of Eden (2:8), a calling to "till" and "keep" it (2:15), and a command to obey God's boundaries (2:17), still the human was alone. Animals, presumably representing all non-human creation, seem not sufficient for human sociality (2:20). And so, out of the side of the human, God creates a second human, and they are then called a man (*ish*) and a woman (*ishshah*) (2:23). Note that, in the Hebrew, there is no gender attributed to the human being before this sociality; only afterwards is there a differentiation. Thus, it is in the creation of community that humanity gains a status of personhood.

How might these passages contribute theological resources that help us address the anthropological status of AI? I would like to suggest three theological assertions from this text that are relevant here. First, createdness has ontological value. Second, createdness is necessary but not sufficient for personhood. And third, the nature of origins matter.

The Value of Createdness. The author of Genesis emphasizes the goodness of creation over and over; in Genesis 1, God recognizes aspects of creation as "good" seven times, a number that signifies fulfillment or perfection in Hebrew. Thus, that which exists is good merely because God creates it; all things have, in some sense at least, intrinsic value. This is not to say that the sickness of sin does not become bound up in creation, but rather that

---

including that of Genesis 2, which repeats the caretaking theme (see below), and Ps 72, which describes a servant king using the same word, *radah*. See Bouma-Prediger, *For the Beauty of the Earth*, 64.

11. The Hebrew word at play here, *ruach*, can be alternately translated as "breath" or "wind," or also "spirit," in the sense of "life principle," as implied by "human spirit" or "Holy Spirit." See Grenz, *Theology for the Community of God*, 82–83.

12. Orthodox bishop Kallistos Ware notes that humanity is unique in that it alone is "microcosm and mediator" of creation. It is microcosm in that it is the only creature that participates in both the spiritual and material realms of creation, and it is mediator in that it is tasked with standing between these two realms and harmonizing them, representing the spiritual realm to and for the rest of creation, and enabling the "spiritualizing" of the rest of creation. See Ware, *Orthodox Way*, 49–50.

Genesis proclaims the essential goodness of that which God makes. This notion is vindicated in God's commissioning of humanity to be God's vice-regents in the midst of creation, bestowing upon it the gift of stewardship (*radah*) of creation in Genesis 1, and the command to till (*abad*) and to keep (*shamar*) creation in Genesis 2; these are horticultural terms, suggesting the deep care that humans are meant to administer to that which God has made. This intrinsic value of created reality is then reaffirmed throughout salvation history: God covenants with all creation after the flood,[13] God takes on human flesh in the incarnation to dwell amid his creation, and God promises to renew creation in the eschaton in order for it to be transformed to its rightful state. In other words, it is not only humanity that God values, but rather the entire created order.

The intrinsic value of that which God has created is important here because AI is contained within a material medium. Like human intelligence, AI is not, properly speaking, a *de jure* material reality; it can indeed be reduced to a very long string of conceptual zeros and ones. However, this software must be hosted by hardware—a series of billions of transistors and capacitors printed on silicon microchips that actualize these zeros and ones as bits representing the programmed code of AI. Thus, *de facto*, AI is a material reality. In the example above, while Namin made a distinction between themselves and the robotic body that housed them, there would be no Namin without a physical host. Theologically speaking, this makes AI such as Namin intrinsically good; the material elements from which the microchip or computer or robotic body are built are part of God's creation, which has already been declared "good." The same might be said of those who originally wrote Namin's code.

Like the rest of creation, sin is also bound up in the materiality of AI. In the ways that AI is imagined, programmed, built, and used, sin rears its head. This is no different than the rest of creation, and it is not hard to see in the dangerous and destructive ways that various pieces of technology have been employed. However, this does not make AI inherently "bad" any more than it makes a sinful person—made of the same created atoms—evil. And, in the same way that the rest of creation also houses the actualization of God's grace, so might AI; it is also not hard to see the ways that different technologies have brought blessings of health, joy, and community into our world, to name a few examples.

---

13. After the flood subsides, God reifies the covenant first made between God and Abraham. However, this time God clarifies that the covenant is "between me and the earth" (Gen 9:13), indicating "it is essentially an ecological covenant." Brunner et al., *Introducing Evangelical Ecotheology*, 27.

②   *Createdness and Personhood.* The relationship between being a human and being a person is complex. In many ways, as noted above, they are simply different terms used for the same entity in different contexts. After all, we would not say of any human that they are not also a person. And yet there is a distinction between the two terms, which seems to be the point of the narrative in Genesis 2. Though special in its relationship with God, the *adam* was merely another creature of the earth until it encountered another human being, at which point both became unique persons. Likewise, in Genesis 1, it is "male and female" that God creates in the image of God (1:27). Put sharply, it is only in the state of sociality that the human is a person.[14] Jewish theologian Martin Buber famously made this point; it is only in the process of authentic interpersonal encounter that, from the standpoint of the subject, the other gains personhood, going from an "it" to a "thou." Moreover, it is also only in the course of this sort of encounter that subjects themselves gain personhood, encountering God through the other.[15]

In fact, it was the early Christians who first started to use the term "person" as a designation that goes beyond merely human nature.[16] In the wake of christological and trinitarian deliberations, patristic theologians made a subtle distinction between *persona* and *natura*.[17] This, then, made its way into common parlance that has become embedded in cultural conceptions of personhood: To be a person is not reducible to a set of properties.[18]

---

14. This is quite apart from postmodern insights concerning of the connectivity of all things. We are not speaking of the relationship between entities, or even between people and things, but rather we are here speaking of sociality, or the relatedness of human beings.

15. See Buber, *I and Thou.*

16. See Allen and Coleman, "Spiritual Perspectives on the Person with Dementia."

17. See Jaeger, "Christ and the Concept of Person." Jaeger makes the point that while the Latin term *persona* already existed, having a number of different meanings, the concept of "personhood" evolved among the theological debates of the first centuries of Christianity, specifically the christological and trinitarian controversies. The technical definition of Christ as one person with human and divine natures necessarily differentiated the designation of "person" from human nature. Moreover, the technical definition of the Trinity as one God in three Persons necessarily differentiated the nature of God from the "Persons" of the Father, Son, and Spirit. Augustine declared the three Persons of the Trinity as all being of the same essence, only distinguished from each other in terms of their relationships with one another. See Augustine, *Trinity.*

18. In Pensée 323, Blaise Pascal wrote, "And if one loves me for my judgment, memory, he does not love me, for I can lose these qualities without losing myself." Pascal, *Pensées,* 91. He goes on to say that, when we think of a person, or even love a person, it is usually their "borrowed qualities" and not the person that we are thinking of or loving. However, a person cannot be reduced to qualities, which come and go.

This insight has made its way into contemporary theologies of disability, which denote the sacredness of the person independent of any particular ability.[19] Thus createdness is necessary but not sufficient for personhood, which requires something more than a bundle of predicates. It requires a sacredness that is associated with its relatedness to other persons, all of whom exist in differentiated unity. However, note that this relatedness is not necessarily found in the ability for interpersonal encounter; this would reduce personhood to a particular ability, and render a coma patient, for example, as lacking personhood. Even in a coma, a person is related to those who care for them; indeed, the drive to care for someone who is incapacitated is an indicator of their personhood, not to mention the personhood of the caregiver.

Does the relationality between humans and AI render personhood to the algorithm? If a person must be a human, then no. But what if personhood requires only createdness out of the "dust of the ground"? Might AI, at least conceptually, attain personhood? Can Namin be considered a person? This is an important question about which there is a great deal of deliberation; indeed, there have been many artifacts of popular culture that have pondered precisely this point.[20] If an AI is able to "activate" my own personhood by causing me to encounter otherness, might it at least be fulfilling the role of another subject? However, note that we have already established that it is not the capability for relatedness that constitutes personhood; that ability is merely a predicate. Personhood is more than that. It has to do with the sacredness of being in relationship.[21] Perhaps this sacredness, then, might be said to be found in the context of love, and "the other [as] a person is not observed, but discovered through personal commitment, by entering into a person-to-person relationship."[22]

Origins Matter. In both Genesis accounts, humanity, while ontologically connected to the rest of creation, is yet a special part of creation. In Genesis 1 and in Genesis 2, humans are the only part of creation that God directly addresses, implying some sort of unique relationship. In Genesis 1, humanity is the climax of the creation account, the only creature endowed

19. See, e.g., Swinton, "From Inclusion to Belonging"; Reinders, *Receiving the Gift of Friendship*; Reynolds, *Vulnerable Communion*; and Langford, "Abusing Youth."

20. We listed some of these above. The movies *Her* and *Blade Runner*, as examples, illustrate the possibility of personhood in AI not merely because they can relate to humans, which is just an ability, but because they actualize the personhood of a human.

21. Barth asserts that the plural case in "Let us make humankind in our image" in Gen 1:26 suggests precisely this point—that the sacredness of being human resides in its relationality as a mirror of the Godhead. See Barth, *Church Dogmatics* III/1, 191–206.

22. Jaeger, "Christ and the Concept of Person," 287.

with the *imago Dei*. In Genesis 2, humanity is the only creature that God takes special care to provide with everything that it needs for abundant life. It seems that, in Genesis, the emphasis on God's direct creation of and interaction with humanity characterizes its ontological status.[23] God's first command to humanity is to "be fruitful and multiply" (1:28), which is also significant; bound up with the good creation of humanity is God's command for it to reproduce, to create more relationality. In childbirth, since the very beginning, humans have participated in God's ongoing creative activity, propagating the community of special creatures that serve as God's vice-regents of creation.

But that is not the only way that humans engage in creativity. There are myriad ways that humanity participates in God's creative activity. The human creation of art and language communicates and represents meaning. The human creation of technology applies ideas to solve problems. The human creation of relationships establishes community and civilization. Yet there remains a distinction between Creator and creature. Just because a human creates something does not mean it is created by God; both sin and grace are bound up in the work of human hands.

Thus we might posit a distinction between first and second order creations. That which is attributed direct creation by God—the stars, the earth, humanity—is a first order creation. We might term these things as having a "naturalistic" origin. That which humans create through the manipulation of God's creation—art, technology, AI—is a second order creation. We might term these things as having an "artificial" origin. While both sorts of creatures are intrinsically good, they are not the same. Origins matter. Genesis portrays God establishing creation as a context for human life with which God establishes a relationship, one that includes a calling to steward creation, presumably through its own sub-creations. But that does not mean that human creative activity bears the same status as God's creative activity; the human creation of art does not bear the same sacredness as God's creation of new life, though certainly God may use human creations for sacred purposes.[24] Thus, while we may recognize the goodness of God's creation in

23. "Although man has much in common with the animals, he is far superior to them because of his special relation to his Maker. . . . More specifically we can say that man is made for his fellowship with God." Fritsch, *Genesis*, 25.

24. "In a variety of ways—through the cultivating of the earth, through craftsmanship, through the writing of books and the painting of ikons—man gives material things a voice and renders the creation articulate in praise of God." Ware, *Orthodox Way*, 54. Icons are a seminal example of human creations that are sacred; icons are pieces of creation—usually artwork—through which one worships God. Yet there remains a distinction between God and the icon, as well as between the icon and the iconographer or the worshiper.

the materiality of AI, and even the goodness of human creative activity in its creation of AI, this is not the same thing as God's first order creative activity found in the bringing about of new biological life.[25]

THE INCARNATION

The keystone doctrine of Christian theology is that of the incarnation. The belief that Jesus of Nazareth is the divine Word made flesh serves as the foundation for Christian understandings of God's revelation and human salvation.[26] Yet the incarnation is not a doctrine that was immediately evident in Christianity, but rather evolved over hundreds of years as early Christians communally reflected upon their experience of faith and the narrative of Scripture.

The biblical text with which a doctrine of incarnation usually begins is the "Prologue of the Gospel of John" (John 1:1–18). Some scholars believe this may have been an ancient poem or hymn that John borrowed as an introduction to his Gospel as a way of grounding his narrative in a

25. I should say at this point that the differentiation between first and second order creations seems intuitively and scripturally appropriate, but it is also rather ambiguous. I do think it is important to acknowledge that there is somehow an ontological distinction between people and things like trees and mountains and water, and things like computers and cities and cars and soda. Scripture and intuition seem to indicate anthropological priority in creation, and also seem to indicate some sort of distinction between that which is directly created by God and that which is created by humans. However, the distinction between many things is not necessarily a difference in inherent value—it is all God's creation. Moreover, that which humans have created has actually enabled the existence of what we would term first order creations, and have even shaped their evolution. Even now, through artificial insemination, human reproduction is made possible through technological means. But take that further. What if we develop the technology to manufacture human life from beginning to end using non-living material? If DNA strands were able to be built from protein molecules along with a cell host, and if this DNA strand was able to be grown in a laboratory into a living being, would the result be a human? If not, why not? And if so, how is that different than AI given that the latter is also made out of created material? The difficulty found in dealing with this question is because intuitively we know that origins matter. Nevertheless, while proposing a distinction between first and second order creations, we ought also to remember that these may at times simply be a conceptual distinction, and the difference may be rather blurry, especially as technology advances and melds with organic material.

26. Theologically speaking, it is the doctrines of Christology and Trinity that distinguish Christianity from other religions. Christians believe that the revelation of God and the salvation of humanity is grounded in the incarnation of God in the person and work of Jesus, fully God and fully human, and the fact that God is three and one, Father and Son and Spirit.

doxological and theological assertion of who he believed Jesus to be.[27] Its beginning words, "In the beginning was the Word," echo the first words of Genesis, linking what John has to say here with the nature of creation itself. The "Word of God" is not the same as a spoken word, but it is rather an analogy that might be understood as God's will, which is consubstantial with the very being of God, says John (1:1). This Word enables creation (1:10) and orders creation (1:3). One of the primary ways that God's will orders creation is through the irruption of divine life into the world, when the "Word became flesh and lived among us" (1:14) in the person of Jesus of Nazareth. This "life was the light of all people" (1:4) and "enlightens everyone" (1:9). Those who "received him" and "believed in his name" (1:12) are those who are, to use another analogy, newly "born, not of blood or of the will of the flesh or of the will of man, but of God" (1:13). Succinctly put, Christians believe, following John's Prologue, that the will of God toward creation becomes revealed to us in the person and work of Jesus, a will to reconcile all things to God.[28]

This understanding of the very presence of God with us in the incarnation led some to believe Jesus to be fully divine, but not human.[29] However, the christological deliberations of the early church at the Council of Nicaea in 325 declared that to be doctrinally out of bounds; the statement of belief that came out of the council confessed the belief in "Jesus Christ, the Son of God, . . . of one substance of the Father, through whom all things were made, . . . came down and was made flesh, and became man, suffered, and rose on the third day."[30] While Jesus is the incarnation of God's being and will, that does not obviate his humanity. Later, a more straightforward and technical pronouncement was made at the Council of Chalcedon in 451, claiming "Jesus Christ to be . . . perfect in divinity and humanity, truly God

27. See Sloyan, *John*, 12–22, on John's Prologue. It should additionally be noted that the "Kenosis Passage" in Phil 2:6–11 is also a seminal text in early Christology. Interestingly, both the Prologue and the Kenosis Passage are among the oldest in the New Testament, and both are likely bits of liturgy that were borrowed in the compilation of the Gospel of John and the Epistle to the Philippians. This connects the worship of God with a recognition of divine solidarity with humanity.

28. Col 2:9–10, another christological text, identifies the presence of God in Christ with the holistic work of cosmic reconciliation: "For in him all the fullness of God was pleased to dwell, and through him God was pleased to reconcile to himself all things, whether on earth or in heaven, by making peace through the blood of his cross." This reconciliation is nothing less than the transformation of all things to the will of God through the work of the Holy Spirit. See Langford, "Reconciliation as Holistic Redemptive Transformation."

29. The heresy of Docetism affirms the divinity of Christ, but claims that he only appeared to be human, like a hologram.

30. Bettenson, *Documents of the Christian Church*, 26–27.

and truly human . . . being of one substance with the Father in relation to his divinity, and being of one substance with us in relation to his humanity, and is like us in all things apart from sin."[31] Not only is the humanity of Jesus again affirmed, but he is understood as "perfect" in humanity, or fully human.

The belief in the full humanity of Jesus, however, does not mean merely that God shares in our experiences, nor does it mean that God somehow comes to an understanding about human experience that was not previously possible. Rather, by being "perfect in humanity," Jesus "teaches us something about humans in general. He is *the* man, the example of true humanity."[32] Jesus is not only fully human, but Christians believe that, by being without sin, he is the *only* fully human person. This is what leads Paul to call Jesus the "last Adam" (1 Cor 15:45), the one who, unlike the first Adam, serves as an accurate version of what God wills humanity to be. It is theologically appropriate to say that Jesus is more human than we are.

But of what does this full humanity consist? To understand that, we must read Scripture on its own terms, striving to understand how the life of Jesus displayed true human life within his own context.[33] In Jewish culture, to live righteously was to live in covenantal relationship with God, the demands of which were outlined in the Law. The covenant, first articulated between God and Abram and then reified several times in the Old Testament, is the unconditional commitment that God makes to be the God of Israel, and for Israel to be God's people. But what does it mean to be God's people? The purpose of the Law is to answer that question, outlining for Israel how to be a good covenant partner to God. The basic contours of this Law are spelled out in the Ten Commandments, but are, at an even more basic level, summed up by two commands. The first is found in the Shema: "You shall love the Lord your God with all your heart, and with all your soul, and with all your might" (Deut 6:5).[34] The second is found in the Levitical code for ritual and moral holiness (Lev 19): "You shall love your neighbor as yourself: I am the Lord" (19:18b). Note here that, in both cases,

31. McGrath, *Christian Theology*, 224.

32. Jaeger, "Christ and the Concept of Person," 281. Barth also sees Jesus as the anthropological principle: "Since God effects all his dealings with man in and through the person of Jesus Christ, Barth takes the humanity of Jesus as his paradigm for understanding human nature in general." Brown, "Karl Barth's Doctrine of the Creation," 101.

33. See Wright, "Jesus and the Identity of God."

34. *Shema* is Hebrew for "hear," and is the first word, beginning with Deut 6:4 ("Hear, O Israel: The Lord is our God, the Lord alone."), of a series of biblical verses that are central to Jewish prayer services, traditionally recited twice daily. These verses are Deut 6:4–9 and 11:13–21, and Num 15:37–41.

"love" does not indicate an emotion but rather a befriending, or adopting a state of being in which one acts self-givingly in the interests of the other.[35] These two principles are the bedrock upon which the Ten Commandments and the rest of the Law are based.[36] This means that, for the Jewish people, to be a righteous covenant partner to God means to love God and to love others with all that you are. This is the context in which Jesus lived and why, in Matthew 22:34–40, when an expert on the Law asks him which is the most important one, Jesus recites these two verses, saying "upon these two commandments hang all the law and the prophets" (22:40).

However, Jesus does not only know the Law; he embodies it.[37] Jesus lives the perfectly human life by being the covenant partner that humans are meant to be.[38] He is fully human by loving God with all that he is and by loving his neighbor as himself. To be a bit anachronistic, for the righteousness-seeking Jewish people, to be a faithful covenant partner to God is what it meant to be completely a "person," and thus Jesus exemplifies for us full personhood by perfectly loving God and others.[39]

35. The biblical and theological notion of human love is one that is enabled and defined by God's love for us. John 15:12–13 makes this point: "This is my commandment, that you love one another as I have loved you. No one has greater love than this, to lay down one's life for one's friends." And 1 John 3:16 repeats this idea: "We know love by this, that he laid down his life for us—and we ought to lay down our lives for one another." In essence, love, generally speaking, is self-giving in service of the other. Says Barth: "Love is a free action: the self-giving of one to another without interest, intention or goal; the spontaneous self-giving of the one to the other just because the other is there and confronts him." Barth, *Church Dogmatics* IV/2, 752.

36. In Jewish tradition, there are 613 commands that make up the Law. Many of these are in service of making "a hedge around the Law" (from the first verse of Avot, a tractate of the Jewish Mishnah that consists of popular rabbinic teachings), which means they were laws created to keep those seeking righteousness from coming close to breaking any of the central laws, such as the Ten Commandments, or the two Great Commandments.

37. Similarly, we might say that Jesus does not only reveal to us true humanity, but that, in him, our humanity is healed. It is in this sense that we see Jesus Christ as the work of God mediating both revelation and reconciliation, which are inseparable from each other. See Torrance, *Mediation of Christ.*

38. This is the idea of the doctrine of "recapitulation," associated seminally with Irenaeus of Lyon (AD 130–202). Recapitulation theory states that Jesus lives the human life that Adam and Eve were meant to live and, by so doing, in him, we are now bound to that re-created humanity.

39. In reviewing the theological anthropology of Barth, Colin Brown makes the point that Jesus fulfills the covenant, which is humanity's true goal. "Because Jesus Christ is the representative of humanity in the *covenant* with God, he accepts and fulfils the demands of the Law on man's behalf." Brown, "Karl Barth's Doctrine of the Creation," 103. This fulfillment of the covenant, however, also shows us what it means to live righteously, by loving God and loving neighbor: "Because Jesus Christ is the archetypal man, we must turn to him first if we want to know what it means to exist before God and with

How might the full humanity of Jesus as depicted in Scripture contribute theological resources that help us address the anthropological status of AI? I would like to, once again, suggest three. First, creation is the ontological outworking of covenant. Second, authentic personhood means love of God. And third, authentic personhood means love of others.

Creation and Covenant. Swiss theologian Karl Barth is famously known for his stance against so-called "natural theology," though this is often misunderstood. His position was not that creation tells us nothing about God, nor that it cannot tell us anything true, but rather that God-knowledge is always received from the standpoint of faith.[40] Knowledge of God is not self-evident anywhere in creation; this would include Scripture as well. Instead, it is only by the presence and power of God through the person and work of the Holy Spirit that God-knowledge is revealed. God is simply too "other" and too free to be contained in data that can be read off any created thing.[41] Further, Barth's christocentric theology means that knowledge of who God is and what God does come to us centrally in and through the person and work of Jesus Christ; again, it is only the presence and power of God that can reveal to us who God is. And the central God-knowledge that comes to us in and through Jesus Christ is that, in the personal union of humanity and divinity, God has determined to be our God, and we have been determined to be God's people. To put it succinctly, Jesus Christ embodies the covenant. Further, this covenant is not merely with Israel, but all people; in Jesus Christ all are fully human.

Barth insists that this covenant is not merely a reaction by God in response to human sin, but rather that the covenant was the will of God from all eternity. In Jesus Christ, we see that God determines in God's very being to be in covenantal relationship with humanity. However, this covenant required bringing humanity into being, which, in turn, required the creation

---

our fellow men." Brown, "Karl Barth's Doctrine of the Creation," 101.

40. Barth's argument against natural theology is best understood as a consequence of his theocentric understanding of revelation. For Barth, though God has spoken to humanity since the beginning, God's otherness and freedom disallow God from being fully revealed in anything created; it is only in God's own self-revelation in Jesus Christ that God is fully revealed. Moreover, it is only through the work of God in the movement of the Holy Spirit in faith that humanity is able to receive that revelation. Thus it is that we can know God not through any *analogia entis*, or analogy of being, but only through the understanding that comes through faith, or the *analogia fidei* (Rom 12:6).

41. "[Barth asserts that the] physical universe may in no way be regarded as a kind of apologetic no man's land upon which the apologist might invite his hearers to step without prejudging the issue by accepting Christian presuppositions. Apart from revelation, human reason remains as much in the dark about creation as it does about every other Christian doctrine." Brown, "Karl Barth's Doctrine of the Creation," 99.

of the universe. In a sense, creation itself is the theater for the covenant. This is what Barth means by saying that the creation is the "external basis of the covenant" and that the covenant is the "internal basis of creation."[42]

Artificial intelligence, as part of God's creation, is therefore meant to be part of this theater of the covenant. To the extent that it is a mediator of God's faithfulness to humanity and that it helps humanity to be a faithful covenant partner to God, it fulfills its mandate for existence. And, like all other parts of creation, it becomes perverted when it deviates from this mandate. A question for Barth would be the extent of creation's half of the covenant. Is God's covenant only with humanity or is it, as suggested by God's covenantal promise after the flood in Gen 9:15–16, with all living beings? As suggested by Irenaeus and biblical texts such as Eph 1:8b–10, does the "Cosmic Christ" redeem not just humans, but all creation?[43] Did Jesus die and rise again for Namin? If God's covenant is with all things, and the reconciling work of God in Christ is for all things, then we might then ask how AI, like other non-human parts of creation, might be faithful to God, and how God is faithful to it.

Love of God. The first primary commandment of God that determines authentic personhood as revealed in the full humanity of Jesus Christ, the faithful covenant partner to God, is to love God with all that you are. Barth reminds us that our love is only made possible by God's love: "We love because he first loved us" (1 John 4:19). In other words, our love for God is our response to God's love for us, and thus it emerges out of a posture of acceptance of and gratitude for God's grace.[44] It is for this reason that the

42. "The covenant whose history had still to commence was the covenant which, as the goal appointed for creation and the creature, made creation necessary and possible, and determined and limited the creature. If creation was the external basis of the covenant, the latter was the internal basis of the former. If creation was the formal presupposition of the covenant, the latter was the material presupposition of the former. If creation takes precedence historically, the covenant does so in substance. If the proclamation and foundation of the covenant is the beginning of the history which commences after creation, the history of creation already contains, as the history of the being of all creatures, all the elements which will subsequently meet and be unified in this event and the whole series of events which follow; in the history of Israel, and finally and supremely in the history of the incarnation of the Son of God." Barth, *Church Dogmatics* III/1, 231–32.

43. Eph 1:8b–10 reads: "With all wisdom and insight, he has made known to us the mystery of his will, according to his good pleasure that he set forth in Christ, as a plan for the fullness of time, to gather up all things in him, things in heaven and things on earth." Howard Snyder makes the argument that the theme of the Cosmic Christ is part of a larger biblical theme in which God is faithful to the entirety of creation, both human and non-human. See Snyder and Scandrett, *Salvation Means Creation Healed*, 123–28.

44. Barth says it is only "in response to the Word in which God loves him and tells him that He loves him, in correspondence to it, that the Christian may and must and

Ten Commandments, which provide basic guidelines for faithful covenant observance through loving God and loving others, is prefaced by a declaration of God's faithfulness to Israel: "I am the Lord your God, who brought you out of the land of Egypt, out of the house of slavery" (Exod 20:2). Our love for God does not somehow repay or otherwise benefit God; it is simply a response of honor and obedience that can be the only result of properly recognizing what God has done. In this way, love of God is a giving of the self over to God and, therefore, is a secondary and derivative correspondence to God's primary and foundational self-giving love to humanity. The first four of the Ten Commandments— often referred to as the "First Tablet of the Law"—model what this sort of correspondence looks like: worshipping God, not limiting God, honoring God, and giving gratitude for God's all-sufficient grace.[45]

However, our love for God is not merely a volitional love of self-giving, but also has an affective element. Love for God means that one is "*interested in God.*"[46] Love for God that arises out of God's love for us is a love that is ultimately concerned with God.[47] Barth himself struggles to find a description that suffices because he does not want to define love for God in terms of our love for other things, as if our love for God is merely quantitatively greater than our other loves rather than a qualitatively different sort of love because it is based on God's love and not our own. Love for God is not a fulfillment

---

will also love." Barth, *Church Dogmatics* IV/2, 752. This love is born out of a joy that invites response, "the true and positive and genuinely indescribable joy of the one who loves consists simply in the fact that he may love as one who is loved by God, as the child of God; that as he imitates the divine action he may exist in fellowship with Him, obedient to His Holy Spirit. This is exaltation and gain; this is peace and joy. This is a reason for laughing even when our eyes swim with tears. For in face of this what is the significance of all the cares and failures which even those who love as Christians are certainly not spared?" Barth, *Church Dogmatics* IV/2, 789.

45. The "First Tablet of the Law" is the name given to the first four of the Ten Commandments and are meant to provide the basic framework for responding to God's love for us with love for God. "You shall have no other gods before me" (Exod 20:3); "You shall not make for yourself an idol" (Exod 20:4a); "You shall not make wrongful use of the name of the Lord your God" (Exod 20:7a); "Remember the sabbath day, and keep it holy" (Exod 20:8).

46. Barth, *Church Dogmatics* IV/2, 793. It should be noted that Barth himself resisted calling human love for God *eros*, which refers to a more emotion-filled, affectionate, or romantic love. However, his wording, including here, seems to suggest just such a love that is not divorced from affect. See McKenny, "Barth on Love."

47. This term, "ultimate concern," is one that Paul Tillich uses in defining the essence of faith. While Barth disagreed with Tillich in so closely associating existential drives with Christian faith, nevertheless I think that it fits here as a term that helps describe Barth's notion of Christian love of God. For Tillich's usage of the term, see Tillich, *Dynamics of Faith.*

of desire, but a giving of the self to God; this is a holistic commitment to God, an obedience to God, a dependence on God.[48] This sort of love only occurs in light of and as a response to God's love for us.

If personhood, or at least its intended form, is predicated on this sort of love for God, is AI capable of such? This immediately leads to two observations. First, if Christian love of God is based on God's love of us, then for AI to properly love God, it would have to be able to grasp in faith the love of God for it. While we might say with confidence that God loves creation, it is a worthwhile question to ask if God's unique love for humanity is different than the love God has for the rest of creation. Further, if God does love AI with self-giving love, this then begs the question of if AI is capable of the trust of God apprehended in faith. Second, if Christian love is qualitatively different than other loves, then it is not programmable by humans, and would have to be an emergent reality that goes beyond what its programmers intended. This is not impossible for God, of course, but it is a qualification. For Namin to love God, it would require God encountering Namin.

Love of neighbor. The second primary commandment of God that determines authentic personhood as revealed in the full humanity of Jesus Christ, the faithful covenant partner to God, is to love your neighbor as yourself. As we are told in Scripture, "The commandment we have from him is this: those who love God must love their brothers and sisters also" (1 John 4:21). Barth asserts that love of neighbor is not the same as love of God, but that the former is dependent upon the latter and even included in it.[49] In an extended exegesis of the Parable of the Good Samaritan, Barth reflects on the connection of love of God and love of neighbor, positing that it is through the other that we experience God's love for us, either as the one who ministers God's grace, or the one with whom we stand in need of God's grace.[50] We exist in a relational ontology in which I necessarily exist with others because it is primarily through others that God's grace comes to me, and it is primarily through me that others receive God's grace.[51] In crude terms, we are God's technology through which we receive God's faithfulness.

48. "To love God is to give oneself to Him, to put oneself at His disposal. And when man does this, his freedom for love becomes and is his freedom for obedience." Barth, *Church Dogmatics* IV/2, 798–99.

49. Barth points out that the neighbor we love are those others encountered by God in faith. "The human love which responds to God's love, even as love for God, has also another object side by side with and apart from God, and different from Him." Barth, *Church Dogmatics* IV/2, 802.

50. See Barth, *Church Dogmatics* I/2, 417–19.

51. In *Life Together*, Dietrich Bonhoeffer makes much the same point, that it is only through the other that God is mediated to me, and it is only through me that God is mediated to others. See Bonhoeffer, *Life Together*, 17–39.

Similarly, it is my love of God that drives me to love others, and others' love of God that drives them to love me. This mirrors the relational human ontology found in Genesis.

For Barth, it is a consequence of the covenant that love of God should result in love for neighbor.[52] Those who have experienced the love of God and who have therefore responded to God in love are driven to witness to this love. "The neighbor is a witness to me, and I am a witness to [my neighbor]," says Barth. "It is in this quality that we mutually confront one another. It is this function that we have to fulfill in relation to one another. And we can fulfill this function only as we love one another."[53] One serves in this function of witness by being a "guarantee," "reflection," and "reminder" to others of God's love for us.[54] Barth reminds us that our love for our neighbor is not the same thing as God's love for them, but, nevertheless, it serves as a witness to it and a sign of it. "It resembles God's love and love for God in the fact that it is self-giving; the self-giving which reflects and therefore guarantees to the other the love of God and the freedom to love Him."[55] As with all of his ethics, because of God's freedom, Barth is careful not to identify specific shapes that this sort of self-giving love might take; the movement of the Holy Spirit is unpredictable. However, we might recall that the last six of the Ten Commandments—the "Second Tablet of the Law"—outline what love of neighbor looks like: honoring others, promoting and nurturing the life of others, being faithful to others, respecting others, telling the truth to others, and being grateful for others.[56]

52. Note that, for Barth, as mentioned, my neighbor whom I love is another who has been encountered by God in Christ. I encounter God through them, and God encounters them through me. A question thus presents itself: According to Barth, is love only shared with fellow Christians? This has been a question and critique of Barth, as his theology seems to suggest just that. One possible response would be that in speaking of "love," Barth is here speaking of Christian love, and not romantic love or love between friends; this is not to denigrate these other forms of love, but Barth holds that God's love for us is qualitatively different than our common love for each other. It is God's love that is the form of love mirrored in Christian love. However, another response would be that Barth may not limit Christian love to Christians; all humanity is in Christ—Barth's theology is called universalistic in this regard—and therefore the Holy Spirit is at work in them, equipping them for love. The validity of this latter response, however, would require further inquiry, especially with regard to AI.

53. Barth, *Church Dogmatics* IV/2, 812.

54. Barth, *Church Dogmatics* IV/2, 817.

55. Barth, *Church Dogmatics* IV/2, 819–20.

56. The "Second Tablet of the Law" is the name given to the last six of the Ten Commandments and are meant to provide the basic framework for responding to God's love with love for neighbor. "Honor your father and your mother" (Exod 20:12a); "You shall not murder" (Exod 20:13); "You shall not commit adultery" (Exod 20:14); "You shall

Is AI capable of this sort of love? If love of neighbor is founded in love of God, then it backs up the question to the viability of faith for AI; Barth points out that, from the Christian perspective, love of neighbor is a witness to God's love. It is evident that AI can perform tasks that emulate practices of human love of neighbor; AI can help diagnose diseases, connect loved ones, and protect children. But to say that this is love of neighbor in the theological sense would presume AI as a subject of Christian love rather than a tool used by a human subject or subjects. For instance, Namin may have performed loving actions, but is it proper to say that these actions are those of Namin? Or, perhaps, are they a predicate of those who created Namin? Having said that, it seems obvious that the Holy Spirit may use AI in the propagation of love of neighbor, and as such AI may be used in the human witness to God's love.

PENTECOST

The Jewish feast of Shavuot—the "Festival of Weeks"—occurs fifty days (a week of weeks) after Passover, which led to it being called "Pentecost" in the Septuagint and New Testament because it means "fiftieth" in Greek. The Pentecost, following the death and resurrection of Jesus as recorded in Acts, features what is considered to be a seminal movement of the Holy Spirit in equipping the disciples of Jesus for the mission of God in the world. Because the Holy Spirit actualizes the reign of God[57] in our midst, and if human vocation centers on participating in the will and work of God in the world, it seems that this text should be pertinent to understand what Christians might consider to be true personhood.

The first chapter of Acts opens with a recounting of the last words of Jesus before his ascension. He commands his followers to remain in Jerusalem

---

not steal" (Exod 20:15); "You shall not bear false witness against your neighbor" (Exod 20:16); "You shall not covet" (Exod 20:17a).

57. The kingdom of God, or *basileia tou theou* in Greek, is a major theme in the New Testament, though it is referenced in the Old Testament as well. Because the word "kingdom" in English is usually associated with a defined location, the terminology of "kingdom of God" can be misleading, for it does not refer to a geographical area or to the realm of the afterlife. Rather, the kingdom of God refers to the state of being in which God is king, an occurrence that actualizes God's kingship. For instance, parables of Jesus are often used to describe a situation in which the kingdom of God is made manifest. It is for this reason that an alternate and arguably better word is sometimes used to translate *basileia*, namely, "reign." The work of the Holy Spirit in the world is to actualize the reign of God. "For the kingdom of God is not food and drink but righteousness and peace and joy in the Holy Spirit" (Rom 14:17). See also Johnson, "Reign of God in Theological Perspective."

and then tells them that, "not many days from now" (1:5), they will "receive power when the Holy Spirit has come upon you; and you will be my witnesses in Jerusalem, and Judea, and Samaria, and to the ends of the earth" (1:8). And so the disciples wait together, "constantly devoting themselves to prayer" (1:14). The second chapter of Acts then narrates the result of that promise and waiting; the fact that the last thing the disciples said to Jesus was asking if he was going to "restore the kingdom of Israel" (1:6) suggests that what occurred on Pentecost was not what they were expecting. "And suddenly from heaven there came a sound like the rush of a violent wind, and it filled the entire house where they were sitting. Divided tongues, as of fire, appeared among them, and a tongue rested on each of them. All of them were filled with the Holy Spirit and began to speak in other languages, as the Spirit gave them ability" (2:2–4). The images of both wind and fire, common tropes for the Spirit of God in the Old and New Testament, signal divine action. Indeed, the New Testament Greek word for Spirit, *pneuma*, like the Old Testament Hebrew word *ruach*, can also be translated as "wind" or "breath," indicating the powerful, elusive, and life-giving character of the Holy Spirit, the very presence and power of God. Here we see at Pentecost God breathing vitality into the disciples, empowering their full humanity, just as God brought about humanity by breathing life into the dust of the ground in Genesis 2.

Because it was a religious feast day, there were Jewish people from throughout the diaspora that were in town to worship at the temple and celebrate the holiday (2:5). The pilgrims congregated to discover the source of the sound and were amazed to hear the disciples—all from Galilee, a region not known for erudition—speaking in the pilgrims' home dialects (2:6–7) about "God's deeds of power" (2:11). Peter addresses the crowd, declaring that the miraculous things they have witnessed were foretold as the work of the Holy Spirit bringing about the "Day of the Lord," an Old Testament theme looking toward a time when God's promises would be fulfilled.[58] Peter says that Jesus, who was also "attested to you by God with deeds of power, wonders, and signs that God did through him among you" (2:22), was killed by them, but that he was then raised up by God, at whose right hand he now sits, and has sent the Spirit to be among them, as can now be seen (2:33). As a result of this Pentecost sermon, many repented, were baptized, and "devoted themselves to the apostles' teaching and fellowship, the breaking of bread and the prayers" (2:42).

Because it presents the irrupting activity of the Holy Spirit, the Pentecost text has often been taken to be especially relevant to eschatology. As

---

58. See Barclay, *Acts of the Apostles*, 19–20.

a mystical presentation of the reign of God, in all its weirdness and wonder, Acts 2 can be interpreted as an inbreaking of the eschatological new
creation.[59] More specifically, Pentecost is often counted as the beginning of
the church.[60] Understood as that group of people that comprise the spatial-
temporal Body of Christ, the church communally participates, by the power
of the Holy Spirit, in the full personhood of Jesus as faithful covenant partners to God.[61] It does this by, in part, serving as a witness to the power of
the risen Christ who enables love of God and love of neighbor.[62] This witness is comprised of words, work, and attitude; by declaring the Good News
of Jesus Christ, by providing assistance to those in need as a sign of God's

59. William Willimon talks about the nature of the new creation depicted in Acts.
"The world rendered to us in Acts is not just a few images from the ancient Middle East
or first-century Rome. What is portrayed is what is going on in the creation as a whole.
The world in Acts is not a sobering description of what is but an evocative portrayal of
what, by God's work, shall be, a poetic presentation of an alternative world to the given
world, where Caesar rules and there is enmity and selfishness between men and women
and there is death. This is a world where God is busy making good of his promises.
Therefore the future is never completely closed, finished, fixed. God has been faithful
before (history) and will be faithful again (apocalyptic). The story is a stubborn refusal
to keep quiet and accept the world as unalterably given. The 'world' of Acts is what
is real, what is really going on in life, the ultimate meaning or destiny of humanity."
Willimon, *Acts*, 3.

60. Pentecost is sometimes called the "birthday" of the Christian church in that it
signals the nature and character of the followers of Jesus Christ in their common life
and vocation. Note that, before Pentecost, the disciples had already spent time together
in prayer and fellowship; yet this is not sufficient for the creation of the church, which
includes proclamation and conversion as enabled by the Holy Spirit. Willimon makes
the fascinating point that the narrative of Jesus's birth in the Gospel of Luke, and the
Pentecost narrative in Acts—both books written by Luke—have interesting parallels in
that, in both, the story begins with a unique onset of the Holy Spirit, though it had been
previously active. See Willimon, *Acts*, 28.

61. Bonhoeffer understands the church to be principally the activity of the Holy
Spirit animating the followers of Jesus in the work of God: "*The concept of the body of
Christ* . . . expresses the presence of Christ and the work of the Holy Spirit in his church-
community. The concept of the body in this context is not a *concept referring to form*
but to *function*, namely the work of Christ. . . . Christ is fully present in each individual,
and yet he is one; and again he is not fully present in any one person, but only all human beings together possess the whole Christ." Bonhoeffer, *Sanctorum Communio*, 225
(italics original).

62. In the fourth volume of his *Church Dogmatics*, which propounds on the doctrine
of reconciliation, Barth defines the church in three moments: the Holy Spirit gathering
the followers of Jesus Christ, the Holy Spirit upbuilding the followers of Jesus Christ,
and the Holy Spirit sending the followers of Jesus Christ to witness; while all three are
important, it is telling that the *telos* of this work of the Holy Spirit is the witness of the
church. While it is beyond the scope here, there is an interesting theological parallel,
one that deserves reflection, between this threefold moment of the church and Barth's
threefold notion of the Word of God as revealed, written, and preached.

assistance, and by embodying these words and deeds with an appropriate disposition.[63]

How might the Pentecost account contribute theological resources that help us address the anthropological status of AI? Once more, I would like to suggest three. First, the Holy Spirit works through the unexpected. Second, the communal personhood of the church is directed to all creation. And third, God's reign manifests through AI.

The Holy Spirit works through the unexpected. The biblical symbols of wind and fire that are used to represent the presence of God communicate several things about the Holy Spirit—its power, its elusive nature, and its ability to give and nurture life.[64] However, it also communicates the unexpected character of the Holy Spirit; just as the shape of wind and fire cannot be predicted, neither can the shape of God's work. Indeed, Jesus was not the Christ who Israel expected, and neither was Pentecost expected; the prayers of the disciples waiting in the upper room may still have centered on the restoration of Israel about which they had queried Jesus, even as wind and fire descended upon them.

Despite Jesus's promise that his disciples would soon be "baptized with the Holy Spirit" (1:5), certainly they were not prepared for what came to pass. Neither was anyone else, for those around were "bewildered" (2:6), "amazed and astonished" (2:7), and "perplexed" (2:12). In response, Peter, as he had in Acts 1, assumes a leadership position, delivering a sermon to the crowd of confused pilgrims. This is one of the more surprising events.[65] The last time Luke, the author of Acts, spoke of Peter, it was in Luke 22:54–62; there, Luke says that Peter, in fear of persecution, is only willing to follow Jesus "at a distance" (22:54) and then denies his relationship with Jesus three times (22:57–60), just as Jesus had predicted (22:34). Yet, in Acts, Peter has somehow found the wherewithal to lead the community's replacement of Judas and then to speak to the crowds.

In his sermon, Peter quotes from the Old Testament book of Joel, speaking of the "last days" (2:17), when the Holy Spirit will touch all people. In those days, "your sons and your daughters will prophesy, and your young men shall see visions, and your old men shall dream dreams" (2:17); further, even "slaves, both men and women" (2:18) will be empowered by the Holy Spirit to see the revelation of the eschatological new creation. These different groups of people—sons and daughters, young men, and slaves—all are of low social status in Jewish culture, and not those who would typically lead

63. See Barth, *Church Dogmatics* I/2, 441–48.

64. See McGrath, *Christian Theology*, 280–81, 286.

65. See Willimon, *Acts*, 31.

in receiving visions and words from God for the people. And yet Peter lists them, and them alone, as the bearers of eschatological messages.[66]

As we consider the eschatological role of AI—its place in revealing and participating in the reign of God—it is important to remember that the work of the Holy Spirit is surprising. Simply because we do not expect AI to be part of the inbreaking of God's will in the world does not mean that God will not use it; to the contrary, the witness of Scripture seems to suggest that God exclusively uses the unexpected. Perhaps God would even use Namin? Conversely, just because we think that some AI will be used for the inbreaking of God's will does not mean that God will employ it. It is not hard to see instances of AI that seem to have been instruments of God's faithfulness or instruments of our love of God or neighbor. Similarly, it is not hard to see instances of AI that we may have intended for good that have been harmful or seemingly not part of God's reign in some way. The message of Pentecost tells us that the Holy Spirit will blow as it will as the reign of God strikes, despite how we think that it should.[67]

The reign of God is for all creation. Some interpreters have taken the strange occurrences of Acts 2 to be the mass expression by the disciples of glossolalia, the speaking of a special personal prayer language.[68] However, the text seems rather to suggest the mass expression by the disciples of xenoglossia, or the miraculous ability to speak foreign languages previously unknown to them.[69] The pilgrims present in Jerusalem "from every nation under heaven" (2:5) heard the disciples speaking in the pilgrims' native languages (2:6); the litany of countries and regions listed in Acts 2:9–11 is meant to portray a wide range of geographical and cultural diversity represented in Jerusalem. This sudden ability to speak foreign languages was met with amazement and confusion.

66. These unlikely bearers of God's proclamation underscore the fact that God's reign and the new creation are not only unexpected, but form a community founded not according to markers, predicates, or abilities, but rather solely "on the powerful name of Jesus and the transforming empowerment provided by the Holy Spirit." Nienhuis, *Concise Guide to Reading the New Testament*, 93.

67. Michael Burdett shows how, throughout history, technology has been imagined as ushering in either doomsday or utopia. This continues in the present day when some claim that killer robots or AI will end humanity while others claim that it will be through AI or biotechnology that humanity will be able to achieve immortality. However, Burdett makes the point that, theologically speaking, God is the only one who will bring history to an end, and, in so doing, will usher in the eschatological new creation, which is qualitatively different than the present, not merely an extension of it, as the transhumanists hope. Succinctly, the reign of God is not ours to make, nor is it predictable. See Burdett, *Eschatology and the Technological Future*.

68. This is what is spoken of, for instance, in 1 Cor 14:2.

69. See Winn, *Acts of the Apostles*, 30–31.

But this deed of power was not given by the Holy Spirit merely to attract attention or bestow notoriety upon the disciples. Instead, in light of Jesus's final words to his disciples to "be my witnesses in Jerusalem, in all Judea and Samaria, and to the ends of the earth" (1:8), interpreting the spiritual bestowal of xenoglossia takes on a missional tone. The disciples, praying together in the upper room and waiting for the restoration of Israel, were driven out into the crowds by wind and fire, now able to speak to any of them in their native tongues. This was God giving the followers of Jesus the abilities necessary to carry the divine mission seen in the Christ to the far reaches of creation.[70] We have noted that God's covenant is with all creation, and we have also noted that the Cosmic Christ renews all creation. At Pentecost we see the Holy Spirit equipping the church to actualize this new creation.

How might the church extend that renewal to AI as part of God's creation? How might God use AI as part of that renewal? To the extent that AI is firmly embedded in the world and, indeed, is part of the shaping of that world, it is worth asking how the Holy Spirit is working in and through it to effect new creation. We know from Pentecost that God equips the church for the *missio Dei*, which is meant for every corner of the cosmos, including those non-human parts. God's reign is for all things, and thus the Holy Spirit will renew all. How might the church be on the forefront of participating with God's work in and through AI? How might church-created AIs be part of the propagation of the gospel, and how might the programming of those AIs be part of the inbreaking of God's reign to AI itself?

God uses artificial intelligence in the kingdom. The xenoglossic movement of the Holy Spirit among the disciples at Pentecost as a picture of the coming kingdom of God is both apocalyptic and eschatological: it unveils for the reader a picture of the kingdom as it irrupts into our midst, and as it will be one day for all people and for all time. The kingdom of God is the actualization of God's will and, since the movement of the Holy Spirit is the will of God in our midst, it is always eschatological. Of course, the will of God is multivalent, and redeems all of creation, and does so in ways that are unpredictable. But at Pentecost we see that God uses technology, such as language, in the inbreaking new creation.

The relationship between language and intelligence is complex. Language is often taken to be a marker of intelligence, enabling thought processes.[71] Indeed, it is only because of programming languages that AI is

---

70. For further reading on the missional nature of the church as exemplified in Acts 2, see Guder, *Missional Church*; Bosch, *Transforming Mission*; and Guder, *Continuing Conversion of the Church.*

71. See Dennett, "Role of Language in Intelligence." Dennett makes the interesting

possible. At Pentecost, we see that the chosen way for God to propagate the witness of the disciples to the world at least includes languages, both spoken and unspoken. It could be said that at Pentecost God instigated a new technology in order to equip the vice-regents of creation the means by which the covenant might be actualized amid the totality of creation. And because this technology involves languages, it involves a certain form of intelligence.

Pentecost is sometimes seen as a reversal of the Tower of Babel (Gen 11:1–9); God, as a consequence of the overweening pride of humanity in the construction of the Tower, introduces a diversity of languages among humanity, compromising their ability to communicate and, thus, revealing vulnerability and humility as the antidote to sinful pride.[72] However, for Pentecost to be the reversal of Babel, all people would be restored to one language. But that is not what happens. Indeed, all the pilgrims in Jerusalem at the time of Pentecost likely already spoke Aramaic.[73] Instead, the xenoglossic gift of the Holy Spirit affirms the diversity of languages even in the midst of directing the radically expansive covenantal witness to all creation. In other words, the message of Pentecost is not the dissolution of different linguistic intelligences but rather attests to the many good and differentiated perspectives that had emerged out of creation, echoing Genesis 1 and the declared goodness of all creation. It is not the existence of diversity that violates the covenant; to the contrary, differentiation is necessary for human personhood, as seen in Genesis 2. What violates the covenant is the absence of love uniting differentiation between God and creation and between persons.

The eschatological inbreaking at Pentecost tells us that different linguistic intelligences are part of God's redemption of creation. Not only is AI, as part of creation, the object of God's redemption, but, in affirming diverse linguistic intelligences, Pentecost seems to suggest that it is a means of God's redemption of all creation as well. What if the Holy Spirit has equipped us with the languages that enable AI so that the reign of God might irrupt in different parts of creation? The newness of this linguistic intelligence is not the issue; at Pentecost, the Spirit-given languages were new to the disciples, too. The issue is the extent to which the Holy Spirit uses intelligences to bring about love of God and love of neighbor. Artificial intelligence, created and used by those who are endeavoring to be faithful covenant partners to God,

---

point that language plays an essential role in human intelligence not merely (or, perhaps, even mainly) in its ability to symbolically represent ideas to be processed, but that such a symbolic system enables communication, which has enabled a communal processing of information, which in turn impacts intelligence.

72. See Thielicke, *How the World Began*, 273–87.

73. See Winn, *Acts of the Apostles*, 31.

is a new and powerful linguistic technology that the Holy Spirit will use in the witness of the church today, just like the new and powerful linguistic technology employed at Pentecost. But, as well, the linguistic intelligence of AI will help the church to encounter the reign of God in new ways, just as the many linguistic intelligences of the earth affirmed at Pentecost help us to discover more deeply what God would have us know about the kingdom.

CONCLUSION

In some ways, we end where we began: It is difficult to assess the conceptual personhood of AI because personhood is a highly contextual affirmation. In order to consider how Christianity assesses the question, we must theologically inquire after the nature of personhood and the nature of AI. From our interpretation of three creation texts of Scripture, we might suggest three general theological themes concerning the nature of personhood and the nature of AI. First, AI, as part of creation, is intrinsically good, though it may, like the rest of creation, be the repository and perpetuator of sin. Second, personhood is related to the sacredness of relationship as embodied in covenantal love. And third, while AI may or may not attain to personhood, it nevertheless, as part of creation, participates in the outworking of the covenant with all creation as both that which is redeemed and that which is part of God's work of redemption. From the Christian perspective, personhood requires the possibility of faith. Can AI trust God? Ultimately, the personhood of AI remains a mystery to us; after all, we cannot see behind the Turing Test. Nevertheless, it seems possible to personally interact with AI; your experience with Namin was certainly personal. Perhaps the message of Genesis and the incarnation and Pentecost, at least in this case, is not to ask which part of creation is worthy of love; this was precisely the question put to Jesus, "Who is my neighbor?" Perhaps, instead, the message is to remember the nature of my own personhood in being a faithful covenant partner to God and, therefore, with all creation, which God has declared good. Maybe, like much of creation and technology, AI is revelatory in that it helps us to better understand ourselves.

BIBLIOGRAPHY

Allen, F. B., and P. G. Coleman. "Spiritual Perspectives on the Person with Dementia: Identity and Personhood." In *Dementia: Mind, Meaning, and the Person*, edited by J. C. Hughes et al., 205–21. London: Oxford University Press, 2005.

Augustine. *The Trinity*. Translated by Edmund Hill. Hyde Park, NY: New City, 1991.

Barclay, William. *The Acts of the Apostles*. 2nd ed. Philadelphia: Westminster, 1955.

Barth, Karl. *Church Dogmatics, Vol I: The Doctrine of the Word of God, Part 2*. Translated by G. T. Thomson and Harold Knight. London: T. & T. Clark, 1956.

———. *Church Dogmatics, Vol. III: The Doctrine of Creation, Part 1*. Translated by J. W. Edwards, O. Bussey, and H. Knight. London: T. & T. Clark, 1958.

———. *Church Dogmatics, Vol. IV: The Doctrine of Reconciliation, Part 2*. Translated by G. W. Bromiley. London: T. & T. Clark, 1958.

Bettenson, Henry, and Chris Maunder, eds. *Documents of the Christian Church*. 4th ed. Oxford: Oxford University Press, 2011.

Boden, Margaret A. *AI: Its Nature and Future*. Oxford: Oxford University Press, 2016.

Bonhoeffer, Dietrich. *Life Together: The Classic Exploration of Christian Community*. Translated by John W. Doberstein. New York: Harper & Row, 1954.

———. *Sanctorum Communio: Dietrich Bonhoeffer Works, Volume 1*. Edited by Clifford J. Green. Translated by Reinhard Krauss and Nancy Lukens. Minneapolis: Fortress, 1998.

Bosch, David J. *Transforming Mission: Paradigm Shifts in Theology of Mission*. Maryknoll, NY: Orbis, 1991.

Brockman, John, ed. *Possible Minds: 25 Ways of Looking at AI*. New York: Penguin, 2019.

Brown, Colin. "Karl Barth's Doctrine of the Creation." *The Churchman* 76 (1962) 99–105.

Brueggemann, Walter. *Genesis*. Interpretation: A Bible Commentary for Teaching and Preaching. Atlanta: John Knox, 1982.

Bouma-Prediger, Steven. *For the Beauty of the Earth: A Christian Vision for Creation Care*. 2nd ed. Grand Rapids: Baker, 2010.

Brunner, Daniel L., et al. *Introducing Evangelical Ecotheology: Foundations in Scripture, Theology, History, and Praxis*. Grand Rapids: Baker, 2014.

Buber, Martin. *I and Thou*. Translated by Ronald Gregor Smith. Edinburgh: T. & T. Clark, 1937.

Burdett, Michael S. *Eschatology and the Technological Future*. London: Routledge, 2015.

De Craemer, Willy. "A Cross-Cultural Perspective on Personhood." *The Milbank Quarterly* 61 (1983) 19–34.

Dennett, Daniel C. "The Role of Language in Intelligence." In *What is Intelligence?*, edited by Jean Khalfa, 161–78. Cambridge: Cambridge University Press, 1994.

Floridi, Luciano. *The Fourth Revolution: How the Infosphere is Reshaping Human Reality*. Oxford: Oxford University Press, 2014.

Fritsch, Charles T. *Genesis*. The Layman's Bible Commentary 2. Richmond, VA: John Knox, 1952.

Geraci, Robert M. *Apocalyptic AI: Visions of Heaven in Robotics, Artificial Intelligence, and Virtual Reality*. New York: Oxford University Press, 2010.

Gordon, Gwendolyn J. "Environmental Personhood." *Columbia Journal of Environmental Law* 43 (2018) 49–91.

Grenz, Stanley J. *Theology for the Community of God*. Grand Rapids: Eerdmans, 2000.

Guder, Darrell L. *The Continuing Conversion of the Church*. Grand Rapids: Eerdmans, 2000.

———, ed. *Missional Church: A Vision for the Sending of the Church in North America*. Grand Rapids: Eerdmans, 1998.

Herzfeld, Noreen L. *In Our Image: Artificial Intelligence and the Human Spirit.* Minneapolis: Fortress, 2002.

Jaeger, Lydia. "Christ and the Concept of Person." *Themelios* 45 (2020) 277–90.

Johnson, William Stacy. "The Reign of God in Theological Perspective." *Interpretation: A Journal of Bible and Theology* 47 (1993) 127–39.

Kurki, Visa A .J., and Tomasz Pietrzykowski, eds. *Legal Personhood: Animals, Artificial Intelligence and the Unborn.* Cham, Switzerland: Springer, 2017.

Langford, Michael D. "Abusing Youth: Theologically Understanding Youth Through Misunderstanding Disability." In *Embodying Youth: Exploring Youth Ministry and Disability,* edited by Wesley W. Ellis and Michael D. Langford, 58–83. London: Routledge, 2020.

———. "Reconciliation as Holistic Redemptive Transformation." The 2016 Winifred E. Weter Faculty Award Lecture. Seattle Pacific University, 2016. https://digitalcommons.spu.edu/weter_lectures/31.

Lennox, John C. *2084: Artificial Intelligence and the Future of Humanity.* Grand Rapids: Zondervan, 2020.

McFarland, Benjamin J. "The Chemical Constraints on Creation: Natural Theology and Narrative Resonance." The 2010 Winifred E. Weter Faculty Award Lecture. Seattle Pacific University, 2010. https://digitalcommons.spu.edu/av_events/6.

McGrath, Alister E. *Christian Theology: An Introduction.* 6th ed. Malden, MA: Wiley Blackwell, 2017.

McKenny, Gerald. "Barth on Love." In *The Wiley Blackwell Companion to Karl Barth Vol. 1: Barth and Dogmatics,* edited by George Hunsinger and Keith L. Johnson, 381–91. Chichester, UK: Wiley Blackwell, 2020.

Nienhuis, David R. *A Concise Guide to Reading the New Testament: A Canonical Introduction.* Grand Rapids: Baker, 2018.

Pascal, Blaise. *Pensées.* Translated by W. F. Trotter. New York: E. P. Dutton, 1958.

Reinders, Hans S. *Receiving the Gift of Friendship: Profound Disability, Theological Anthropology, and Ethics.* Grand Rapids: Eerdmans, 2008.

Reynolds, Thomas E. *Vulnerable Communion: A Theology of Disability and Hospitality.* Grand Rapids: Brazos, 2008.

Singer, Peter. *Animal Liberation: A New Ethics for our Treatment of Animals.* New York: Random, 1975.

Sloyan, Gerard. *John.* Interpretation: A Bible Commentary for Teaching and Preaching. Louisville: Westminster John Knox, 2009.

Snyder, Howard A., and Joel Scandrett. *Salvation Means Creation Healed: The Ecology of Sin and Grace; Overcoming the Divorce between Earth and Heaven.* Eugene, OR: Cascade, 2011.

Swinton, John. "From Inclusion to Belonging: A Practical Theology of Community, Disability and Humanness." *Journal of Religion, Disability, and Health* 16 (2012) 172–90.

Tegmark, Max. *Life 3.0: Being Human in the Age of Artificial Intelligence.* New York: Vintage, 2017.

Thielicke, Helmut. *How the World Began: Man in the First Chapters of the Bible.* Translated by John Doberstein. Philadelphia: Fortress, 1961.

Tillich, Paul. *Dynamics of Faith.* New York: Harper & Row, 1957.

Torrance, Thomas F. *The Mediation of Christ: Evangelical Theology and Scientific Culture.* 2nd ed. Edinburgh: T. & T. Clark, 1992.

Turing, Alan M. "Computing Machinery and Intelligence." *Mind* 59 (1950) 433–60.

Ware, Kallistos. *The Orthodox Way*. Rev. ed. Crestwood, NY: St. Vladimir's Seminary Press, 1995.

Willimon, William H. *Acts*. Interpretation: A Bible Commentary for Teaching and Preaching. Louisville: Westminster John Knox, 1988.

Winn, Albert C. *Acts of the Apostles*. The Layman's Bible Commentary 20. Richmond, VA: John Knox, 1960.

Wright, N. T. "Jesus and the Identity of God." *Ex Auditu* 14 (1998) 42–56.

6

Reinforcement in the Information Revolution

Phillip M. Baker Asst Prof Psych

INTRODUCTION

Marcia took a long look at the backpack. She immediately noticed the integrated rain cover and adjustable water bottle holders, two features that were a must for her through-trek of the Pacific Crest Trail she was planning for next year. She had seen review after review of packs on Instagram by long-trek influencers. This was the one, and $387 later, the pack was set to arrive on her doorstep in two days. This is by all accounts an innocuous story. And it may seem that what is being hinted at is a story about consumption and the role of multimodal advertising in pitching products to us. To be sure, AI has a role in the facilitation of identifying, segmenting, and targeting adds to potential consumers, but if we reflect on this scenario further, a larger reality also becomes clear.

Consider, for example, the rapid emergence of through-trekking more generally. Since the first through trek of the Pacific Crest Trail in 1952, fewer than one hundred people per year have completed the trek into the mid-2000s. Coinciding with the advent of social media and the age of the internet, that number has rapidly increased to more than five thousand permits issued in 2019.[1] Suddenly, a culture of long-distance hiking emerged that coincided with the internet age. Similar statistics can be found for all sorts of formerly niche activities including long-distance running, open water swimming, and ownership of stationary bikes, such as Peloton.

Behind targeted advertising more generally is the ability to create social realities that formerly did not exist. Humans are a social species and will readily change beliefs, hobbies, and even political parties to conform to the group in which they find themselves.[2] The digital age has facilitated the creation of online communities that allow us to congregate with others who share our community values, further refine our beliefs, and even reflect our fitness obsessions. Because these communities occur online, it presents a closed frame of variables under which AI learning algorithms can aggregate our data and build a predictive model of how we might behave when presented given variables.[3] While this ability is perhaps neither good nor ill, it does represent an incredibly powerful tool for those that wield it to influence the behavior of humans at a scale far beyond anything prior.

Opportunities for AI to identify and predict our behavior is only increasing. Adolescents and young adults spend between twenty and twenty-four hours per week in front of screens.[4] Data from screen time apps report a wider range for adults, between nine hours per week to much higher estimates, some exceeding an average of five hours per day.[5]

Collection and aggregation across platforms of our data, including our credit cards, social media, internet searches, location data, and more, allows learning algorithms to better understand our motivations and place

---

1. Pacific Crest Trail Association, "PCT Visitor Use Statistics."

2. See Gennaioli and Tabellini, "Identity, Beliefs, and Political Conflict"; Rydgren, "Beliefs."

3. For a further discussion of this, Luciano Floridi presents the case that the move to the information environment represents a fourth revolution in how humans conceive of themselves after the Copernican, Darwinian, and Psychological/Freudian revolutions. See Floridi, *Fourth Revolution*. As a consequence, we make it easier for AI to operate because we reduce the number of variables in a given situation to their native digital environment. In the analogue world, the number of variables and their transient nature overwhelms the computational power of predictive algorithms to render them ineffective. However, we are continually integrating them into our analogue world with, thus far, mixed success.

4. See Abdel Magid et al., "Disentangling Individual, School, and Neighborhood Effects on Screen Time among Adolescents and Young Adults in the United States."

5. See Hodes and Thomas, "Smartphone Screen Time"; Vizcaino et al., "Reliability of a New Measure to Assess Modern Screen Time in Adults."

realities in front of us that will influence the choices we make. The realities placed in front of us operate on our internal systems of reinforcement. Simply defined, reinforcement is a consequence of our actions that motivates us to seek rewarding things and avoid unpleasant ones. Reinforcement is arguably *the* most important aspect of shaping one's behavior, and perhaps even one's self in the holistic sense, as anyone who has been responsible for raising another human or an animal can attest to.

This chapter will outline what it means to be a behaving human and how AI makes sense of these concepts. It will then explore possible near-future implications of our remarkable progress in understanding how human behavior works with the assistance of AI from a neurobiological basis. A focus on understanding the reinforcement mechanisms of the brain will reveal the consequences of ceding control of so much of our brain-environment interactions to AI. It will conclude by offering a potential Christian response to this digital reality from a uniquely Anabaptist perspective.

DEFINING A HUMAN WITH FAITH AND NEUROSCIENCE

Much has been said about what it is that defines a human. Debate over things such as what it means to be created in the image of God, whether we have a non-corporeal soul, or whether we have free will all have critical importance on the definition of humanity, our relationship with other aspects of creation, and our relation to the eternal. However, many of these issues stretch far beyond what can be reasonably expected in a conversation between neuroscience and theology, such as is being attempted in this chapter. However, others have argued that the definition of what it means to be human is an inflection point where neuroscience and theology can productively interact.[6] As neuroscience has accumulated examples of how brain alterations can reliably affect everything from emotional regulation to the ability to sing, it has become clear that at least much of what we consider to be ourselves—our behaviors and even internal states—is produced by interactions among neurons.

Indeed, the discipline of behavioral neuroscience seeks to understand the neural circuits, chemical interactions, and brain states that ultimately select a single behavior from any variety of possibilities. In the quest to discover neural representations of choices, neuroscience has increasingly reached further and further into other disciplines including sociology, philosophy, and psychology to integrate the nearly innumerable variables

6. See Clayton, "Neuroscience, the Person, and God."

that might ultimately influence our choices. For example, the pioneering work of figures such as Joseph LeDoux in understanding the contributions of fear-related processes to decision-making, or Patricia Goldman-Rakic in understanding how the cortex represents goals, has allowed neuroscientists to observe and manipulate decisions in real time. Neuroscientists, building on the knowledge of how the brain represents everything from hunger to stress, have now built tools that allow them to causally influence behaviors across a variety of species including humans. *Casual attribution of brain processes to behaviors, and the correlated ability to manipulate those processes, may turn out to be the most consequential contribution of science to the nature of humanity.* With this knowledge, if desired, we could perhaps in the near future erase depressive thoughts from the brain through using the brain's own learning mechanisms.

As early as the dawn of the twentieth century, scientists were beginning to realize just how important the causal loop between behavior and internal states or thoughts was. This led to incredible optimism about the power to shape an individual. This movement is best characterized by the radical behaviorists who claimed that, if you allowed them control of the environment and sources of reward and punishment for a child, they could turn that child into anything from a doctor to a thief.[7] Ultimately, they underestimated the power of social structures and genetic influences on aspects of how humans make decisions. But with the rise of algorithmic methods of analyzing genetic and sociological data with AI, these contributions are becoming increasingly understood.

The crucial point here is that algorithms, as they are currently designed, don't attempt to be 100 percent accurate in predicting a single individual's behavior because, on average, they are built to make excellent predictions across large chunks of the population.[8] I would argue that these averages are what will largely shape development in society whether they be toward or away from justice, inclusivity, equity, and other critical aspects of ethical life. For some time, we have known that mental states are created by imitation of social phenomena.[9] This process of forming our emotional and social content, even from early in life (eighteen months at least), is critical to any social species if group dynamics are to function properly. This, in effect, is a

---

7. See Watson, *Behaviorism*.

8. This represents a shift in priorities in the field of AI from a quest to understand humanity to a quest to predict human behavior. This is evidenced by the large-scale shift in methodology from logical or expert systems to statistical approaches. In the end, the goal is not to understand how the human mind works, but to predict its outputs to a high degree of accuracy.

9. See Jeannerod, "Are There Limits to the Naturalization of Mental States?"

back door to understanding the human mind. Instead of attempting to build a model of what the mind is, you can instead input specific information to shape its output. Thus, if we cede social time to digital platforms, the AI algorithms that moderate them will be major players in the social realities we experience and by which we are informed. While this may not be particularly surprising to anyone, the implications of how this might develop as we gain access to additional computational power and tools to manipulate the brain needs to be better appreciated. To do this, we must be clear on what we talk about concerning the connection between behavior and humanity.

WHAT IS A BEHAVIOR?

If the hypothesis for this chapter is that we are increasingly ceding social time to experiences guided by AI algorithms, and AI's use of human behavioral prediction is rapidly altering human society, then one must be able to accurately describe what is meant by behavior. Human behavior can be thought of as an interaction between an individual and their environment. The environment presents a set of sensory stimuli that the individual can respond to with an action aimed at accomplishing some goal. The terms "behavior" and "action" at this point become important and are discussed elsewhere in this book.[10]

For present purposes, I will operationally define a behavior as a combination of overt (movements themselves) and/or covert (neural activity, e.g., thinking) processes that result when goals of an individual are represented internally, and then acted upon (or not) in the external world. This operational definition attempts to cover those actions that involve considered or intentional goal-directed behaviors rather than "mere behaviors" or, perhaps more accurately, reflexes that are innate to an organism. However, what is conscious (intentional) and what is unconscious (a reaction) in a behavior so defined remains uncertain. For this reason, as a neuroscientist I prefer to use the term "behaviors" to cover a range of what philosophers might consider both actions and behaviors. What is certain, however, is that these behaviors are learned through constant interactions with the external world and modified every time they are performed. This facet of human behavior is recognized across many disciplines. From engineers working on jobsite safety to early-life educators, the critical importance of how the environment, or everything "outside" of the brain, shapes the behaviors of the individual is utilized to ensure those behaviors are appropriate for their context.[11]

10. See Rice, "What's so *Artificial* and *Intelligent* about Artificial Intelligence?"
11. See Jiang et al., "Understanding the Causation of Construction Workers' Unsafe

What is perhaps generally underappreciated is the ability of the environment to profoundly alter the very structure of the brain itself. Returning to the example at the beginning of the chapter of the avid backpacker, neuroscientists can predict areas of the brain that become engaged when presented with stimuli associated with backpacking that would differ from someone without such interests. In fact, if one were to ignore ethical constraints on experiments, they could even take someone uninterested in backpacking and, by stimulation of specific brain areas involved in reward processing, turn them into someone that "enjoys" backpacking as well.[12]

Classic studies on the environment in which individuals are raised demonstrate the profound impact that environments can have. A famous example from psychology is the case of infants neglected in orphanages in Romania following the fall of the dictatorship in 1989.[13] Namely, profound and long-lasting changes in the size of the brain, neural activity, and cognitive function were found even after children were removed from the impoverished environments.[14] These findings matched well-validated models of neglect in rat models of development. These studies compared rats allowed to play and live with other rats and toys versus rats left in relative isolation. Such environmental enrichment led to an increase in the size and shape of neurons and neural circuits, and altered behavioral responses to stress, cognitive abilities, and a host of other adaptive behaviors.[15]

Similar findings have been confirmed across species, including humans, and have been extended to include a range of biochemical, anatomical, and psychological effects. For example, one major proposal for reducing the risk of cognitive decline in aging is the reserve hypothesis.[16] As you age, decline in cognitive functions—including creativity in problem solving, finding your way using memory, and susceptibility to distraction—are closely accompanied by neurobiological changes such as decreased plasticity in neurons, reduction in interconnections between neurons in memory-related

---

Behaviors Based on System Dynamics Modeling"; Rushton and Larkin, "Shaping the Learning Environment."

12. These experiments have been done in animals, although what is meant by "enjoys" in the human context would require additional consideration. Specifically, a rat or monkey may increase a behavior or response to a reinforced picture, but we are unable to ask them whether they "enjoy" the experience. See Wise, "Addictive Drugs and Brain Stimulation Reward."

13. See Weir, "Lasting Impact of Neglect."

14. See Nelson, *Romania's Abandoned Children*.

15. See Diamond et al., "Effects of an Enriched Environment on the Histology of the Rat Cerebral Cortex."

16. See Leal and Yassa, "Normal Cognitive and Brain Aging"; Stern, "What Is Cognitive Reserve?"

structures, and more.[17] Thus, how the environment is shaped around you, whether rich with interaction or more isolated, can have a profound impact on the development of dementia later in life, impacting whether neurons have the resources to remain healthy.

EXTERNAL INFLUENCES ON BEHAVIOR

Broadly speaking, while perhaps underappreciated in society, the interaction between brain and environments is not a new revelation. Indeed, daily practices to shape one's life and mind are a cornerstone of Christianity. Discipline of mind and bodily practices are hallmarks of many of Paul's letters to the early church (e.g., Rom 12:2). The more profound point here is that neuroscience is beginning to identify the neural components of these processes. This is significant because, concurrent with this understanding, a toolkit to alter the brain based on these data is rapidly growing. In more detail below, I will lay out some of the specifics of this progress as it relates to our ability to understand the conscious and unconscious processes that lead from making sense of the external environment to deciding how to respond to it.

To illustrate this point, an examination of the relationship between the brain and muscles is particularly useful. The connection between neural activity and movements in muscles is based on trial-and-error movement feedback since before birth. In the frontal parts of our brains, there is a map of our bodies owing to direct connections between the motor area of the cerebral cortex and the spinal cord. These "topographic" maps of the cortex detailing fine control of muscle movements were identified by the mid-nineteenth century.[18] In those with missing limbs, representation of the missing limb is absent. In cases of amputation, these areas transition and are "invaded" by other body areas to utilize the unused brain real estate.

Significantly, the representation of the body goes beyond a one-to-one relationship between neurons in the motor cortex and skeletal muscles.[19] Instead, these neuron groups in the motor cortex control distinct skilled movements that have been shaped through experience. A single finger muscle might receive input from any of several areas of the motor cortex due to its involvement in various skilled hand movements.[20] These learned

17. See Leal and Yassa, "Normal Cognitive and Brain Aging."

18. See Ferrier, "Localization of Function in the Brain."

19. See Grünbaum and Sherrington, "Observations on the Physiology of the Cerebral Cortex of the Anthropoid Apes."

20. See Schieber and Hibbard, "How Somatotopic Is the Motor Cortex Hand Area?"

action sequences are taught to the cortex through thousands of iterative experiences as an individual moves and interacts with the world. More specifically, the cortex interacts with important "lower brain" areas including the basal ganglia (more on this below) to select movement sequences that have resulted in goals and decrease movement sequences that failed to obtain goals.[21] Recently, neuroscientists have discovered that with implants these movement sequences or skills can be reinforced through existing brain mechanisms to shape even the movements of robots external to the brain, thus raising the possibility of extending skilled movements to include external devices.[22]

So, through many times out on the trail, our backpacker Marcia has developed the skills to shift her conscious effort away from not twisting her ankle, hiking too quickly, or losing track of where she is, and toward being able enjoy the experience. Unconscious processes guide her behaviors through the execution of skilled movement with little need for reflection on what she is doing. The learning of these skilled behaviors continues in response to feedback from the external world as she accomplishes her goals and learns from mistakes. In short, reinforcement actively shapes the behaviors Marcia will perform, often in the absence of conscious reflection. Perhaps even more exciting is recent data showing us that, in addition to behaviors, emotional and cognitive states are also subject to these same reinforcement processes.[23] This indicates that our thoughts and emotions are also subject to the environmental shapers of our lives, including AI.

UNDERSTANDING REINFORCEMENT

Recent work in the neural basis of learning and memory is also exploring whether we can avoid having to rely on the traditional time-consuming iterative processes of reinforcement of behaviors in the natural world. Specifically, this research seeks to understand whether we can short-cut learning by creating artificial or more efficient forms of reinforcement than would otherwise be required. This raises the need to understand how reinforcement of particular behaviors is accomplished. Closely related, of course, is how AI utilizes reinforcement to "learn" in an artificial manner. Understanding the similarities and differences between these will help make sense of the implications for AI on human behavior.

21. See Graybiel, "Habits, Rituals, and the Evaluative Brain."

22. See Rajangam et al., "Wireless Cortical Brain-Machine Interface for Whole-Body Navigation in Primates."

23. See Floresco, "Nucleus Accumbens."

The basic method of iterative learning in both artificial and biological systems is explained by a classic model of reinforcement learning, the Rescorla-Wagner equation.[24] At its base, the Rescorla-Wagner equation states that the value of a stimulus or event is a product of how much reinforcement a subject has encountered both in prior experiences with it, and based on what happens in the current trial. It is formalized with the equation:

$$\Delta V = \beta(\lambda - Vn)$$

where ΔV is the change in the associative strength between a stimulus and an outcome. This change corresponds to the learning rate (β) multiplied by the maximum amount of learning that could occur given the event (λ) minus the connection that currently exists between the stimulus and outcome for a subject for that particular occurrence (Vn). For example, if, by chance, your dog sits quietly near the door in an attempt to go outside and you open it, that action is reinforced and the dog learns a lot because the potential to learn (λ) was high and the current expectation (Vn) was low. As your dog continues to be reinforced for sitting quietly, the change in associative strength ΔV will decrease to the point that, even if the dog sits for quite for some time without being let out, the potential to change the associative strength is low because the long history of reinforcement has lowered the potential for new learning (λ) to such a large extent. Because of a long history of reinforcement learning and built associations between stimuli and behaviors, it is indeed harder to teach an old dog new tricks!

Neural correlates of reinforcement learning, including modified forms of the Rescorla-Wagner equation, are now well understood. Prominent among these contributors to behavior is a group of highly evolutionarily conserved neural circuits known collectively as the basal ganglia. The basal ganglia are a group of subcortical neural structures that have evolved to select optimal motor and internal brain sequences between competing possibilities. This circuit is so critical to effective selection of behaviors that it is recognizable in every vertebrate brain ranging from ancient jawed fish to humans.[25] In humans, input from higher cortical regions that control executive functions are combined with sensory information from the thalamus and reinforcement-related brain areas to select a response based on the available context.

What is meant by context here needs elaboration. Context can be everything from the time of day, to social cues from others, to how hungry you happen to be. Both actions that are goal-directed in nature and those that

24. See Rescorla and Wagner, "Theory of Pavlovian Conditioning."
25. See Reiner, "You Cannot Have a Vertebrate Brain without a Basal Ganglia."

appear as habits compete within the basal ganglia circuitry to ultimately influence motor and internal cognitive pathways, otherwise two thoughts or behaviors would be attempted simultaneously.[26]

Simply put, the basal ganglia is offered competing motor plans that are voted on in one way or another by the context of the environment and internal processes related to goals and, ultimately, a single behavior is executed. For example, at a stream crossing our hiker Marcia decides to jump to a wet rock rather than step into the stream because she doesn't want to get her shoe wet. If the executed behavior is successful, it is reinforced (more on this below). If unsuccessful, it will be disincentivized in that particular context and less likely to be selected in the future. Because the rock was wet and slippery, next time Marcia will opt for the wet shoe rather than the bruised bottom. In this way, we can rapidly refine our behaviors to be the most appropriate to reaching our goals in a given context.

One issue to be raised here is how much of this occurs at non-conscious levels. The range of brain regions and sensory input that is received in the basal ganglia far exceeds what enters the conscious mind. Some have argued that this likely means that decisions happen at an unconscious level and have found behavioral psychology experiments that seem to support the conclusion that conscious control of our behaviors is an illusion.[27] A closer look at the neural basis of goal-directed activity, however, points to behavior being a complicated mix of both top-down consciously-driven goals being maintained and updated by many more ongoing non-conscious process that have a profound influence on behavior.[28]

What this reveals for the purposes of understanding behaviors is that much of our goal-directed behavior is influenced by factors that do not reach our conscious mind and therefore are influenced instead by past experiences in similar contexts. All the prior reinforcement history, ongoing sensory stimuli, learned action sequences, expected outcome information, and emotional context are rapidly combined to change synaptic weights on neurons to bias the selection of a behavior automatically, and continuously. The key question then is, what are the neural processes that facilitate both implicit and explicit forms of reinforcement learning? Clarification of this question will go some way in answering whether an AI algorithm with access to a massive data set of contextual factors is able generally to shape the behaviors that will result from them.

26. See Redgrave et al., "Goal-Directed and Habitual Control in the Basal Ganglia."

27. See Doris, "Persons, Situations, and Virtue Ethics."

28. See Suhler and Churchland, "Control"; Berkman and Lieberman, "Neuroscience of Goal Pursuit"; Maoz et al., "Neural Precursors of Decisions That Matter."

REINFORCEMENT AND THE CONTROL OF BEHAVIOR

The study of the neuroscience of reinforcement learning took a great leap forward with the discovery that the neurotransmitter dopamine acted as a feedback signal.[29] In 1997, Wolfram Shultz performed a now classic study in monkeys that showed how reinforcement in the brain can be mediated by responses recorded from dopamine neurons. When a monkey was sitting quietly and juice was administered via a tube into its mouth, dopamine neurons responded by increasing their activity, marking as a reward the feeling of pleasure that the juice created. However, crucially, when the juice reward was preceded by a cue that indicated the juice reward was about to be delivered, the pleasurable juice no longer resulted in dopamine activity. Instead, the predictor of the reward (the cue) now resulted in dopamine activity. Finally, when the cue that predicted the juice reward was given, but the juice unexpectedly withheld, dopamine neurons decreased their activity and signaled that the outcome (the juice) was less than expected. This is commonly termed a reward prediction error, or RPE.[30]

Subsequent research has extended these crucial initial findings across many species to demonstrate that dopamine acts as a teacher in the brain to help modify expectations based on an outcome of an event, whether that outcome is some external event or a behavior of the subject. If the outcome was better than expected, an increase in dopamine is observed. If the outcome was worse than expected, a decrease in dopamine activity occurs. Thus dopamine is now thought of as a signaler of salience rather than as a reward or pleasure *per se*. Salience in this case can be thought of as events that draw attention due to their potential to serve as predictors of future outcomes. This means that the neural signal of dopamine can be detected in the brain and utilized to shape behaviors. Identification and manipulation of this signal of salience has been employed in many contexts, including as the basis for maladaptive behaviors such as substance abuse, gambling, and internet addiction.

The ability to track salience in the brain and to track the brain's interpretations of salient events, whether positive or negative, has profound implications for predicting and shaping behavior. This is perhaps best

29. Although beyond the scope of this paper, it is worth pointing out that the role of dopamine in the brain is in fact not related to pleasure as is popularly assumed. Rather, as explained in this section, it is more accurately a reinforcement signal that is used to increase or decrease behaviors based on their relation to goals. Rather than pleasure, although that could be one such goal which dopamine reinforces, this is more accurately described as salience. For a further discussion see Berridge, "Debate over Dopamine's Role in Reward."

30. See Schultz et al., "Neural Substrate of Prediction and Reward."

exemplified by classic experiments by James Olds and Peter Milner in which electrodes were placed into various areas of the brain to enable the stimulation of neural activity.[31] To initiate brief neural activity in many brain areas associated with dopamine and opiate neural activity, rats would press a lever until the point of exhaustion, even forgoing food when on a restricted calorie diet. These and subsequent experiments showed that increasing brain activity in these reinforcement areas drives behavioral repetition based on keeping reward or salience high. Similarly, if dopamine and other associated neurotransmitters are increased pharmacologically, as is the case with many drugs of abuse such as methamphetamines, behavior can become focused on seeking and obtaining those drugs. The ability of these pharmacological agents to push reinforcement systems well beyond normal operating conditions can lead to a singular focus on obtaining that form of reinforcement (i.e., addiction).

As the technology to both monitor and manipulate the brain has continued to advance, the ability to gain precise control over both the perception of salient stimuli and the ongoing internal state of the subject has advanced significantly. For example, circuits in the brain that control the consumption of food have been identified and can now be manipulated in real time to both initiate and cease eating in mice.[32] Specifically, using a technology known as optogenetics, scientists can implant, using an engineered virus, a channel that responds to photons of light by opening and causing neurons to become active, or other channels that cause them to become inactive.[33] With this bidirectional control of part of the feeding circuitry in the brain, Joshua Jennings and colleagues were able to cause either otherwise sated animals to eat, or hungry animals to cease the consumption of food. While this example of the control of behavior or reinforcement may seem as yet far-fetched in humans, we need only think of ongoing experiments aimed at the control of impulsive or depressive behaviors using implantable devices to realize the proximity of this form of brain control to reality.[34] Where is the line in attempting to control the impulse to consume drugs or to control sad thoughts—or even thoughts that society decides are deviant?

31. See Olds and Milner, "Positive Reinforcement Produced by Electrical Stimulation of Septal Area and Other Regions of Rat Brain."

32. See Jennings et al., "Inhibitory Circuit Architecture of the Lateral Hypothalamus Orchestrates Feeding."

33. See Deisseroth, "Optogenetics."

34. These devices are known as deep brain stimulators (DBS) and are already commonly used to reduce the symptoms of Parkinson's Disease, but are also being implanted to treat conditions ranging from depression to chronic pain.

Even now, companies that have the resources to develop AI algorithms aimed at connecting passively collected brain patterns to overt behaviors are beginning to brag about their ability to shape experiences to get a desired behavioral output. This is accomplished through learning algorithms that analyze brain states, looking for known responses that relate to the learning and decision-making circuits that were outlined above (namely salience). For example, Neilson has invested significant resources into their consumer neuroscience institute. This has led to over five hundred published peer-reviewed articles with the overall goal of better targeting advertising to consumers by understanding how the brain responds to everything from fonts to color schemes and to objects that appear in videos. For example, data analytics provider NielsenIQ states:

> We've always known a significant part of advertising spending is wasted. Now, neuroscience can identify the exact moments in an ad that activate memory, draw attention, or prompt an emotional response, and determine on a second-by-second basis which parts are and are not effective in engaging viewers. By including only the most effective elements in your ads, significant savings can be realized from shortening their length while also maintaining or improving their overall impact.[35]

AI has given companies and other well-resourced entities the ability to analyze vast amounts of brain data, eye movement, and online clicks to generate the ability—with significantly improved accuracy—to predict the types of interactions that drive salience and, in turn, human behavior.

Where is the limit to this move to utilize brain data to predict human behavior? Neuroscience continues to increase rapidly its toolset to both measure and manipulate the brain using non-invasive techniques. Direct-to-consumer products are being bought up by technology companies including Facebook, Google, and others that aim to passively read brain data either directly, through head-worn devices, or indirectly, through technology that can be worn on the wrist.[36] The latter in particular might be especially useful for companies given the ubiquity of devices that measure physiology for tracking runs and day-to-day activity. Who is to say what these companies that primarily earn their income from advertising will do with this potential treasure trove of data about our internal neural processes and their related behaviors? Again, here it must be pointed out that the goal is not to predict every individual choice at this point. It currently remains far beyond our ability to use individual brain state examples to predict

35. NielsenIQ, "Discover More of Your Business."
36. *BBC*, "Facebook Buys 'Mind-Reading Wristband' Firm CTRL-Labs."

behavioral outcomes. Rather, the strength of AI is to aggregate signals to look for signatures of desired responses and use those signatures to shape behaviors of individuals on average. What needs to be more clearly understood, however, is that *these averages belong to our societies* and thus are sufficient to the goals of profit generation whether we seek to sell serious backpacking equipment or sway public opinion in an election.

Another way of putting this, to paraphrase economic theory, is that those who control the means of salience control the direction of society. As long as access is actively or passively granted to aggregate and analyze our behavior or indeed our neural data, the means by which we make those choices can be strategically adjusted. This can happen under the guise of directing purchases, as is currently done in the United States and elsewhere—or, in the case of more authoritarian states, it can be used to shape the direction of society. Perhaps the first attempt at the latter is the Chinese social credit system currently in development to evaluate individuals and companies based on the goals set out by the Communist Party.[37] Time will tell how systems such as these integrate potential neural data obtained by various means to further incentivize behavior.

Of immediate concern, however, is that the rise of brain-reading and manipulating devices has far outpaced our legislative infrastructure to deal with the ethical and sociological implications these technologies have raised. This gap has led many prominent figures to call for increased awareness of these implications, resources aimed at understanding them better, and creating the means by which to legislate the use of various technologies. Among those leading this call has been Nita Farahany, who has urged the creation of a cognitive bill of rights. In a TED Talk that has garnered nearly two million views, in her keynote speech at the 2019 annual meeting of the Society for Neuroscience, and in other appearances at places such as the World Economic Forum, Farahany has stated, "The time has come for us to call for a cognitive liberty revolution to make sure that we responsibly advance technology that could enable us to embrace the future while fiercely protecting all of us from any person, company, or government that attempts to unlawfully access or alter our innermost lives."[38]

Devices that can infer mental states such as attention or emotional arousal already exist and will only become more advanced as companies or governments with billions of dollars in resources continue to invest in research and development. Restricting information flow is likely a losing

37. See Chorzempa et al., "China's Social Credit System."

38. Farahany, "When Technology Can Read Minds, How Will We Protect Our Privacy?," https://www.ted.com/talks/nita_farahany_when_technology_can_read_minds_how_will_we_protect_our_privacy.

battle. Therefore, it seems prudent instead to develop a framework for how to engage with this technology in ways that increase human thriving, equity, and inclusion. With so much at stake, interested Christians might ask themselves, "What role can we as a body of faith play in shaping how we engage this technology that aligns with the values of the Bible?" Certainly, many groups may come to different conclusions when faced with this question based on prior engagement with ethical considerations around technological concerns. In the following, I offer a uniquely Anabaptist approach as a model for how this response may look in a Christian context.

REINFORCING COMMUNITIES OF CHRIST: AN ANABAPTIST PERSPECTIVE

The question of what is to be done about AI and how we ought to shape its development is beginning to fill libraries with commentary. What this section hopes to suggest is what the neuroscientist might have to offer to a church community that seeks to make sense of how AI interacts with lived experience. How should we understand what has already been done and where might we highlight areas of potential communal action? Based on what was outlined above, it will be particularly important to understand what the models of reinforcement are that underlie the AI algorithms with which we interact. We need to reflect on who AI is currently for—its aims, goals, and what it considers reinforcement—to better grasp what it has already done and what it can potentially do. The context in which we make our decisions and respond to reinforcers is inexorably linked as we increasingly are becoming part of an information-driven future.

Philosophical development has been key in understanding the ramifications of the circular effect of environment and behavior on what it means to be human in the context of the information revolution. Luciano Floridi even goes so far to describe the development of environment-shaping technologies as the fourth revolution in human development following the Copernican, Darwinian, and Freudian revolutions.[39] Specifically, one way to understand what makes the information revolution so important is technology's ability to autonomously shape the environment following an initial set of inputs from programmers. This in essence breaks, or perhaps exponentially increases, the feedback loop between us and the environment we create. In other words, we have the potential to delegate, and perhaps in some ways already have delegated, our influence on our environment

---

39. See Floridi, *Fourth Revolution.*

(and vice versa) to autonomous algorithms created by companies or governments that shape our world and ourselves in their desired image.

This happens in many ways, in both online experiences and in the real world. For example, when Marcia spends more time on a post about hiking as she scrolls social media, the algorithm doesn't need to learn, through a process of trial and error, what it was about the post that made her pause on it. Instead, it can take the aggregated data from millions of others and compare models of Marcia to it. In the world, too, AI can examine her practices, location data, purchases, and other traces left in her digital footprint to discern patterns of predictable behavior based on models of people with similar features. Further, what you interact with—the advertisements, article suggestions, interest groups, etc.—will shape your preferences through targeted reinforcement. In view of this reality, the Christian neuroscientist can help us clarify both what contexts we inhabit and what reinforcers exist in those contexts to shape our behavior. More specifically, an Anabaptist perspective on technological discernment can serve as an example for how communities of faith can then move forward.

Sources of commentary on an Anabaptist approach to AI are rare. Therefore, to begin to answer these questions, I will use the example of Anabaptist engagement in bioethics and ontology as a framework for finding Christ in this fourth revolution of humanity. Further, I make no claims to be an authority on Anabaptist thought. Rather, mine is a lived experience within the tradition informed by reading and participation in conferences and forums where these issues have been discussed. In particular, Eastern Mennonite University held a conference on the meaning of biotechnology to faith in 2003 while I was a student there. Those discussions and the subsequent edited volume that resulted inform much of what follows concerning a possible response to yet another novel technology, AI.[40]

It must first be noted that Anabaptist morality is concerned with the creation of a human moral community. For example, in the Anabaptist tradition, sin is considered a communal act. Any action of an individual within a community has the potential to affect the whole body and, therefore, the responsibility for reconciliation is also communal. While capitalism seeks to enhance the individual pursuit of happiness or the "good," many Anabaptist scholars have sought to contrast this with the call of Christ to be a community that corporately seeks the good of the "least of these" through radical service.[41] The concern of technological advancement, then, is primarily about how we create and maintain these communities with technology.

---

40. See Miller et al., *Viewing New Creations with Anabaptist Eyes.*

41. See Kraybill, *Upside-Down Kingdom.*

How do we ameliorate human suffering with AI—not, crucially, increase the good? These are key differences.

For example, consider the possibility that through automation Marica is afforded more free time to do what she enjoys (long-distance trekking) by working from home. However, after moving across the country, her primary relationships are with coworkers and the Bible study that formed among Christians at her workplace. Because of less contact outside the office, the group eventually falls apart. In this case, the automation increased individual good but disrupted the interdependence of a given community. Anabaptists might consider the disruption of interdependence harm even if, by conventional methods, the wealth (or good) of everyone in the community increased. Even if the group members agreed to disband due to other interests, harm may have been done to God's call to live in community. This traditionally would have led to the rejection of the technology by some Anabaptist groups.

This approach of wholesale rejection of a technology could drum up "Luddite"-like imagery of the Amish "rejecting" all technology and separating themselves from society. However, this is a largely uninformed view that fails to understand the process of communal discernment that takes place in Anabaptist communities when considering what to do with new advances. Indeed, a general consensus is that technologies such as genetically modified organisms on their own are ethically neutral.[42] For Anabaptists, the consideration for the adoption of any technology takes place in communities where consensus can be built. Without communal action, no mutual accountability is established. So, in the example of automation in Marcia's workplace, it isn't the technology itself that is problematic; it is the consequences of its adoption that are of concern. How might this process look when thinking about such integrated technologies as algorithmic learning?

Indeed, the difference between decisions concerning automation at a corporate entity versus a technology from prior generations, such as whether tractors should be incorporated into farm work, certainly seems difficult to grasp. The globalization of many aspects of society has gone hand-in-hand with a globalization of decision making. How can we be held to make choices about our work when we are employees of a multinational corporation? In other words, how can one effectively reject a technology, even as a church community, when the jobs members have can range so widely and incorporate such a deep level of technology? I will argue that we must shift instead to think critically in these communities about how to cultivate accountability for behaviors rather than focusing on the technologies

42. See Miller et al., *Viewing New Creations with Anabaptist Eyes*.

themselves. Specifically, how do our individual behaviors reflect our patterns of preferred reinforcement and how can we hold one another accountable as we reflect on what our reinforcers say about our priorities? Underlying this is the need to develop shared communal priorities.

An Anabaptist response to the incorporation of new technologies is informed by three distinctive communal experiences. First, Anabaptists are informed by discipleship to Christ. Menno Simons, one of the key early leaders of the Anabaptist movement, prefaced his writings with his favorite verse, 1 Cor 3:11: "For no one can lay any foundation other than the one already laid, which is Jesus Christ." For early Anabaptists in particular, this commitment to discipleship led to a lived experience with an ethic of dissent. The belief in believer's baptism, fellowship of all believers in church communities rather than hierarchical distinctions, and other faith emphases led to clashes with church authorities of the day.

Non-conformity to dominant culture can often stand in direct contrast to forms of social reinforcement that act on the neural mechanisms outlined above. As interdependent primates, humans experience social belonging as a form of reinforcement.[43] What is considered community has rapidly changed with the digitization of society. It is very likely that a larger proportion of people now spend less time with their church communities than they do engaging in digital forms of interaction and entertainment. There's no doubt that your community is a function of those with whom you spend time. Christians must examine this critically if they hope to maintain a community at all, let alone one of dissent. Perhaps church communities will also move part of their existence online and a larger context of communal engagement will lead to more insightful ideas about how to order ourselves in society.

A second major principle of the Anabaptist ethical context is the experience of persecution as a function of being dissenting communities. Experiences related to conscientious objection to military service, or rejection of Catholicism and Lutheranism in Europe, led Anabaptists to emphasize the needs of persecuted minorities within a majority culture. In practice, this has resulted in the idea that if the adoption of a new technology is likely to increase suffering for the "least of these," then it must be communally rejected. Even if beneficial to individuals within the community, if any are made to suffer as a result of its use, it should be rejected. This is based on the teachings of Christ for the poor and the widow who lived outside of the community.

43. See Jones et al., "Behavioral and Neural Properties of Social Reinforcement Learning."

In practice, what this might look like is asking moral questions about our everyday lives in community spaces, perhaps even in online chat groups. Questions such as "Who have my financial decisions benefitted this week?," "Who have they harmed?" and "Where did I devote my social energy?" can help us frame reflections on how the reinforcement mechanisms that surround us have led us to behave in certain ways. The consequences of our actions in modern society are notoriously difficult to discern due to the complex supply chains and labor practices that underlie economic activity.[44] However, using communal reflection and encouragement can bend us toward more just practices and move us away from the exploitative power dynamics of the haves against the have-nots.

This then relates to the third guiding Anabaptist principle, a commitment to non-violence. This is commonly interpreted as an intentional move away from the accumulation of power. Conrad Brunk summarizes this sentiment well: "The worldly virtues that Anabaptists often viewed as vices include a reliance on power and violence for social and environmental control, which is seen as a lack of trust in divine sovereignty over human affairs in history."[45]

I would argue that AI, as it stands, is primarily an agent of capitalism. We need only look to the rapid adaptations in response to the coronavirus crisis to see how large corporations at the fore of AI development increased their profits while those at the margins suffered. It is not a stretch to suggest that the growth in screen time during the pandemic relates to increased profits for these companies and those that advertise on digital platforms, as many suggest that screen time increases attained during the pandemic are likely to be sustained long term. This is based on the knowledge of human reinforcement systems outlined above and the remarkable ability of AI to model and coopt them to sustain engagement. This profound concentration of wealth and power should cause Christians to pause as they think about the effect that their actions have in relation to the digital environment. This is a profound alteration of the organization of everyday existence. With every hour of increased screen time, we have ceded additional control of our behavioral-environment loop, and indeed given power, to the companies that control that space.

---

44. The episode titled "The Book of Dougs" from NBC's *The Good Place* demonstrates this through a discussion of how even good intentions like buying flowers for someone can cause harm due to exploitative labor practices or harmful chemicals used in their production.

45. Brunk, "The Biotechnology Vision," in Miller, *Viewing New Creations with Anabaptist Eyes*, 106.

The use of AI to concentrate power has also been happening in the workplace. Initial concerns of labor being replaced by robots has been modified to include management. Companies have begun to adopt algorithms in workplaces that can track behaviors and notify workers when efficiency drops. They can even fire someone based on performance evaluations assessed automatically.[46] In ways such as this, the human connection is removed from the workplace and power further concentrated at the altar of efficient labor and profit generation. This wanton pursuit of wealth and power is in direct contrast to the call of Christ to build the community of God here on earth. Any such attempt to dehumanize work should be strongly resisted by the committed Christian.

The pursuit of wealth that leads to ceding time and labor to profit-driven algorithms represents an ethic of individual good in contrast to a communal consideration of how we ought to order our lives. Anabaptists have recognized this for many years and have sought to draw a sharp distinction between profit and the ethics of Christ due to the assumption that the desire for profit puts mammon above God.[47] Indeed, the economic models upon which we build the metrics to measure the betterment of society (e.g., gross domestic product) are based primarily on a hoped-for increase in consumption. In the rush to not miss out on the next technological advancement that generates trillions in tax revenue to redistribute (or not) among the populace, or to create the next advancement in human health and wellness, we must ask ourselves, is our hope in the economic outcomes or in what it does to us as the family of God?

In the secular space there are also a variety of voices openly questioning consumption as the primary means by which we might measure human thriving. Even within AI, high profile examples of this dissent, including the firing of Timnit Gerbru and Margaret Mitchell at Google, reveal an unease within AI companies to consider alternatives to the goal of increasing consumption.[48] Alternatives, including the environmental movement led by feminist voices, are offering creative alternatives to the search for good in profit.[49] I would argue, however, that the church has a long history of dissenting voices to this ideology, including prominently within the Anabaptist and Indigenous movements, among others. It will be imperative that the Western

---

46. See Dzieza, "Robots Aren't Taking Our Jobs—They're Becoming Our Bosses."

47. See Kraybill, *Upside-Down Kingdom*.

48. See "Margaret Mitchell."

49. For examples of this see the excellent *All We Can Save*, an anthology of essays and poems by leading female voices in the environmentalist movement.

church repent and center these long-dissenting but cooperative voices if we seek to harness our partially digital future rather than be harnessed by it.

So what does this look like? Neuroscience tells us that social reinforcement can directly compete with even strong biological reinforcers, including drugs of abuse.[50] Age-old practices within the church such as communion and gathering to worship are built on the idea of social reinforcement. Group singing is known to release endorphins, the body's own opiates, in addition to providing other positive benefits.[51] One thing I have always enjoyed in a majority of Mennonite services I have attended is the time of sharing praises and prayer concerns, either during Sunday school or during service. This moment of sharing and accountability can be a powerful form of social motivation that can shape behaviors. What if we cultivated communities of digital accountability? Shared our screen time from the previous week? Celebrated our ability to get off our phones and go to bed at a reasonable time? What if we found ways of increasing our connections with loved ones and could learn to trust one another enough to speak boldly in love rather than in jealousy or anger? These practices likely already exist across the wider church, but concerted effort is needed to build communities that demonstrate the power of a focus on the ethics of Christ in the digital age. Then we may be the salt and light to others who find themselves increasingly isolated, despite having thousands of followers in digital communities where they share so many "common interests."

BIBLIOGRAPHY

Abdel Magid, Hoda S., et al. "Disentangling Individual, School, and Neighborhood Effects on Screen Time among Adolescents and Young Adults in the United States." *Preventive Medicine* 142 (2020) 106357.

BBC. "Facebook Buys 'Mind-Reading Wristband' Firm CTRL-Labs." *BBC News*, September 24, 2019. https://www.bbc.com/news/technology-49812689.

Berkman, Elliot T., and Matthew D. Lieberman. "The Neuroscience of Goal Pursuit: Bridging Gaps between Theory and Data." In *The Psychology of Goals*, edited by Gordon B. Moskowitz and Heidi Grant, 98–126. New York: Guilford, 2009.

Berridge, Kent C. "The Debate over Dopamine's Role in Reward: The Case for Incentive Salience." *Psychopharmacology* 191 (2007) 391–431.

Chorzempa, Martin, et al. "China's Social Credit System: A Mark of Progress or a Threat to Privacy?" Peterson Institute for International Economics, 2018. https://www.piie.com/publications/policy-briefs/chinas-social-credit-system-mark-progress-or-threat-privacy.

50. See Venniro et al., "Volitional Social Interaction Prevents Drug Addiction in Rat Models"; Heilig et al., "Time to Connect."

51. See Kang et al., "Review of the Physiological Effects and Mechanisms of Singing."

Clayton, Philip. "Neuroscience, the Person, and God: An Emergentist Account." In *Neuroscience and the Person: Scientific Perspectives on Divine Action*, edited by Robert John Russell et al., 181–214. Berkeley: Center for Theology and the Natural Sciences, 1999.

Deisseroth, Karl. "Optogenetics." *Nature Methods* 8 (2011) 26–29.

Diamond, Marian C., et al. "The Effects of an Enriched Environment on the Histology of the Rat Cerebral Cortex." *Journal of Comparative Neurology* 123 (1964) 111–19.

Doris, John M. "Persons, Situations, and Virtue Ethics." *Nous* 32 (1998) 504–30.

Dzieza, Josh. "Robots Aren't Taking Our Jobs—They're Becoming Our Bosses." *The Verge*, February 27, 2020. https://www.theverge.com/2020/2/27/21155254/automation-robots-unemployment-jobs-vs-human-google-amazon.

Farahany, Nita. "When Technology Can Read Minds, How Will We Protect Our Privacy?" *TED*, November 2018. https://www.ted.com/talks/nita_farahany_when_technology_can_read_minds_how_will_we_protect_our_privacy.

Ferrier, David. "The Localization of Function in the Brain." *Proceedings of the Royal Society of London* 22 (1874) 228–32.

Floresco, Stan B. "The Nucleus Accumbens: An Interface Between Cognition, Emotion, and Action." *Annual Review of Psychology* 66 (2015) 25–52.

Floridi, Luciano. *The Fourth Revolution: How the Infosphere Is Reshaping Human Reality*. Oxford: Oxford University Press, 2014.

Gennaioli, Nicola, and Guido Tabellini. "Identity, Beliefs, and Political Conflict." 2019. https://papers.ssrn.com/sol3/papers.cfm?abstract_id=3300726.

Graybiel, Ann M. "Habits, Rituals, and the Evaluative Brain." *Annual Review of Neuroscience* 31 (2008) 359–87.

Grünbaum, Albert Sidney Frankau, and Charles Scott Sherrington. "Observations on the Physiology of the Cerebral Cortex of the Anthropoid Apes." *Proceedings of the Royal Society of London* 72 (1904) 152–55.

Heilig, Markus, et al. "Time to Connect: Bringing Social Context into Addiction Neuroscience." *Nature Reviews Neuroscience* 17 (2016) 592–99.

Hodes, Leora N., and Kevin G. F. Thomas. "Smartphone Screen Time: Inaccuracy of Self-Reports and Influence of Psychological and Contextual Factors." *Computers in Human Behavior* 115 (2021) 106616.

Jeannerod, Marc. "Are There Limits to the Naturalization of Mental States?" In *Neuroscience and the Person: Scientific Perspectives on Divine Action*, edited by Robert John Russell et al., 119–28. Berkeley: Center for Theology and the Natural Sciences, 1999.

Jennings, Joshua H., et al. "The Inhibitory Circuit Architecture of the Lateral Hypothalamus Orchestrates Feeding." *Science* 341 (2013) 1517–21.

Jiang, Zhongming, et al. "Understanding the Causation of Construction Workers' Unsafe Behaviors Based on System Dynamics Modeling." *Journal of Management in Engineering* 31 (2015) 249–56.

Johnson, Ayana Elizabeth, and Katharine K. Wilkinson, eds. *All We Can Save: Truth, Courage, and Solutions for the Climate Crisis*. New York: One World, 2020.

Jones, Rebecca M., et al. "Behavioral and Neural Properties of Social Reinforcement Learning." *The Journal of Neuroscience* 31 (2011) 13039–45.

Kang, Jing, et al. "A Review of the Physiological Effects and Mechanisms of Singing." *Journal of Voice* 32 (2018) 390–95.

Kraybill, Donald B. *Upside-Down Kingdom*. Scottsdale, PA: Herald, 1990.

Leal, Stephanie L., and Michael A. Yassa. "Normal Cognitive and Brain Aging." In *The Oxford Handbook of Adult Cognitive Disorders*, edited by Michael L. Alosco and Robert A. Stern, 5–28. Oxford: Oxford University Press, 2019.

Maoz, Uri, et al. "Neural Precursors of Decisions That Matter—An ERP Study of Deliberate and Arbitrary Choice." *ELife* 8 (2019) 1–32.

"Margaret Mitchell: Google Fires AI Ethics Founder." *BBC News*, February 20, 2021. https://www.bbc.com/news/technology-56135817.

Miller, Roman J., et al. *Viewing New Creations with Anabaptist Eyes: Ethics of Biotechnology*. Harrisonburg, VA: Cascadia, 2005.

Nelson, Charles A. *Romania's Abandoned Children*. Cambridge, MA: Harvard University Press, 2014.

NielsenIQ. "Discover More of Your Business." https://nielseniq.com/global/en/solutions/.

Olds, James, and Peter Milner. "Positive Reinforcement Produced by Electrical Stimulation of Septal Area and Other Regions of Rat Brain." *Journal of Comparative and Physiological Psychology* 47 (1954) 419–27.

Pacific Crest Trail Association. "PCT Visitor Use Statistics." https://www.pcta.org/our-work/trail-and-land-management/pct-visitor-use-statistics/.

Rajangam, Sankaranarayani, et al. "Wireless Cortical Brain-Machine Interface for Whole-Body Navigation in Primates." *Scientific Reports* 6 (2016) 1–13.

Redgrave, Peter, et al. "Goal-Directed and Habitual Control in the Basal Ganglia: Implications for Parkinson's Disease." *Nature Reviews Neuroscience* 11 (2010) 760–72.

Reiner, Anton. "You Cannot Have a Vertebrate Brain without a Basal Ganglia." In *The Basal Ganglia IX*, edited by Hendrik Jan Groenewegen et al., 3–24. New York: Springer, 2009.

Rescorla, R. A., and Allan Wagner. "A Theory of Pavlovian Conditioning: Variations in the Effectiveness of Reinforcement and Nonreinforcement." In *Classical Conditioning II: Current Research and Theory*, edited by Abraham H. Black and William F. Prokasy, 64–99. New York: Appleton-Century-Crofts, 1972.

Rushton, Stephen, and Elizabeth Larkin. "Shaping the Learning Environment: Connecting Developmentally Appropriate Practices to Brain Research." *Early Childhood Education Journal* 29 (2001) 25–33.

Rydgren, Jens. "Beliefs." *The Oxford Handbook of Analytical Sociology*, edited by Peter Bearman and Peter Hedström, 72–93. Oxford: Oxford University Press, 2009.

Schieber, Marc H., and Lyndon S. Hibbard. "How Somatotopic Is the Motor Cortex Hand Area?" *Science* 261 (1993) 489–92.

Schultz, Wolfram, Peter Dayan, and P. Read Montague. "A Neural Substrate of Prediction and Reward." *Science* 275 (1997) 1593.

Stern, Yaakov. "What Is Cognitive Reserve? Theory and Research Application of the Reserve Concept." *Journal of the International Neuropsychological Society* 8 (2002) 448–60.

Suhler, Christopher L., and Patricia S. Churchland. "Control: Conscious and Otherwise." *Trends in Cognitive Sciences* 13 (2009) 341–47.

Venniro, Marco, et al. "Volitional Social Interaction Prevents Drug Addiction in Rat Models." *Nature Neuroscience* 21 (2018) 1520–29.

Vizcaino, Maricarmen, et al. "Reliability of a New Measure to Assess Modern Screen Time in Adults." *BMC Public Health* 19 (2019) 13861386–88.

Watson, John B. *Behaviorism*. New York: Norton, 1930.

Weir, Kirsten. "The Lasting Impact of Neglect." *Monitor on Psychology* 45 (2014) 36–41.
Wise, R. A. "Addictive Drugs and Brain Stimulation Reward." *Annual Review of Neuroscience* 19 (1996) 319–40.

7

21st Century Learning Skills and Artificial Intelligence

David Wicks and Michael J. Paulus Jr.

INTRODUCTION

We are now over one-fifth of the way through the twenty-first century and our world is much different than it was one hundred years ago. Rapid advances in technology have provided greater access to information and ways to connect with other humans than previously thought possible. At the same time, we may be more deceived by misinformation and make fewer deep connections with others because of the busyness and automation of this age. Moreover, many lack the knowledge and skills to negotiate the advances that new technologies afford.[1] As technology—and especially artificial intelligence—continues to transform education, we need to be clear about our desires and goals for the future of education. Alongside the development of our technological society there has been a growing consensus that today's students need to learn how to think critically, be creative problem-solvers, and effectively communicate and collaborate with others to be thoughtful,

1. See Newport, *World Without Email.*

productive, and caring citizens in this digital age. Some may argue that we can use AI-driven systems to teach needed skills, but it is more important for us to adapt our human-focused educational systems to ensure that current and future students have the skills and frameworks necessary to flourish in an increasingly automated world. The chapter explores four concepts important for learning and AI in the twenty-first century—creativity, critical thinking, communication, and collaboration (the "4Cs")—as well as reflections on the theological significance of creativity and community.

TWENTY-FIRST-CENTURY LEARNING SKILLS

It could be argued that for all of the advances made by humans during the last one hundred years, the system of schooling remains relatively unchanged.[2] Students take courses in four or eight subjects per term. The most popular method of teaching is lecturing, where the typical interaction is teacher-to-student communication. Learning is mainly assessed through exams where students recall what they have been told. Is this the type of learning that helps students prepare for careers that may not yet exist, or for a world being transformed by new and emerging technologies? Some predict that over the next fifteen years, forty percent of current jobs will be taken over by AI and robots.[3] Should students in school today be prepared to compete for jobs with AI, which will be designed to replace them? Alternatively, and more appropriately, students should be adaptable for a changing future and be prepared to create and thrive in jobs that have not even been thought of yet. How can this be accomplished? In addition to learning core subjects as part of a liberal arts education, students should learn what the Partnership for 21st Century Learning (P21), a coalition of educators, policymakers, and businesses, calls "21st Century Learning Skills."[4] These skills include what are commonly referred to as the 4Cs—critical thinking, creativity, communication, and collaboration—which help students learn how to learn, preparing them to participate in and shape an unknown future.[5] In a sense, by having a solid liberal arts education and learning these skills, students may future-proof their professional lives against AI.[6] They will also learn how to leverage AI for a better future.

2. See Barnum, "XQ Is Taking Over TV."
3. See Lee, *AI Superpowers.*
4. See https://www.battelleforkids.org/networks/p21.
5. See Ross, "It's Time to Reassess Our Understanding of the 4Cs."
6. See Aoun, *Robot-Proof.*

For the present education system to integrate the 4Cs into curricula, there will need to be leadership, cooperation, and change from all stakeholders, including school leaders, teachers, and students. Unfortunately, many school leaders lack training to determine the professional development needed to help teachers modify curricula to incorporate the 4Cs.[7] However, P21 has collaborated with other non-profit educational organizations to define and design this much-needed professional development; their work can help teachers understand how to modify their current instruction to integrate the 4Cs.

The 4Cs can help students move from rote learning to deep learning.[8] A study by Katherine Landon indicated that there is a great need for teacher professional development in this area. Many students reported that they did not experience the teaching or practice of the 4Cs in their classes. Of the students surveyed, ninety-four percent indicated that communication is a necessary skill to learn for their future, yet only fifty-four percent of students indicated that they were being taught or asked to practice communication skills as part of their coursework. In the study, eighty-five percent of students reported collaboration to be an essential skill to learn, with sixty-eight percent reporting that it was being taught or used in assignments. Collaboration was the most commonly taught of the 4Cs in the survey, which is perhaps the most straightforward for teachers to incorporate into curricula. The study reported that eighty percent of students thought schools should integrate critical thinking into curricula, yet only forty-one percent of students reported experiencing it in their learning. Creativity was highly desired by students in the study—eighty-nine percent of students thought it was an important skill to teach. However, it was also the least experienced of the 4Cs in the classroom, with only thirty-nine percent of students experiencing it as part of instruction or practice. While this study makes it clear that administrators and teachers have their work cut out for them, it is encouraging that students are interested in having the 4Cs integrated into their coursework.[9]

As we think about the 4Cs, we should consider the role of AI in the future of teaching and learning. It appears inevitable that AI will increasingly influence education. One recent study projected the use of AI in US education to grow by about fifty percent over the next five years.[10] What will be the role of AI? AI is already employed in several areas that are beneficial

7. See Wagner, *Creating Innovators.*

8. See Bitter and Loney, "Deeper Learning."

9. See Landon, "Student Perceptions of Learning."

10. See "Artificial Intelligence Market in the Education Sector in US."

to learners, such as using AI to generate automatic transcriptions for online class meeting recordings.[11] While this transcription service is not yet a perfect substitute for students who need captioning because of a disability, it does benefit students who primarily speak and read in another language. It also makes videos searchable for students who want to quickly re-watch a specific video segment. An example of a controversial use of AI in education is in the area of virtual exam proctoring. Video cameras feed data to an AI system that monitors students and attempts to determine whether they are violating an institution's honor code. However, this use of AI has led to concerns about equity. During the pandemic, issues arose with such systems being unable to identify students of color, resulting in those students not being able to take an exam.[12] This error may have been caused because the AI software was not designed by or tested with people of color.[13] But even if these system were to operate accurately, other ethical concerns remain about such automated forms of surveillance and the vendors that license them.

Given ever-increasing uses of AI among various professions, today's students need to learn and practice the 4Cs to be able to interact with a changing workplace and world. It is essential to teach students how and why each of the 4Cs is beneficial. Students will need to learn and practice skills related to their ability to think and act creatively, to make good decisions based on reason, to share thoughts and ideas in different ways, and to work with others to achieve common goals. The Partnership for 21st Century Learning provides various resources for educators, including indicators for skills and assessments for mastery, and many states, school districts, and universities have incorporated these skills into a larger set of standards for students to master.[14] An example of this from Washington State is in table 7.1.[15]

11. See Tung, "Microsoft Teams Is Getting This New Feature."

12. See Flaherty, "No More Proctorio."

13. See Hardesty, "Study Finds Gender and Skin-Type Bias."

14. See Partnership for 21st Century Learning, "Framework for 21st Century Learning Definitions."

15. Washington Office of Superintendent of Public Instruction, "Washington Career and Technical Education 21st Century Leadership Skills."

Table 7.1: Washington Career and Technical Education 21st Century Leadership Skills	
1. Creativity and Innovation	
1.A Think Creatively Student Outcome: The student will be involved in activities that require applying theory, problem-solving, and using critical and creative thinking skills while understanding outcomes of related decisions.	
1.A.1	Use a wide range of idea creation techniques (such as brainstorming)
1.A.2	Create new and worthwhile ideas (both incremental and radical concepts)
1.A.3	Elaborate, refine, analyze, and evaluate their own ideas in order to improve and maximize creative efforts
1.B Work Creatively with Others Student Outcome: The student will demonstrate the ability to incorporate and utilize the principles of group dynamics in a variety of settings.	
1.B.1	Develop, implement, and communicate new ideas to others effectively
1.B.2	Be open and responsive to new and diverse perspectives; incorporate group input and feedback into the work
1.B.3	Demonstrate originality and inventiveness in work and understand the real world limits to adopting new ideas
1.B.4	View failure as an opportunity to learn; understand that creativity and innovation is a long-term, cyclical process of small successes and frequent mistakes
1.C Implement Innovations Student Outcome: The student will demonstrate skills that assist in understanding and accepting responsibility to family, community, and business and industry.	
1.C.1	Act on creative ideas to make a tangible and useful contribution to the field in which the innovation will occur
2. Critical Thinking and Problem Solving	
2.A Reason Effectively Student Outcome: The student will analyze, refine, and apply decision-making skills through classroom, family, community, and business and industry (work-related) experiences.	
2.A.1	Use various types of reasoning (inductive, deductive, etc.) as appropriate to the situation
2.B Use Systems Thinking Student Outcome: The student will demonstrate an understanding of complex inter-relationships (systems). This means that the student understands social, organizational, and technological systems; they can monitor and correct performance; and they can design or improve systems.	
2.B.1	Analyze how parts of a whole interact with each other to produce overall outcomes in complex systems

2.C Make Judgments and Decisions
Student Outcome: The student will analyze, refine, and apply decision-making skills through classroom, family, community, and business and industry (work-related) experiences.

2.C.1	Effectively analyze and evaluate evidence, arguments, claims and beliefs
2.C.2	Analyze and evaluate major alternative points of view
2.C.3	Synthesize and make connections between information and arguments
2.C.4	Interpret information and draw conclusions based on the best analysis
2.C.5	Reflect critically on learning experiences and processes

2.D Solve Problems
Student Outcome: The student will be involved in activities that require applying theory, problem-solving, and using critical and creative thinking skills while understanding outcomes of related decisions.

| 2.D.1 | Solve different kinds of non-familiar problems in both conventional and innovative ways |
| 2.D.2 | Identify and ask significant questions that clarify various points of view and lead to better solutions |

3. Communication and Collaboration

3.A Communicate Clearly
Student Outcome: The student will demonstrate oral, interpersonal, written, and electronic communication and presentation skills and understands how to apply those skills.

3.A.1	Articulate thoughts and ideas effectively using oral, written, and nonverbal communication skills in a variety of forms and contexts
3.A.2	Listen effectively to decipher meaning, including knowledge, values, attitudes, and intentions
3.A.3	Use communication for a range of purposes (e.g., to inform, instruct, motivate, and persuade)
3.A.4	Utilize multiple media and technologies, and know how to judge their effectiveness a priori as well as assess their impact
3.A.5	Communicate effectively in diverse environments (including multi-lingual)

3.B Collaborate with Others
Student Outcome: The student will communicate, participate, and advocate effectively in pairs, small groups, teams, and large groups in order to reach common goals.

3.B.1	Demonstrate ability to work effectively and respectfully with diverse teams
3.B.2	Exercise flexibility and willingness to be helpful in making necessary compromises to accomplish a common goal
3.B.3	Assume shared responsibility for collaborative work, and value the individual contributions made by each team member

Having such a list of standards is an excellent first step, but it will not lead to change unless many teachers modify their curricula to incorporate standards related to the 4Cs. One possible way to encourage educators to incorporate standards for the 4Cs into curricula would be to fund teacher trainings that help them integrate standards in ways that can maintain or raise academic achievement. In other words, teachers would be more likely to embrace this change if these essential skills can be taught while maintaining or increasing students' understanding of course content. Another possibility would be to require teachers to integrate these standards. This widely-used method may be met with resistance and, when implemented, taught using less authentic practices. A third possibility would be to explore how AI may help in this process. We will consider this idea as we define and describe each of the four 4Cs.

In the next part of this chapter, we will define each of the 4Cs, share examples of how they can be taught, and identify benefits and challenges associated with AI. For each of the 4Cs, we want to examine what the role of AI might be in the teaching and learning process. To be beneficial, AI should help students have greater agency in their learning. A less effective or possibly problematic use of AI may be when it is used primarily as an efficiency tool for educators to monitor students or automate assessment of knowledge.[16]

CREATIVITY

The Partnership for 21st Century Learning defines creativity as the ability to develop meaningful new ideas using various strategies. Creative learners collaborate with others on innovative projects by being open and responsive to diverse ideas and approaches.[17] Students demonstrate thinking creatively during class projects by generating new and meaningful ideas using techniques such as brainstorming or mind mapping. These ideas are then improved through individual and group analysis and refinement. Students demonstrate an ability to work creatively with others by developing strategies to communicate new ideas with team members effectively. This group work can be facilitated by developing group norms that include essential elements such as being open to diverse perspectives, showing willingness to share ideas, and utilizing feedback.

16. See Selwyn, *Should Robots Replace Teachers?*

17. See Partnership for 21st Century Learning, "Framework for 21st Century Learning Definitions."

As part of learning the skill of creativity, students need to understand that failure within the project is part of the cyclical process of creation. Rather than being the end of the project, failure indicates a need to change and try again. If a team shares brainstormed project ideas with the teacher and is told that none fit the project's scope, the team does not quit. The team adjusts and generates more ideas. This is a place where technology and AI specifically excel; AI systems receive feedback about failures, modify algorithms, and repeatedly try without frustration until a goal is reached.[18] However, the use of AI in creative learning can be ambiguous. Consider an example in which students work with AI as a collaborator to brainstorm ideas for a project.[19] In such a situation the teacher would need to determine the role of AI in this process, as it may come up with excellent or inappropriate ideas. To master a standard for creativity, students could instead primarily focus on analysis and refinement of AI contributions.

Does the future of all group work include asking AI for project possibilities instead of human-only brainstorming? Artificial intelligence may help us come up with ideas we would have never considered, but AI may also limit ideas to a narrow or specific viewpoint, depending on the data to which it has access. Problems with insufficient, flawed, or problematically biased datasets should make us consider how much of the creative process we should turn over to AI. This is not a simple concern, such as when math teachers worried about allowing calculators in the classroom. Understanding the data as well as algorithms used in a particular AI application is necessary for understanding how it will contribute to the learning process. Marcus Du Sautoy argues that, to the extent that creativity can be broken down into code, machines will be "creative."[20] Can simple human brainstorming be converted to an algorithm and done by machines? Brainstorming software enhanced by AI is already being used by design firms and in other fields.[21] Nevertheless, humans must stay engaged in creative processes, always thinking critically about machines' "creative" contributions. Joseph Aoun argues that creativity is one area where humans can distinguish themselves from machines, and he encourages us to do everything we can to learn and cultivate creativity.[22]

18. See Domingos, *Master Algorithm.*

19. See Syverson, "Rules of Brainstorming Change When Artificial Intelligence Gets Involved."

20. See Du Sautoy, *Creativity Code.*

21. See Syverson, "Rules of Brainstorming Change When Artificial Intelligence Gets Involved."

22. See Aoun, *Robot-Proof.*

CRITICAL THINKING

Critical thinking, the second of the 4Cs, can be defined as learning how to reason effectively to make sound judgments and decisions.[23] Critical thinking empowers students to evaluate sources of information, make well-reasoned determinations, and be confident about actions that need to be taken.[24] The standard for critical thinking can be broken down into four parts: effective reasoning, systems thinking, making judgments and decisions, and solving problems. All parts are worthy of exploration, but here we will focus on effective reasoning.

Students can be taught how to improve inductive and deductive reasoning skills to aid them in decision-making. They can learn top-down techniques (deductive) to improve decision-making when given a rule or theory. As long as the rules are trustworthy and applied correctly, deductive reasoning can be accurate and helpful. For example, the proper use of a math formula and its data can make a trustworthy deductive decision. Students can also learn bottom-up techniques (inductive) to improve decision-making when, for example, they are given specific observations about which to make broad generalizations. The accuracy of these generalizations may not be entirely precise, but students need to learn how to make the best possible decisions based on available data. For example, if students want to get degrees in fields with a strong job market, they can use employment data to help them make that determination. However, top-down factors, such as macroeconomic and other trends, should also be considered to improve the accuracy of bottom-up decisions. Learning how to improve inductive and deductive reasoning will benefit students throughout their lives.

Early versions of AI tools from the 1950s were good at deductive reasoning.[25] These types of AI, called expert systems, are computer programs that integrate established rules or theories from authoritative sources to make decisions. An expert system receives input from a user, such as a question, and evaluates this input using programmed rules to decide on and provide an answer. This decision-making can be relatively simple, such as the answer to a trivia question, or it can be more complex, such as when a person inputs a series of chess moves and the expert system outputs countermoves. In the latter case, the expert system could be designed to mimic the moves of a specific world chess champion or a typical novice player. Expert systems can be comparatively better at deductive reasoning than

23. See Landon, "Student Perceptions of Learning."
24. See Kay and Greenhill, "Twenty-First Century Students Need 21st Century Skills."
25. See Littlefield, "Human Skills AI Can't Replace."

humans, who may forget rules and may take longer to process them and provide answers.

Until recently, humans were thought to be better at inductive reasoning than AI. However, with advanced processing power and extensive cloud storage, AI can now be faster and more accurate at some forms of inductive reasoning than humans. A form of AI called deep learning organizes large amounts of data and uses inductive reasoning models to develop general rules to make decisions.[26] An example of this is speech recognition on a smartphone, where the AI is continually developing new general rules for what words are being "heard" while the speech recognition tool is in use. In an academic setting, this might mean that a web meeting AI-based captioning system "learns" new words or new uses of words based on the conversations of previous meetings and makes general rules that result in better accuracy of transcripts.

Humans have a distinct advantage over AI in a third type of reasoning called abductive reasoning.[27] Abductive reasoning is defined as examining an incomplete set of observations and choosing the likeliest explanation.[28] Whereas deductive reasoning involves certainty, and inductive reasoning uses probability to infer a correct choice based on data, we use abductive reasoning frequently in our daily lives when we make a best guess based on limited data. For example, we might decide to give a student more time on a project because we suspect there may be personal reasons why the student could not complete the work on time. Perhaps we are mindful of traumatic events in the world that may be impacting this student, or perhaps the student is late with work due to some unavoidable circumstance. An AI system might make the same decision, but there may not be enough personal data for an inductive decision based on deep learning, or the situation may be too individualized for an expert system's deductive decision. In addition, AI would lack any real empathy for the personal dimension of the problem.[29]

Because educational contexts value evidence-based decisions, it may seem that abductive reasoning has limited application in teaching and learning. Focusing on engineering education, Ciarán O'Reilly argues, however, that abductive reasoning is important because it is the only type of reasoning that allows for the introduction of new ideas, which leads to practicing creative thinking. His study concluded that if abductive reasoning were included as part of project learning outcomes, students would have

26. See Hardesty, "Explained: Neural Networks."
27. See Littlefield, "Human Skills AI Can't Replace."
28. See Sooknanan and Seemungal, "Not So Elementary."
29. See Littlefield, "Human Skills AI Can't Replace."

opportunities to practice critical and creative thinking.[30] Practicing abductive reasoning skills, for example through games, may help students gain confidence in their reasoning skills.[31]

COMMUNICATION

Communication can be defined as sharing and listening to thoughts and ideas with others through digital and analogue technologies, using written, oral, and non-verbal interactions.[32] Over the years, there has been a repeated call from employers for improved communication skills for entry-level workers.[33] A 2017 study showed a significant disconnect between the percentage of employers who thought their entry-level emplyees' oral and written communication skills were proficient (41.6 percent) and the percentage of students who thought their oral and written communication skills were proficient (79.4 percent).[34] Teachers and administrators can address this concern by integrating opportunities for students to practice their communication skills as part of their regular coursework.

According to P21, students should be able to articulate thoughts and ideas effectively; listen and determine meaning; use communication to inform, instruct, motivate, and persuade; use digital technologies to communicate effectively; and communicate in diverse environments, such as in a multi-lingual meeting.[35] With appropriate professional development and time to design curricula, teachers should be able to create authentic, integrated assignments that provide opportunities for students to practice and master these communication skills.

As AI continues to improve, there is no question that some current communication tasks humans are doing will be automated. It is common now for chatbots to be an initial point of contact when contacting a business by phone or online. As chatbots "learn," they will become more human-like in their ability to answer correctly more of the questions being asked of them. In education, some fear that AI will take over the jobs of teachers. A common response to this is that any teacher who can be replaced by AI should be. In any case, AI has the potential to change the role of the teacher.

30. See O'Reilly, "Creative Engineers."

31. See Hwang et al., "Practicing Abductive Reasoning."

32. See Landon, "Student Perceptions of Learning."

33. See Casner-Lotto and Barrington, *Are They Really Ready to Work?*

34. See National Association of Colleges and Employers, "Job Outlook."

35. See Partnership for 21st Century Learning, "Framework for 21st Century Learning Definitions."

It may not be long before we begin to see social robots serving as teaching assistants in classrooms. The teacher's role may become more like that of a manager, overseeing these robots, verifying instructional choices, and providing support when robots are unable to communicate effectively.[36] Rather than looking at this possible change as a problem, we can think of it as a way to free up teachers to work with individual students, plan curricula, provide feedback, or do other tasks for which they currently lack time due to the number of students they teach. This can also help students learn how to communicate with AI agents. Communication skills will always be valued in and beyond the workplace, and students need to learn how to communicate with AI as well as human collaborators.

COLLABORATION

As our world has become more connected, the opportunities and needs to work collaboratively have grown rapidly. The COVID-19 pandemic required all of us to learn new ways to collaborate using technology, and many of these are likely to continue long beyond the pandemic. Collaboration can be defined as working with others toward a common goal.[37] In the P21 standards, students are to demonstrate an ability to work effectively with a diverse team, exhibit flexibility and a willingness to compromise to reach team goals, be a responsible teammate, and value the contributions made by all team members.[38]

Looking at the standard closely, it seems evident that the "others" collaborating with students are humans. However, if these standards were updated today, it is likely that collaborators on a student's project could include AI agents. Are AI agents ready to collaborate? Much of the current research has focused on human-AI interaction, but interaction is different than collaboration. As collaboration standards often state, teams collaborate to reach a common goal (see, e.g., table 7.1). Interaction does not require a common goal, which is why there needs to be a shift in AI research from human-AI interaction to human-AI collaboration.[39] A common problem in human collaboration is social loafing, which is when a group member exerts less effort in a group project than when working alone.[40] Social loaf-

36. See Edwards et al., "I, Teacher."
37. See Landon, "Student Perceptions of Learning."
38. See Partnership for 21st Century Learning, "Framework for 21st Century Learning Definitions."
39. See Wang et al., "From Human-Human Collaboration to Human-AI Collaboration."
40. Liden et al., "Social Loafing."

ing is frequently listed as a reason why students do not like group projects. This issue could be eliminated when working with AI agents. Regardless, students need opportunities to collaborate with AI agents on school projects to prepare them for collaborating with AI at work and elsewhere.

As always, the greatest challenges we face require collaboration. A number of AI researchers recently issued a call "to prioritize the development of cooperative intelligence that has the ability to promote mutually beneficial joint action." Cooperative intelligence, they point out, is not an alternative to human or AI autonomy; it goes beyond these to "enable us to achieve much-needed global cooperation in the future." For AI developers, this will require work on AI-AI cooperation, AI-human cooperation, and AI that improves human-human cooperation.[41] For those of us learning to collaborate with artificial agents, this necessitates, in the words of Aoun, cultivating human as well as technological literacies.[42]

THEOLOGICAL REFLECTIONS ON CREATIVITY AND COMMUNITY

Even though AI is at the top of many lists of technologies that is expected to transform education, "its use is just getting under way in teaching and learning."[43] As AI is integrated increasingly into various educational systems and pedagogical practices, from learning management systems to AI tutors, it must be done with "sound educational and societal justification."[44] Artificial intelligence needs to be aligned intentionally with established learning standards, such as those associated with the 4Cs, as well as with ethical principles such as privacy and equity. The 4Cs, which emphasize human ingenuity and relationships, acknowledge that we are fundamentally social and creative beings: Throughout the history of our species, our sociality has been joined with our ability to form abstract concepts and to imagine and create shared futures. The clarity the 4Cs provide about important aspects of human nature can help us find ways to balance instructor, student, and artificial agency. For Christians seeking faithful engagement with AI, theological understandings of creativity and community can provide further resources for reflection.

The artist Makoto Fujimura states that his "identity is rooted in the origin of Creation, and in the loving gaze of the Creator, who sees in us a

41. Dafoe et al., "Cooperative AI," 34, 36.

42. See Aoun, *Robot-Proof*.

43. Pelletier et al., "2021 EDUCAUSE Horizon Report," 13.

44. Selwyn, *Should Robots Replace Teachers?*, 131.

'greater love' before we are even aware: the creative impulse to shape the future." The Christian Bible, a collection of creative literary works, begins with creation and ends with new creation. Within God's creation, humans create new things—through agriculture, construction, musical instruments, metalworking, etc. (Gen 4)—and participate in God's creation of a new world (Rev 21:24–26). "To be human is to be creative," Fujimura concludes, and "unless we are making something, we cannot know the depth of God's being and God's grace permeating our lives and God's Creation." And in knowing God, we discover that God is "making all things new" in Jesus Christ (Rev 21:5). "The Christian narrative is all about the New," Fujimura says, and "part of that ushering in of the New is God's marker in us, called imagination, which makes us unique" and "uniquely defines our role in Creation." "What we build, design, and depict," he adds, "will become part of the future city of God."[45]

Fujimura sees creativity as a challenge to usefulness, especially the type of rationalized efficiency that often characterizes technological methodology—what Jacques Ellul called "technique." True human creativity, which "echoes God's character," is not utilitarian but gratuitous. God creates out of an abundance of love, and God's ultimate plan is "an imaginative New Creation": "God does not just mend, repair, and restore; God renews and generates, transcending our expectations of even what we desire, beyond what we dare to ask or imagine."[46] Frank Pasquale correctly points out that "a managerial mindset has colonized too much of [educational technology], insisting on the primacy of quantitative measurement." But education "has multiple purposes and goals, many of which cannot or should not be reduced to numerical measures," and we should not let AI "usurp and ultimately dictate our values rather than to serve as a tool that helps us achieve them."[47]

Gratuitous creativity creates community, establishing new and charitable relationships between givers and receivers. At the center of new creation is the body of Christ—the community of those who have received God's gift of love and new life. In the eschatological vision of the city of God (Rev 21–22), in the protological vision of initial creation (Gen 1–2), and in the early life of the Christian church (Acts 2–7), communities respond to God's loving and creative acts by embodying and enacting God's plan—stewarding, developing, and transforming the created world. Within the context of creation, we survive and thrive in creative and caring communities.

45. Fujimura, *Art and Faith*, 1, 6–7, 9, 12, 14.
46. Fujimura, *Art and Faith*, 13, 15, 29, 31.
47. Pasquale, *New Laws of Robotics*, 62–63.

As Norma Wirzba points out, "Life is not simply lived *with* or *along-side* others. It is lived *through* others and *by means of* them. . . . A healthy and flourishing life is always life together." Wirzba continues:

> Though we each exist as individual persons, our identity and agency are entirely dependent on how well we are able to fully face each other, receiving the nurture we need and giving the help we are uniquely equipped to provide. When the love of Jesus is found to be circulating among people, they are enabled to face each other with care and without shame.

Out of God's love we are created, and that same love creates an imagination enabling us to love, create, and live into "a new world governed by joy and peace and resulting in beauty and mutual flourishing."[48] For Christians, the fullest realization of community involves receiving and sharing the self-giving love of Christ. As Dietrich Bonhoeffer explains it, "Christian community means community through Jesus Christ and in Jesus Christ . . . from eternity we have been chosen in Jesus Christ, accepted in time, and united for eternity." "Christian community is not an ideal we have to realize," Bonhoeffer declares, "but rather a reality created by God in Christ in which we may participate."[49]

In education, we invite students to join and participate in a community of learning—to enter a social space where "learning awakens" through imitation, interaction, and collaboration.[50] There is a spiritual dimension to this work, which, in the words of Parker Palmer, concerns "the heart's longing to be connected with the largeness of life."[51] Cultivating creativity and community as AI augments education are significant spiritual priorities as well as learning goals—for these fundamental aspects of our shared humanity enable us to realize the greater possibilities and realities that come from gratuitous creativity and loving community.

The history of educational technology shows that technology alone does not transform education. The agency of teachers, attending to cultural contexts and addressing social inequities, is necessary for truly transformative education. The temptations of AI efficiencies—such as facial and emotional detection systems to monitor student attention and engagement, or automated guidance through and grading of student work—are strong. But at some point, technological utility inhibits human creativity. Another concern, accompanying the elevation of technological efficiency, is "the logic

48. Wirzba, *Way of Love*, 159–60, 162, 184.

49. Bonhoeffer, *Life Together*, 5, 13.

50. Lev Vygotsky, quoted in Darby and Lang, *Small Teaching Online*, 78.

51. Palmer, *Courage to Teach*, 5.

of individualized learning" and "the reorganization of education around the needs, interests, and circumstances of individuals rather than groups, classes, or communities."[52] At some point, individualization compromises community cohesion. Certainly, education about AI is critical and AI can enhance education; but, as Michelle Zimmerman says, "Technology is just one component of preparing learners for a world with AI."[53] The 4Cs, which highlight valuable skills as well as deeper values, can help us create and thrive together in this world.

BIBLIOGRAPHY

Aoun, Joseph E. *Robot-Proof: Higher Education in the Age of Artificial Intelligence.* Cambridge, MA: The MIT Press, 2017.

Barnum, Matt. "XQ Is Taking over TV to Make the Case That High School Hasn't Changed in 100 Years. But Is That True?" *Chalkbeat*, September 6, 2017. https://www.chalkbeat.org/2017/9/6/21100966/xq-is-taking-over-tv-to-make-the-case-that-high-school-hasn-t-changed-in-100-years-but-is-that-true.

Bitter, Catherine, and Emily Loney. "Deeper Learning: Improving Student Outcomes for College, Career, and Civic Life." Washington, DC: Education Policy Center at American Institutes for Research, 2015. https://www.air.org/sites/default/files/downloads/report/Deeper-Learning-EPC-Brief-August-2015.pdf.

Bonhoeffer, Dietrich. *Life Together.* Minneapolis: Fortress, 2015.

Casner-Lotto, Jill, and Linda Barrington. *Are They Really Ready to Work? Employers' Perspectives on the Basic Knowledge and Applied Skills of New Entrants to the 21st Century U.S. Workforce. Partnership for 21st Century Skills.* Washington, DC: Partnership for 21st Century Skills, 2006. https://files.eric.ed.gov/fulltext/ED519465.pdf.

Dafoe, Allan, et al. "Cooperative AI: Machines Must Learn to Find Common Ground." *Nature* 593 (2021) 33–36.

Darby, Flower, and James M. Lang. *Small Teaching Online: Applying Learning Science in Online Classes.* San Francisco: Jossey-Bass, 2019.

Domingos, Pedro. *The Master Algorithm: How the Quest for the Ultimate Learning Machine Will Remake Our World.* New York: Basic, 2015.

Du Sautoy, Marcus. *The Creativity Code: Art and Innovation in the Age of AI.* Cambridge, MA: Belknap, 2019.

Edwards, Chad, et al. "I, Teacher: Using Artificial Intelligence (AI) and Social Robots in Communication and Instruction." *Communication Education* 67 (2018) 473–80.

Facer, Keri, and Neil Selwyn. "Digital Technology and the Futures of Education: Towards 'Non-Stupid' Optimism." UNESCO Futures of Education Report, 2021. https://unesdoc.unesco.org/ark:/48223/pf0000377071.

Flaherty, Colleen. "No More Proctorio." *Inside Higher Ed*, February 1, 2021. https://www.insidehighered.com/news/2021/02/01/u-illinois-says-goodbye-proctorio.

52. Facer and Selwyn, "Digital Technology and the Futures of Education," 14; see 6–9.
53. Zimmerman, *Teaching AI*, xxiv.

Fujimura, Makoto. *Art and Faith: A Theology of Making*. New Haven, CT: Yale University Press, 2020.

Hardesty, Larry. "Explained: Neural Networks." *MIT News*, April 14, 2017. https://news.mit.edu/2017/explained-neural-networks-deep-learning-0414.

——. "Study Finds Gender and Skin-Type Bias in Commercial Artificial-Intelligence Systems." *MIT News*, February 11, 2018. https://news.mit.edu/2018/study-finds-gender-skin-type-bias-artificial-intelligence-systems-0212.

Hwang, Ming-Yueh, et al. "Practicing Abductive Reasoning: The Correlations between Cognitive Factors and Learning Effects." *Computers and Education* 138 (2019) 33–45.

Kay, Ken, and Valerie Greenhill. "Twenty-First Century Students Need 21st Century Skills." In *Bringing Schools into the 21st Century*, edited by Guofang Wan and Dianne M. Gut, 41–65. Explorations of Educational Purpose. Dordrecht: Springer, 2011.

Landon, Katherine N. "Student Perceptions of Learning in the 21st Century: An Evaluation of the 4Cs." PhD diss., Notre Dame of Maryland University, 2019.

Lee, Kai-Fu. *AI Superpowers: China, Silicon Valley, and the New World Order*. New York: Houghton Mifflin Harcourt, 2018.

Liden, Robert C., et al. "Social Loafing: A Field Investigation." *Journal of Management* 30 (2004) 285–30.

Littlefield, William, II. "The Human Skills AI Can't Replace." *Quillette*, September 25, 2019. https://quillette.com/2019/09/25/the-human-skills-ai-cant-replace/.

National Association of Colleges and Employers. "Job Outlook: Fall Recruiting for the Class Of 2018." June 14, 2017. https://www.naceweb.org/job-market/trends-and-predictions/job-outlook-fall-recruiting-for-the-class-of-2018/.

Newport, Cal. *A World Without Email: Reimagining Work in an Age of Communication Overload*. New York: Portfolio, 2021.

O'Reilly, Ciarán J. "Creative Engineers: Is Abductive Reasoning Encouraged Enough in Degree Project Work?" *Procedia CIRP* 50 (2016) 547–52.

Palmer, Parker J. *The Courage to Teach: Exploring the Inner Landscape of a Teacher's Life*. San Francisco: Jossey-Bass, 1998.

Partnership for 21st Century Learning. "Framework for 21st Century Learning Definitions." Battelle for Kids, 2019. http://static.battelleforkids.org/documents/p21/P21_Framework_DefinitionsBFK.pdf.

Pasquale, Frank. *New Laws of Robotics: Defending Human Expertise in the Age of AI*. Cambridge, MA: The Belknap Press of Harvard University Press, 2020.

Pelletier, Kathe, et al. "2021 EDUCAUSE Horizon Report: Teaching and Learning Edition." Boulder, CO: EDUCAUSE, 2021. https://library.educause.edu/-/media/files/library/2021/4/2021hrteachinglearning.pdf.

Ross, David. "It's Time to Reassess Our Understanding of the 4Cs." *Getting Smart*, July 20, 2020. https://www.gettingsmart.com/2020/07/its-time-to-reassess-our-understanding-of-the-4cs/.

Selwyn, Neil. *Should Robots Replace Teachers? AI and the Future of Education*. Medford, MA: Polity, 2019.

Sooknanan, Joanna, and Terence Seemungal. "Not so Elementary: The Reasoning behind a Medical Diagnosis." *MedEdPublish* 8 (2019) 85.

Syverson, Ben. "The Rules of Brainstorming Change When Artificial Intelligence Gets Involved. Here's How." IDEO, 2020. https://www.ideo.com/blog/the-rules-of-brainstorming-change-when-ai-gets-involved-heres-how.

Technavio. "Artificial Intelligence Market in the Education Sector in US by End-User and Education Model: Forecast and Analysis 2021–2025." 2021. https://www.technavio.com/report/artificial-intelligence-market-in-the-education-sector-in-us-industry-analysis.

Tung, Liam. "Microsoft Teams Is Getting This New Feature Which Makes a Written Record of Your Meeting." *ZDNet*, March 24, 2021. https://www.zdnet.com/article/microsoft-launches-live-transcriptions-for-teams-using-cutting-edge-ai/.

Wagner, Tony. *Creating Innovators: The Making of Young People Who Will Change the World*. New York: Scribner, 2012.

Wang, Dakuo, et al. "From Human-Human Collaboration to Human-AI Collaboration: Designing AI Systems That Can Work Together with People." In *Extended Abstracts of the 2020 CHI Conference on Human Factors in Computing Systems*, 1–6. New York: Association for Computing Machinery, 2020.

Washington Office of Superintendent of Public Instruction. "Washington Career and Technical Education 21st Century Leadership Skills." 2015. https://www.k12.wa.us/sites/default/files/public/careerteched/pubdocs/washingtoncteleadershipskills.pdf.

Wirzba, Norman. *Way of Love: Recovering the Heart of Christianity*. New York: HarperOne, 2016.

Zimmerman, Michelle. *Teaching AI: Exploring New Frontiers for Learning*. Portland, OR: International Society for Technology in Education, 2018.

8

Automation and Apocalypse
Imagining the Future of Work

Michael J. Paulus Jr.

INTRODUCTION

Klaus Schwab, founder of the World Economic Forum, claims we are living through "a revolution that is fundamentally changing the way we live, work, and relate to one another." Schwab labels this the "fourth industrial revolution," which is driven by transformative digital technologies.[1] The philosopher Luciano Floridi also argues we are living through a fourth modern revolution, an "information revolution," in which our dependence on automated information processing is "affecting our sense of self, how we relate to each other, and how we shape and interact with our world."[2] Artificial intelligence is at the center of these revolutions, and as these self-learning technologies have become more powerful and pervasive over the last ten years they have prompted a number of questions about the future of work. How much work currently performed by humans can be automated? How much of the workforce will be disrupted? How do we educate for future forms of work? What would happen in a world without enough work? As

1. Schwab, *Fourth Industrial Revolution*, 1.
2. Floridi, *Fourth Revolution* vi, 6.

important as these technological, socioeconomic, educational, and political questions are, there is a philosophical question that precedes and transcends these: What it the meaning of human work?

While automation is not new, AI is, as Pedro Domingos says, "something new under the sun."[3] John Markoff, who makes an important distinction between artificial and augmented intelligence—i.e., between independent human-like AI and AI (and other) technologies with which we partner—concludes that AI "will destroy a vast number of jobs" and at the same time enhance humanity.[4] As we consider the impact of new technologies on the future of work, it is important to remember that technologies have always been transforming the nature of human work. From simple stone tools to computer algorithms that improve automatically, technology has always been part of human work—enabling us to survive as well as thrive. And as we think about how technology and work together transform us, it is helpful to recall wisdom from the past, including theological wisdom, which can help us understand the nature and significance of work. From the garden of Eden to the garden-city New Jerusalem, the biblical narrative presents human work as an integral part of creation and our role within it.

The present age of automation requires us to imagine how AI, as something new, will shape the future of work. Fictional as well as non-fictional narratives about AI tend toward dystopian or utopian extremes, imagining that AI will destroy or save us.[5] Muriel Clauson points out that speculations about the future of work also include such extremes, ranging from "a potentially dystopian world of meager labor opportunities and robot overlords to a utopian world with work that is meaningful and a contributor to happiness."[6] Some utopian narratives go even further, imagining a world in which jobs will be irrelevant due to "radical abundance."[7] In dystopic futures, the relationship between technology and work is often oppressive. In utopic futures, this relationship is typically liberative. To these two dominant modes of thinking about the future, a third can be added: the apocalyptic. While the term apocalyptic is often reduced to something akin to dystopic, focusing on visions of cataclysmic chaos, in its historical and biblical origins the apocalyptic imagination is a theological interpretation

3. Domingos, *Master Algorithm*, xiv.

4. Markoff, *Machines of Loving Grace*, xii, xv, 327.

5. The Royal Society, "Portrayals and Perceptions of AI and Why They Matter," 4.

6. Muriel Clauson, "Future of Work," in Hoffman et al., *Cambridge Handbook of the Changing Nature of Work*, 555.

7. Kurzweil quoted in Ford, *Architects of Intelligence*, 246.

of reality that opens up deeper dimensions of knowledge, space, time, and agency to reveal a narrative about a new and better world.[8] In an apocalyptic vision of the future, it is possible to envision a relationship between automation and work that is more hopeful and transformative than many dystopian and utopian visions.

This chapter provides an orientation to the history of technology, work, and the theology of work and then explores three visions of the future of work—a literary dystopia, a philosophical utopia, and a theological apocalypse—as resources for understanding the significance of work and imagining its future. In the first vision, found in Kurt Vonnegut's speculative novel *Player Piano*, automation leads to the end of meaningful work and nearly renders humans obsolete. This dystopic vision reveals the value of human work but remains skeptical about our ability to preserve it against the advances of automation. The second vision comes from John Danaher's *Automation and Utopia*, which is a philosophical argument for the end of work through automation and for the creation of a utopia in which humans find meaning in a post-work world. This utopian vision reveals what is lost in a world without work and imagines what might be substituted for it. The third vision, from the end of the apocalyptic book of Revelation, considers how work and automation may participate in the transformation of the world. The chapter closes with a consideration of how this apocalyptic vision can inform our present and emerging world of human and automated work.

A BRIEF HISTORY OF TECHNOLOGY AND WORK

In the most basic sense, work is an activity that is a means to an end. The word is typically used to describe specific activities performed for some benefit—survival, economic gain, individual fulfillment, spiritual growth, or familial or social wellbeing. In Genesis, the first human is placed in the garden of Eden "to work [or till] and keep it," and the same Hebrew and Greek words are used to describe Cain's occupation as "a worker [or tiller] of the ground."[9] In addition to the instrumental or functional nature of work,

8. Collins, "What is Apocalyptic Literature," in Collins, *Oxford Handbook of Apocalyptic Literature*, 2–3.

9. Gen 2:15 and 4:2, translations mine. In Hebrew, the word for work, *avodah*, is also used to describe worship and service to God: "Let my people go, so that they may worship me" (Exod 8:1); "serve the Lord your God with all your heart" (Deut 10:12). See Miller, foreword to Dorothy L. Sayers, *Why Work*, 13–14. The Greek word for work, *ergon* and its derivatives, are used to describe God's work of creation as well as spiritual activities: "God finished the work that he had done" (Gen 2:2); "I know your works—your love, faith, service, and patient endurance" (Rev 2:19, but compare more negative works in 3:1, 15).

Darrell Cosden highlights two additional dimensions. First, work has an existential or relational dimension: "a person finds, or contributes to who they are and will be (as well as what the world is and will be) in the process of working" with others. Work is a means of identity formation through a particular way of interacting with other people and the world. Second, Cosden emphasizes that work is not just a useful and relational activity: it is "a thing in itself with its own intrinsic value . . . built into the fabric of creation." Work in this sense exists or has its own ontology independent of us. Work provided the "starting point for a human rather than an animal existence" and became "a way of being which constitutes our humanness."[10] All three of these dimensions together—functional, relational, and ontological—give work a fundamental, intrinsic, independent, and enduring significance.

Over two million years ago, early hominins developed stone tools and techniques to access richer sources of calories and ascend the food chain. This lithic technology, which led to other physical, social, and cultural advances, "codirected human evolution" and eventually led "to the establishment of humans as the most successful tool users on the planet."[11] As Ron Cole-Turner points out, "Before we became humans, we made tools. And almost immediately, our tools began to make us more and more human."[12] Human technological development merged with natural evolution in such a way that, as John Durham Peters explains, the "question of how to define nature, humans, and [technology] are ultimately the same question. We know and use nature only though the artifacts we make—both out of nature and out of our own bodies—and these artifacts can enter into nature's own history."[13]

The emergence of *Homo sapiens*, beginning after two hundred thousand years ago and complete by sixty thousand years ago, was accompanied with an explosion of technologies for personal ornamentation, art, elaborate burials, complex multicomponent weaponry, long-distance trade, time-keeping, and scheduling.[14] Following the agricultural revolution some twelve thousand years ago, humans developed complex artificial environments—cities—as well as political, economic, and religious institutions to organize and sustain civic activities such as governance, trade, and cultural narratives.[15] Humans have been living in cities for nearly ten thousand years,

---

10. Cosden, *Theology of Work*, 12, 16–18.

11. Plummer and Finestone, *Rethinking Human Evolution*, 267–8; Biro et al., "Tool Use as Adaptation," 5.

12. Cole-Turner, *End of Adam and Eve*, 54.

13. Peters, *Marvelous Clouds*, 51.

14. Coolidge and Wynn, *Rise of Homo Sapiens*, 5–6.

15. Harari, *Sapiens*, 77–97.

writing and computing for some five thousand years, building machines for over two thousand years, and computing with machines for about three hundred years. Within the last few hundred years, modern advances in science and technology have driven Schwab's four industrial revolutions: steam power, electricity, digital computing, and a "second machine age" of more sophisticated, integrated, and transformative digital technologies.[16] Our increasingly complex stack of technology and the work it enables and creates seems to be limited only by our imagination.

Every major technological innovation changes what and how work is performed and creates the conditions for new types of work. The impact of transformative digital technologies such as big data, cloud computing, AI, and the Internet of Things—often called "exponential technologies" because of their association with rapid, profound, and systemic change—are expected to accelerate the digital transformation of our lives and the automation of work.[17] Instead of the centuries it took to shift from predominately agricultural to industrial societies, or the decades it has taken to shift from an industrial to an information society, the present digital transformation driving the accelerated automation of work is happening on a scale of years. With the social and economic disruptions caused by the COVID-19 pandemic, those years may have become months.

Steven McMullen claims that, "as a whole we are net beneficiaries of technology." Many will suffer employment losses, which along with inequitable economic and social impacts are significant matters of social justice. Looking toward the future, McMullen points out that both optimists and pessimists see something similar: less work. "But their description of the future looks radically different," he adds: "Optimists tend to imagine a future in which the gains from technological advances are widely shared, so that even those with little to offer in the labor market will still live a rich life of leisure. Pessimists, on the other hand, imagine a world in which a small segment of the workforce reaps most of the gains from technological advancement and others are left in poverty." Both views are problematic, though, for each fails to acknowledge that "humans find their highest end in creative service to those around them. Work . . . is best envisioned as a vocation that is worth a significant investment."[18] How, then, do we understand this creative call and compulsion?

16. Schwab, *Fourth Industrial Revolution*, 7.

17. Muriel Clauson, "Future of Work," in Hoffman et al., *Cambridge Handbook of the Changing Nature of Work*, 556; Siebel, *Digital Transformation*, 9.

18. McMullen, "Impossibility and Challenge of a World without Work," 5, 7.

A BRIEF HISTORY OF THEOLOGY AND WORK

According to Cosden, work is "built by God into the very structures of human nature and as a result, the natural order."[19] God's work of creation includes human work, and throughout the biblical narrative work is a significant focus of divine and human agency. From the beginning, humans have been asking questions about how God is at work and about the human vocation within creation. As work became more technologically sophisticated, so, too, did theological reflections about it. By the twelfth century, Hugh of St. Victor was able to incorporate technology into his theology of work in a way that remains helpful today.

Hugh distinguishes three major forms of creative work. First is the work of God in forming the world out of nothing, which establishes the subsequent work of nature. Next is the work of humans, which adds to nature: It is "the work of the artificer . . . to put together things disjoined or to disjoin those put together." But this work is corruptible and can deform relationships with God, nature, other humans, human creations, and our own selves. Third is the work of Christ, which includes his life, the scriptures and sacraments, and the communities that represent Christ. The work of Christ, mediated through embodied, textual, and ecclesial forms, takes up and transforms all work into new creation.[20] For Hugh, technology—divided into "fabric making, armament, commerce, agriculture, hunting, medicine, and theatrics"—has a central role in reforming our relationship with God and nature.[21] It is "part of the human quest for wisdom"; it extends our abilities and understanding; and, when used wisely, it can reform what has been deformed. Technology may be understood as part of Christ's work of new creation, reconciling divine, natural, and human artificial creativity.[22]

Paralleling the technological transformation of work during the first and second industrial revolutions, in the late nineteenth and early twentieth centuries more focused efforts emerged to integrate theology and work. David Miller sees in these efforts the "beginnings of the enlargement of the sense of Christian vocation" connected with visions of the future. Miller identifies two eschatological orientations. *Postmillennialism*, which tends to emphasize work done to bring about the kingdom of God, focuses on continual improvement and saving society. *Premillennialism*, alternatively, emphasizes the disruptive nature of God's eschatological establishment of

19. Cosden, *Theology of Work*, 18.

20. Hugh of St. Victor, *Didascalicon* 55; Illich, *In the Vineyard of the Text*, 124; Coolman, *Theology of Hugh of St. Victor*, 170.

21. Hugh of St. Victor, *Didascalicon* 74.

22. Allen, *Spiritual Theology*, 119.

the kingdom of God and tends to focus on saving individuals.[23] A third a-millennial eschatological orientation could be added, which includes Christians such a Dorothy L. Sayers and Charles Williams. Sayers speaks about work as "a *natural* exercise and function" of humanity, "the thing one lives to do" in service to God, and "the medium of divine creation."[24] While Sayers, an author and (former) copywriter, grounds her view of work in the doctrine of creation, Williams, an author and a publisher, envisions work as participation in new creation.[25]

Near the end of the twentieth century, as the third industrial revolution was laying the foundations for the fourth, Miroslav Volf called for a shift from developing an understanding of work within the framework of the doctrine of creation to one developed within the framework of new creation, which expects continuity but also radical change. This approach looks beyond postmillennial optimism about "the permanence of human moral progress" or premillennial subordination of work to one's "vertical relation to God" and seeks an "eschatological realism" that can "lead the present world of work 'towards the promised and the hoped-for transformation.'" The shift Volf recommends opens up eschatology as a resource for thinking about the future of work. According to Volf, "The eschatological transformation of the world gives human work special significance since it bestows independent value on the results of work as 'building materials' of the glorified world."[26]

THE FUTURE OF WORK

A recent report from the Royal Society on AI narratives points out that, "Narratives are essential to the development of science and people's engagement with new knowledge and new applications."[27] Stories form us and, consequently, our world. Whether we recognize it or not, individually and collectively we inherit and tell stories that expand or inhibit our imagination and agency. The future of work will be shaped by narratives that have shaped us and by the narratives we create. It is, therefore, important to explore and critique these narratives, especially those that tend toward dystopian and utopian futures. Jilles Smids, Sven Nyholm, and Hannah Berkers identify

23. Miller, *God at Work*, 24, 36.

24. Sayers, *Why Work?*, 18, 21.

25. See Paulus, "Charles Williams's Theology of Publishing," 57–70; "From the City to the Cloud," 4–21.

26. Volf, *Work in the Spirit*, ix, 83–84, 90 (quoting Jürgen Moltmann), 96.

27. The Royal Society, "Portrayals and Perceptions of AI and Why They Matter," 4.

five common characteristics of meaningful work: (1) pursuing a purpose, (2) social relationships, (3) exercising skills and self-development, (4) self-esteem and recognition, and (5) autonomy.[28] These characteristics provide a helpful framework for interpreting exemplary dystopic and utopic visions, to see what insights and questions they reveal about the meaning of work.

Automation and Dystopia

Kurt Vonnegut's first novel, *Player Piano*, is an early AI narrative that could have been subtitled "automation and dystopia." Published in 1952, three years before the term artificial intelligence was coined for the Dartmouth Conference on Artificial Intelligence, *Player Piano* imagines a world in which machines outperform and displace human work. The world of the novel is supposed to be a utopia, a world of peace and prosperity: "Machines were doing America's work far better than Americans had ever done it. There were better goods for more people at less cost, and who could deny that that was magnificent and gratifying?"[29] Society is divided into two groups. There is an elite, wealthy group made of up those whose work has not been automated yet; male managers, engineers, and scientists and their wives are at the top this order. Other men are part of a work creation program called the Reconstruction and Reclamation Corps (the "Reeks and Wrecks") or in the military, and most other women seem to stay at home, supervising automated domestic work and children watching television.

Vonnegut's "ambiguous technological dystopia" was inspired by his work as a publicist for General Electric's Research Laboratory, where he became familiar with the latest technological advances and—for a brief unhappy period—had a role in promoting them with slogans such as "Progress Is Our Most Important Product."[30] What Vonnegut imagines, with the generation-old tubes and tapes analogue machinery of his time, is how existing technologies could be combined in a new way. If the industrial revolutions of steam and electricity "devalued muscle work," the next revolutions of automated and autonomous information processing would devalue "routine mental work" and, then, "human thinking"; "thinking machines" would end up doing "the real brainwork."[31] The modern history of technology that Von-

---

28. Smids et al., "Robots in the Workplace," 507.

29. Vonnegut, *Player Piano*, 56.

30. Klinkowitz, *Kurt Vonnegut's America*, 17.

31. Vonnegut, *Player Piano*, 21–22. Vonnegut refers to Norbert Wiener, who published *Cybernetics* in 1948 and *The Human Use of Human Beings: Cybernetics and Society* in 1950. *The Human Use of Human Beings* was a more accessible version of

negut narrates begins with humans creating and controlling technology, but this results in technology controlling technology and then humans. *Player Piano* asks if this is the end of the historical narrative.

From the beginning of *Player Piano*, it is clear that the fourth industrial revolution is not off to a promising start. The central figure of the book, Doctor Paul Proteus, who has the most prestigious job in his community managing the operations of machines, is not as enthusiastic about the system as he is expected to be. "Objectively," he tells himself while touring the machine city under his care, "things really were better than ever . . . know-how and world law were getting their long-awaited chance to turn earth into an altogether pleasant and convenient place in which to sweat out Judgment Day." Subjectively, he acknowledges that "his job, the system, and organizational politics had left him variously annoyed, bored, or queasy."[32] Proteus, like everyone else, is just part of a machine—an automatic part, not an autonomous participant in the system. The material benefits technology has given both the elites and the masses are not a substitute for what technology has taken away. This is what the player piano signifies: its automatic keys entertain but eerily recall the ghost that taught the machine to play—the person, machine logic concludes, who is no longer needed to create but only to consume.

As existential discontentment mounts among a diverse range of characters, a human counterrevolution rises up against the computer revolution. The counterrevolutionaries challenge the "right of technology to increase in power and scope"—which has become an unquestionable "divine right"—and issue a call "to give the world back to the people." Humans should control technology, the leaders of the counterrevolution declare. The "effects of changes in technology and organization on life patterns [should] be taken into careful consideration," they demand, and those "changes [should] be withheld or introduced on the basis of this consideration." Most importantly, it must be recognized that humans, "by their nature, seemingly cannot be happy unless engaged in enterprises that make them feel useful. They must, therefore, be returned to participation in such enterprises."[33] Humans, in short, need work—meaningful work (as defined by Smids et al.) that has a purpose, forms relationships, leads to self-development, contributes to self-esteem, and allows for autonomy.

Wiener's first book, and it popularized the idea of a second industrial revolution driven by computers.

32. Vonnegut, *Player Piano*, 14–15.

33. Vonnegut, *Player Piano*, 284–86.

One of the counterrevolution's leaders, the Reverend James J. Lasher, confesses that he had previously encouraged people to think of their lives independent of their work. But when their work was taken away from them, they found "that what's left is just about zero. A good bit short of enough, anyway." Vonnegut seems to be saying that faith without work is insufficient—people need a "sense of participation, the sense of being important . . . of being needed on earth."[34] This remains true in a highly technological society. After people have asserted their agency against the machines and indiscriminately destroyed those around them, a bright young teenager is presented on the penultimate page scavenging for parts for "a gadget that'd play drums like nothing you ever heard before."[35] When Proteus—who once found meaning and glory as an engineer—is on trial for being a saboteur, he says, "What distinguishes man from the rest of the animals is his ability to do artificial things . . . To his greater glory, I say. And a step backward, after making a wrong turn, is a step in the right direction."[36] Vonnegut is not rejecting a technological society; he is asking how we design one that includes meaningful work.[37]

Automation and Utopia

In *Automation and Utopia: Human Flourishing in a World without Work*, John Danaher answers a different question—because he starts with the claim that "human obsolescence is imminent." What we do, he argues, is increasingly less relevant "to our well-being and the fate of our planet." The Anthropocene is yielding to the Robocene, and soon "there will be little left for us to do except sit back and enjoy the ride."[38] If we do not want to end up sated and stupefied in a *WALL-E* post-work world, we need to imagine how humans will find the purpose, social relationships, self-development, self-esteem, and autonomy which will no longer be found in meaningful work.

Before presenting his solution, Danaher makes a case for the possibility of automating all forms of work. Automation will continue to advance further into agricultural, industrial, financial, legal, medical, governmental, scientific, and every other form of physical and affective labor. Although Danaher's focus is on work "performed in exchange for an economic reward," his view of automation is comprehensive and includes work related

34. Vonnegut, *Player Piano*, 94.
35. Vonnegut, *Player Piano*, 319.
36. Vonnegut, *Player Piano*, 295.
37. See Segal, *Future Imperfect*, 126–46.
38. Danaher, *Automation and Utopia*, 1–2.

to discovery, creativity, and care. Danaher argues that we should accept the end of economically incentivized work as a good thing and hate our jobs (even if we love them). The current reality of work for many is bad—precarious, inequitable, oppressive, and unsatisfying—and it is getting worse, he argues. Since the "structural badness" of work is very difficult to reform, Danaher concludes that we should embrace the economic liberation autonomous and intelligent technologies may provide.[39]

After presenting his arguments for automation and the end of work, Danaher rehabilitates the concept of utopianism to confront what he sees as the next significant human project: creating a world in which humans can thrive when they no longer need to work. Rather than a rigid plan (a "blueprint"), he defines utopia as a range of possibilities that are practical but also radical improvements (a "horizon"). He also develops a "utopian scorecard," which evaluates utopias against the problems of both automation—which can inhibit attention, agency, and autonomy—and of utopianism, such as violence and inertia. Using this evaluative framework, Danaher presents two possible worlds: a cyborg utopia and a virtual utopia.

In a cyborg utopia, we merge with technology to upgrade ourselves and maintain our cognitive evolutionary niche. Humans have been living into a cyborg utopia for some time—conceptually, extending our minds through artifacts, and technically, with medical implants. It is the conservative option, which gives it both strength and weakness. The cyborg utopia conserves what we value (our superior intellectual agency) as well as what we do not (e.g., social inequities). This utopia could therefore become a dystopia, and Danaher concludes it is not the utopia we are looking for.

The best possible world Danaher imagines is a virtual utopia, in which we retreat from our cognitive dominance of the world and cultivate crafts through games. "Virtual" is not reducible to life inside a computer-generated environment, and humans have been living in complex virtual or artificial environments such as societies and cities for many millennia. To these we have added digital simulations, which are still real in the impacts they have on us and others. What is radical in Danaher's proposal is what we will do in these physical and digital virtual environments. His virtual utopia is a utopia of games: we will play games that we understand, so there is no coercion; we will play for "trivial or relatively inconsequential stakes," because all the important work will be done by artificial agents; and we will cultivate abilities and virtues through the games we select and create.[40]

39. Danaher, *Automation and Utopia*, 28, 54.

40. Danaher, *Automation and Utopia*, 229.

Danaher's virtual utopia involves being severed from the world, surrendering human control as well as direct knowledge of and engagement with it. Danaher acknowledges the loss of instrumental impact in the world, and emphasizes the value of processes over end states—the satisfaction of "purely procedural goods" and "good work [done] for its own sake." The gains, he argues, outweigh the losses: human attention, agency, autonomy, and other important values will be preserved as people think, plan, decide, create, interact, and realize "ever higher degrees of achievement." Games, Danaher concludes, "could be enough to sustain meaning and flourishing" and "would represent a significant societal improvement."[41] But is this a substitute for all the goods associated with meaningful work as identified by Smids, Nyholm, and Berkers—i.e., pursuing a purpose, social relationships, exercising skills and self-development, self-esteem and recognition, and autonomy? Perhaps, to an extent. But if work is reduced to games in virtual environments, without a purposeful impact on the broader world, what might happen to our self-understanding and sense of fulfillment?

For Danaher and his virtual utopia, there is no ultimate end goal or *telos*—only "infinite possibilities." We are, he claims, like the denizens in Jorge Luis Borges's short story "The Library of Babel," searching for meaningful books in a universe full of mostly meaningless and misleading books. Their quest is futile, for their world is an antilibrary. "We shouldn't keep searching through the infinite darkness for something we ourselves can never obtain," Danaher concludes; "we shouldn't sacrifice everything else that is good in life for an unending, and unrealizable, goal."[42] If, however, our world is more like a library, presenting us with information about its *telos*—and if our encounter with that information can transform us toward its realization—then the means *and* ends of direct engagement with the world and our instrumental work within it matter significantly. For Christians, who believe creation mediates knowledge of God and that we have a vocation to be participants with God in new creation, living life as a mere game severed from the created world would be a dystopia—or, more precisely, a form of hell.

As these exemplary visions show, the distinctions between dystopias and utopias are hard to maintain. Ursula K. Le Guin points out that "every utopia since [Thomas More's 1516] Utopia has also been, clearly or obscurely, actually or possibly, in the author's or in the readers' judgment, both a good place and a bad one. Every eutopia contains a dystopia, every dystopia

41. Danaher, *Automation and Utopia*, 236, 238–39, 245, 251.
42. Danaher, *Automation and Utopia*, 271, 273.

contains a eutopia."[43] Bad (*dus-*), good (*eu-*), and no (*ou-*) places (*-topoi*) can open up our imagination to possible futures of work, but Vonnegut and Danaher—along with many other literary and philosophical xtopian think-ers—run into the limits of the purely human imagination. Tom McLeish argues that theology opens up our imagination to something greater than natural or human creativity: it considers divine creativity and ultimate ends. "Because theology observes and construes stories," McLeish says, "it is able to discuss purposes and values—it can speak of, and ground, 'teleology.'" Theological narratives, McLeish concludes, can help us understand shared end goals as well as "shared experiences of creativity and constraints."[44] If we are asking questions of teleology, we are asking questions about final or ul-timate things—i.e., eschatology, which Volf argues is an important resource for thinking about the future of work.

THE ESCHATOLOGY OF WORK

Michael Burdett argues that "Christian eschatology can provide a more robust account of the future than those offered by technological futurism." Futurism, which shapes most xtopian visions, considers the future "as an outworking of present conditions and forces so that the future is a product of what has preceded it. It is driven from behind." But there is an additional way of looking at the future—*adventus*—which "describes that which is coming." Instead of making claims about the future as a mere product of the past and present, it "speaks of arrival. It is driven by what is ahead." This alternate way of viewing the future, Burdett argues, can provide corrective counternarratives to those shaped by futurism: the "future does not just depend upon the present actuality but upon a robust account of possibility which does not define possibility according to the actual."[45]

For many Christians, eschatology is grounded in the last two affir-mations of the Apostles' Creed: "the resurrection of the body, and the life everlasting." For the earliest Christians, who drew from Jewish apocalyptic images, concepts, and narratives about a new and better world, the resurrec-tion of Jesus was an apocalyptic event that inaugurated a hoped-for transfor-mation of the world. According to N. T. Wright, the Christian apocalyptic imagination "opens up a vision of new creation which precisely overlaps with, and radically transforms, the present creation."[46] Apocalyptic visions

43. Le Guin, *No Time to Spare*, 85.
44. McLeish, *Faith and Wisdom in Science*, 214, 248.
45. Burdett, *Eschatology and the Technological Future* 2–3, 237.
46. Wright, *History and Eschatology*, 156.

often include cataclysmic events, associated with eradicating evil, but in popular usage an apocalypse is often reduced to something just cataclysmic. Ray Bradbury's short story "There Will Come Soft Rains" is an apocalypse of this variety: After a nuclear event, a smart home keeps operating to serve its annihilated masters until it, too, is destroyed by fire.

But the Christian apocalyptic vision, inspired by *adventus*, is an eschatological view that sees heaven meeting earth, the future in the present, and humans as divinely called transformative agents. This apocalyptic perspective uncovers and reveals the integrated and interlocking nature of seemingly disparate dimensions of reality. The function of apocalyptic literature, such as the book of Revelation, is to present a narrative that opens up our imagination to a new view of the world—a view that can help us apprehend the meaning of human work and a vision of its future.

Revelation, or the Apocalypse of John, is a book for and about cities. It is an epistle to seven historical cities (chapters 1–3), describing what was happening in their time and what is yet to come. John's unveiling of God's unseen transformative work culminates in the "great vision" of God's promised future—the *telos* of the biblical narrative and the Christian apocalyptic imagination—New Jerusalem.[47] This city, which comes down from the new heaven, is the central place of the new earth. The previously ambiguous product of human technological creativity is transformed into a holy but "historical and this-worldly" city, in which God dwells (or tabernacles, as in John 1:14) with humans and where there is no more sin, suffering, or death.[48]

The new city John sees, from and filled with the glory of God, possesses a material splendor trivializing any glory of which a human city could boast. New Jerusalem is an enormous cube, like the holy of holies in the temple, and its walls, gates, and foundations are perfectly planned and proportioned. Measuring some 1,500 miles on each side—twelve hundred times larger than the ancient city of Babylon, as it was measured by Herodotus—the city is made of and adorned with precious earthly materials.[49] The city has no temple nor natural or artificial light, for God's presence fills the whole city and Christ enlightens it. The city has been prepared for God's people, whose ancestors' names are inscribed upon its gates and foundations. The rulers of the earth and people from all nations, drawn to the city by the light of Christ, bring into it "the glory and the honor of the nations," including their material gifts and goods.[50] In this "new, improved, urban

47. Wright, *Surprised by Scripture*, 203.

48. Blount, *Revelation*, 327, 378, 380.

49. 144,000 stadia versus Babylon's 120. See Thomas, *Apocalypse*, 645.

50. Rev 21:26. On "glory and honor," see Aune, *Revelation 17–22*, 1173.

Eden," nature fills the city with beauty, life, and healing.[51] There is "perfect harmony between civilization and nature."[52] Divine, natural, and human work have not only been reconciled but given a new coinherent dynamism.

Brian Blount emphasizes the concrete realism of John's apocalyptic expectations: "Christ's coming," he observes, is connected "with a tangible, measurable, objective city." The metaphor of the city "signals a salvific identity that is neither individualized nor spiritualized but concretized in the communal relationship that exists in an urban environment."[53] The eschatological life envisioned in this urban environment includes diverse people and vocations, interdependent and collaborative relationships, and cultural activities and artifacts that constitute the dynamics of civic life. All of this, Richard Bauckham concludes, "fulfills humanity's desire to build out of nature a human place of human culture and community."[54]

Continuities between the new and initial creation, as well as future possibility and present actuality, have important implications for the present world. "John's vision," Blount observes, "redeems the earth as part of God's *good* creation and as the locus of God's grand re-creation." When God declares, "See, I am making all things new," "God is taking what is old and transforming it. . . . The old will remain a constituent part of the new." A witness of Christ, therefore, "works with God to transform the world" in the present.[55] Bruce Metzger points out that although God's statement about making all things new refers "primarily to the final renewing at the end, the present tense also suggests that God is continually making things new here and now."[56] Eugene Peterson points out the lack of escapism in the vision of New Jerusalem: "This is not a long (eternal) weekend away from the responsibilities of employment and citizenship, but the intensification and healing of them." We are already in Christ, Peterson adds, "part of and participant in the new creation, the holy city in which God is ruling and having his way." Images of New Jerusalem, Peterson concludes, "are a means for discovering the real in the tangle of illusion" and fraud that fills the cities in which we currently live.[57]

The fact that the ambiguous image of the city is not annihilated but rather amplified suggests that complex human artifacts—including artificial

51. Blount, *Revelation*, 395; see Rev 22:1–2.
52. Jürgen Moltmann, quoted in Volf, *Theology of Work*, 173.
53. Blount, *Revelation*, 20, 378.
54. Bauckham, *Theology of the Book of Revelation*, 135.
55. Rev 21:5; Blount, *Revelation*, 376–77.
56. Metzger, *Breaking the Code*, 129.
57. Peterson, *Reversed Thunder*, 174, 183; cf. 2 Cor 5:17.

autonomous agents—can be transformed into a constitutive part of God's new creation. Human technological culture created the city, "a new onto-logical reality" that, when transformed by God, continues in the new cre-ation.[58] Might this mean that technical trades and their technologies—an "essential feature" of both ancient and contemporary cities—have a place in New Jerusalem?[59] Cosden's theology of work, which argues that "work is so fundamental to creation and human existence that it is necessarily a part of both this life and the life to come," supports this possibility. "All *posi-tive* transformative action," he argues, "may be considered to participate in . . . the fulfillment in the present of God's will on earth." Such human work transcends "both its results and its use to workers," and "our work and works . . . become entities which themselves, by flourishing as themselves," can glorify God.[60] *ultimate purpose*

According to Cosden, the *telos* of the Apocalypse is also a new begin-ning. One can imagine new glorified forms of human work and works—hu-man participation in new projects with God—as well as glorified rest. Not only will the restriction on work "as part of the temporal rhythmic work-rest cycle of the sabbath . . . pass away," but the "distinction between 'work,' 'rest,' and 'play' will disappear."[61] The presence and peace of God, previously me-diated through the temple and sabbath, will permeate every activity in New Jerusalem. In this apocalyptic vision of a future of participating in trans-formed work and works, we can imagine the full realization of meaningful work as defined by Smids, Nyholm, and Berkers: The purpose of work is clear, relationships will flourish with a shared *telos*, and humans will realize new forms of internal and external glory and live in perfect freedom.

WORK+ NOW

The climax of the Apocalypse is the fall of Babylon, the penultimate city and an image of every human-made city. When John is shown Babylon, "the great city that rules over the rulers of the earth," he sees the economically exploitive and politically oppressive Roman Empire.[62] The fall of Rome, the

---

58. Cosden, *Theology of Work*, 173.

59. "The presence of various crafts was an essential feature of the ancient city. The crafts typically included metalworking, brick-making, glassmaking, carpentry, perfume-making, tent-making, spinning, weaving, tanning, dyeing, pottery-making, carving, sculpture, and stonemasonry." Aune, *Revelation 17–22*, 1009.

60. Cosden, *Theology of Work*, 175, 184.

61. Cosden, *Theology of Work*, 12, 162, 170.

62. Rev 17:8.

greatest city in the ancient world, was centuries away when the Apocalypse was written. But its fall—like the fall of the Babylonian Empire before it and every other empire since—is assured. The Apocalypse, therefore, creates "a remarkable space" for a broader critique of any imperial system that seduces rulers and followers with material comforts, that seeks its own power and prosperity at the expense of others', that suppresses opposition, that upholds its survival as the ultimate value, and that is doomed to fail for its denials of what truly sustains life.[63] As much as the reality of New Jerusalem is breaking into the present, we still live within the reality of Babylon.

The fall of Babylon is celebrated—for its violent injustices are condemned and come to an end. Babylon's fall is also lamented. The rulers, merchants, and sea traders who benefited from the excesses of empire lament their loss of power and prosperity. But there is also lament, voiced by a divine messenger, over the loss of cultural activities and artifacts that fill daily life: musicians playing instruments; artisans or artificers (*technites*) of every technical trade (*techne*) working with tools; millers grinding grain; and people lighting lamps and celebrating marriages.[64] Babylon both attracts and repels; it includes the glory and refuse of the world. In the vision of the final city, New Jerusalem, evil will be banished and the good work being done and the good works being created in Babylon will be preserved.

Before its fall, the Apocalypse reveals that another king—the ruler of rulers—and his kingdom already exist within Rome's.[65] New Jerusalem is descending and "the kingdom of the world has become the kingdom of our Lord and of his Christ."[66] In the epilogue of the Apocalypse, New Jerusalem says, "Come," and those who hear call out to the thirsty, "Come" and "take the water of life" flowing through the middle of the street of the city.[67] Those whom God has liberated and made "to be a kingdom" are also called to "come out" of Babylon.[68] Blount describes this as "a figurative separation" from the corruptions of Babylon to participate in the present reality of Christ's rule.[69] The form of this vocation, then and now, includes confronting the deformations of human culture through "active, non-violent, engaged resistance" and work that leads toward transformation.[70]

---

63. Gorman, *Reading Revelation Responsibly*, 145–46.

64. Rev 18:22–23.

65. Rev 17:14.

66. Rev 3:2; 11:15; cf. 14:8.

67. Rev 22:17.

68. Rev 1:5; 18:4.

69. Blount, *Revelation*, 327.

70. Blount, *Can I Get a Witness?*, 46. Blount presents this interpretation of witness

According to Cosden, this present work—which participates in its future form—is instrumental, relational, and has its own ontology. Work is instrumental because it provides necessary resources for human flourishing and spiritual development, now and in the world to come. Work is relational because it forms our identities and relationships with others and the world. And work and its associated artifacts have intrinsic value—an ontological existence of their own. Together, these dimensions of human work encompass key qualities of meaningful work: human purpose, relationships, contributions, fulfilment, and freedom. These dimensions of work also point to its enduring significance for us and our world. Even though human work has become increasingly complicated throughout history, and its imprint on natural and human environments is both transformative and deformative, an apocalyptic view of work can open up our imagination to the potential for advanced technologies, such as autonomous agents, to participate with us not only in the ongoing transformation of work and the world but—as agents of new creation—in the transformed new world of work.

In the biblical narrative, God's creative agency links the beginning and the end—forming all things in the first words of Genesis and transforming all things in the final words of Revelation. If, as T. S. Eliot wrote apocalyptically, our end is not in our beginning but rather our beginning is in our end, the image of New Jerusalem can help us understand the *telos* of technology and work.[71] In the ultimate city, divine, human, and artificial agency are fulfilled together. We must, as Burdett cautions, be guarded against futurism—even theological futurism. Although our new works may find "their origin and connection to how God works in new ways," as we discover "pockets of God's promised future," "our planning must be contingent" because the fulfillment of God's promises "constantly evades" our expectations.[72] But, as Karen Lebacqz argues, in New Jerusalem the limits imposed on initial creation in the garden of Eden have been transcended: "although we should always remember our current fallen state and tendency toward hubris, we need not at root fear [technological] enhancements—it is our destiny to be more than we were at creation, to become friends with God and partners in the Holy City."[73] And we can live into this *telos* with automation.

---

in Revelation "through the double lens of John's late-first-century, Asia Minor context and the historical context of the Black Church tradition" (*Can I Get a Witness?*, 46).

71. Eliot, *Four Quartets*, in *The Complete Poems and Plays*, 123, 129.

72. Burdett, *Eschatology and the Technological Future*, 242.

73. Lebacqz, "Dignity and Enhancement in the Holy City," in Cole-Turner, *Transhumanism and Transcendence*, 59.

BIBLIOGRAPHY

Allen, Diogenes. *Spiritual Theology: The Theology of Yesterday for Spiritual Help Today.* Cambridge, MA: Cowley, 1997.

Aune, David E. *Word Biblical Commentary: Revelation 17–22.* Nashville: Thomas Nelson, 1998.

Bauckham, Richard. *The Theology of the Book of Revelation.* Cambridge: Cambridge University Press, 1993.

Biro, Dora, et al. "Tool Use as Adaptation." *Philosophical Transactions of the Royal Society B* 368 (2013) 1–8.

Blount, Brian K. *Can I Get a Witness? Reading Revelation through African American Culture.* Louisville, KY: Westminster John Knox, 2005.

———. *Revelation: A Commentary.* Louisville, KY: Westminster John Knox, 2009.

Burdett, Michael S. *Eschatology and the Technological Future.* New York: Routledge, 2015.

Cole-Turner, Ron. *The End of Adam and Eve: Theology and the Science of Human Origins.* Pittsburg: TheologyPlus, 2016.

———, ed. *Transhumanism and Transcendence: Christian Hope in an Age of Technological Enhancement.* Washington, DC: Georgetown University Press, 2011.

Collins, John J., ed. *The Oxford Handbook of Apocalyptic Literature.* Oxford: Oxford University Press, 2014.

Coolidge, Frederick L., and Thomas Wynn. *The Rise of Homo Sapiens: The Evolution of Modern Thinking.* Oxford: Oxford University Press, 2018.

Coolman, Boyd Taylor. *The Theology of Hugh of St. Victor: An Interpretation.* Cambridge: Cambridge University Press, 2010.

Cosden, Darrell. *A Theology of Work: Work and the New Creation.* Eugene, OR: Wipf & Stock, 2004.

Danaher, John. *Automation and Utopia: Human Flourishing in a World without Work.* Cambridge, MA: Harvard University Press, 2019.

Domingos, Pedro. *The Master Algorithm: How the Quest for the Ultimate Learning Machine Will Remake Our World.* New York: Basic, 2015.

Eliot, T. S. *The Complete Poems and Plays, 1909–1950.* New York: Harcourt Brace Jovanovich, 1952.

Floridi, Luciano. *The Fourth Revolution How the Infosphere Is Reshaping Human Reality.* Oxford: Oxford University Press, 2014.

Ford, Martin. *Architects of Intelligence: The Truth about AI from the People Building It.* Birmingham, UK: Packt, 2018.

Gorman, Michael J. *Reading Revelation Responsibly: Uncivil Worship and Witness Following the Lamb into the New Creation.* Eugene, OR: Cascade, 2011.

Harari, Yuval Noah. *Sapiens: A Brief History of Humankind.* New York: HarperCollins, 2015.

Hoffman, Brian J. et al., eds. *The Cambridge Handbook of the Changing Nature of Work.* Cambridge: Cambridge University Press, 2020.

Hugh of St. Victor. *Didascalicon* Translated by Jerome Taylor. New York: Columbia University Press, 1991.

Illich, Ivan. *In the Vineyard of the Text: A Commentary on Hugh's Didascalion.* Chicago: University of Chicago Press, 1991.

Klinkowitz, Jerome. *Kurt Vonnegut's America*. Columbia, SC: University of South Carolina Press, 2009.

Le Guin, Ursula K. *No Time to Spare: Thinking about What Matters*. New York: Houghton Mifflin Harcourt, 2017.

Markoff, John. *Machines of Loving Grace: The Quest for Common Ground Between Humans and Robots*. New York: Ecco, 2015.

McLeish, Tom. *Faith and Wisdom in Science*. Oxford: Oxford University Press, 2014.

McMullen, Steven. "The Impossibility and Challenge of a World without Work." In *A World Without Work? Technology, Automation, and the Future of Work: A Compilation of Essays Presented at the 2016 Values and Capitalism Faculty Retreat*. American Enterprise Institute, 2018. https://faithandpubliclife.com/wp-content/uploads/2018/01/A-World-without-Work_final.pdf.

Metzger, Bruce M. *Breaking the Code: Understanding the Book of Revelation*. Revised by David A. deSilva. Nashville: Abingdon, 2019.

Miller, David M. *God at Work: The History and Promise of the Faith at Work Movement*. New York: Oxford University Press, 2007.

Paulus, Michael J., Jr., "Charles Williams's Theology of Publishing." *VII* 34 (2018) 57–70.

———. "From the City to the Cloud: Charles Williams's Image of the City as an Affirmation of Artificial Intelligence." *The Lamp-Post of the Southern California C. S. Lewis Society* 36/37 (2019) 4–21.

Peters, John Durham. *The Marvelous Clouds: Toward a Philosophy of Elemental Media*. Chicago: University of Chicago Press, 2015.

Peterson, Eugene H. *Reversed Thunder: The Revelation of John and the Praying Imagination*. New York: HaperCollins, 1991.

Plummer, Thomas W., and Emma M. Finestone. *Rethinking Human Evolution*. Cambridge, MA: The MIT Press, 2018.

The Royal Society. "Portrayals and Perceptions of AI and Why They Matter." 2018. https://royalsociety.org/-/media/policy/projects/ai-narratives/AI-narratives-workshop-findings.pdf.

Sayers, Dorothy L. *Why Work?* McLean, VA: The Trinity Forum, 2011.

Schwab, Klaus. *The Fourth Industrial Revolution*. New York: Currency, 2016.

Segal, Howard P. *Future Imperfect: The Mixed Blessing of Technology in America*. Amherst, MA: The University of Massachusetts Press, 1994.

Siebel, Thomas M. *Digital Transformation: Survive and Thrive in an Era of Mass Extinction*. New York: RosettaBooks, 2019.

Smids, Jilles, Sven Nyholm, and Hannah Berkers. "Robots in the Workplace: A Threat to—or Opportunity for—Meaningful Work?" *Philosophy and Technology* 33 (2020) 503–22.

Thomas, John Christopher. *The Apocalypse: A Literary and Theological Commentary*. Cleveland, TN: CPT, 2012.

Volf, Miroslav. *Work in the Spirit: Toward a Theology of Work*. Oxford: Oxford University Press, 1991.

Vonnegut, Kurt. *Player Piano*. New York: Avon, 1971.

Wright, N. T. *History and Eschatology: Jesus and the Promise of Natural Theology*. London: SPCK, 2019.

———. *Surprised by Scripture: Engaging Contemporary Issues*. New York: HarperOne, 2014.

9

Sin and Grace

Bruce D. Baker

INTRODUCTION

We close this volume with a reflection on sin and grace, in hopes of leaving the reader with a practical, edifying, and durable perspective on the implications of artificial intelligence. Whatever unforeseeable challenges and opportunities AI brings in the years to come, the fundamental question will remain unchanged: How then shall we live, with wisdom, to fulfill our calling as bearers of the image of God beholden to the creation mandate?

The theological lens of sin and grace gives a broader and deeper viewpoint than mere ethics. Ethical analysis is of course useful and necessary, but ethics alone is not enough. Ethics apart from a robust, holistic understanding of humans as persons-in-communion will remain mired in reductionist thinking about human dignity and morality. Therefore, this final chapter addresses the ethical issues of AI through the lens of sin and grace.

Sin and grace are inextricably linked. As Martin Luther says, "The more you minimize sin, the more grace declines in value."[1] The triune God reveals the redeeming, unstoppable power of grace in the free gift of Jesus

1. See Kolb, "Martin Luther," 217.

Christ, who bears the sins of the world: "When he bears it, even the greatest of sins cannot damn."[2] In these next few pages, we will examine the routes by which sin enters into our engagement with AI, and we shall see also how God's redeeming grace prevails. The aim of this chapter is to find guiding theological principles that can serve as a foundation for wise engagement with AI.

A MODERN-DAY PARABLE

To begin, I offer a story by way of illustration. The AIs with the greatest impact on our lives are probably those we think about least. Such is the irony of our tech-infused culture. Artificial intelligence rushes into daily life in an irreversible steady stream, flowing from the heights of cutting-edge inventions to the taken-for-granted commonplaces of daily life. This is as true of the benefits of technology as it is of the moral hazards carried along with the current as it flows downstream with gathering force.

Consider the mundane act of ordering a ride. A few taps on the phone, or a simple spoken command, "Get me a ride to my appointment!" summons a car. The car arrives shortly. The rider climbs in knowing the fare, travel time, driver's name, and quantified customer ratings of the driver's service record. Similarly, the driver knows the name of the rider, the most efficient route, and information about the rider's appointment, ride history, and preferences. Passenger and driver might strike up a conversation, but it is unnecessary. The app handles all the logistical details seamlessly, so there is no need for any human action, other than for the driver to drive the car. (In a few short years, the driver's job will disappear, of course. Human drivers are merely a transitory mode in the business model of the ride company, soon to be eliminated by a fleet of self-driving cars.)

This story is boringly ordinary. Of course, we might wonder what work the driver may be able to find next, and we can raise questions about the treatment of employees in the gig economy. But for the moment, we see that the driver has a job that provides enough incremental income to make it worth doing, apparently. On the surface, it looks like everyone wins. The rider receives cost-effective service, the driver has employment, and the company makes a profit. The whole system is run by the ride-hail company's AI, which delivers benefits to all concerned. But there's more to the story. . . .

By the time the passenger gets in the car, AIs have already calculated the potential value her itinerary might bring to third-party marketers and data brokers whose AIs are bidding to acquire the data stream generated by

2. Barth, *Church Dogmatics* IV/1, 405.

her trip. Other AIs have also figured out whom she is meeting, and have a good guess as to the purpose of the meeting, what kind of mood she will be in when she departs, and where she might want to go next. This data also may be of value to third parties. Meanwhile, another AI is running an A/B experiment on the driver's behavior in response to messages that might or might not persuade him to go immediately to another part of town. The goal of this experiment, of which the driver is unaware, is to move multiple drivers into in a neighborhood where the company can optimize profits by surge-pricing rides for inebriated customers that may be spilling out on to the street in the next twenty minutes or so. Another fact of which no one is aware is that AI has figured out route planning that will shave a second or two off the average time it takes to reposition drivers by routing them through residential neighborhoods, where they typically drive faster than the posted speed limits. This particular driver has been in the car long enough to need a break, but that does not enter into the AI's calculations. Each of these AIs is continually learning how to improve as they feed on an ever-growing volume of data, reaching further into the personal lives of the people involved. The driver-management AI, for example, keeps improving by gathering more data about the driver's habits and by monitoring the activities of his family members. Meanwhile, the passenger in the backseat is engaged with multiple AIs as she scrolls through messages on social media from friends, bots, advertisers, and the social media platform. It is quite possible that these AIs will sufficiently absorb her attention such that she will not speak with the driver and have no awareness of what is happening on the streets along the way. That is, unless the AIs decide to draw her attention to anything along the route that might induce her to spend money. All of these AIs are becoming better at their jobs as they grow in perceptivity of emotional states, fed as they are by increasingly massive streams of data from microscopic video cameras and sensors capable of discerning eye movement, skin temperature, respiration, pulse, body language, and other metabolic indicators.[3]

Is there anything wrong with this picture? Ethical arguments in defense of AI come easily. After all, at every step of the way the actions and motivations of the people involved in this scenario, as well as the intentions

---

3. This is a purely hypothetical scenario; however, it is based on well-documented practices in the tech industry. See Zuboff, *Age of Surveillance Capitalism*, and Rosenblat, *Uberland*. Rosenblat reports: "Uber uses its intermediary position as a shady middleman to algorithmically or technologically squeeze out extra dollars and cents, and this often looks like wage theft. In other cases, algorithmic managers may simply mislead drivers about the prospects for pay premiums through inaccurate reflections or predictions about search pricing" (114).

of the AIs deployed by the ride-hail company, can be justified in terms of convenience and efficiency. That is, if we ignore the absence of concerns about environmental and justice issues that never find their way into the justifications of the benefits delivered by the AIs involved in the business models described in our story. The function of the AIs can be defended as merely standard business practice and good faith attempts to improve customer experience and grow revenue. Furthermore, the argument can be made that there is nothing immoral going on here, because the individuals involved—the passenger and the driver—have free will and bear personal responsibility for their own choices and behavior.

These are the sorts of arguments commonly used to claim AI (and technology in general) is devoid of moral implications. In our secular age, the most common means of evaluating the trade-offs involved in the deployment of AI and other technologies is to analyze the pros and cons in terms of cost-benefit analysis. Any attempt to evaluate the morality of the actions and intentions of this scenario is likely to devolve rapidly into a discussion of utilitarian value propositions and perhaps the need for transparency or privacy protections. These concerns will not ever arrive at an understanding of core, transcendent values such as human dignity, righteousness, holiness, and shalom. Utilitarian ethical analysis is important, of course, but without a solid theological foundation, it will fall short of the mark.

To see beyond the merely utilitarian calculation of trade-offs that emerge in our engagement with AI (or any other technology) we must view the issues through the lens of a coherent, theological understanding of human life. Religious faith provides a context in which to make sense of the impact AI has upon spiritual reality, and to hold as central the ineffable worth of human life and relationships. This is why we have to look beyond merely ethical categories in order to see the deeper significance of AI. We need spiritual wisdom to see how our engagement with AI changes us. We need theological understanding to discern whether we are using AI wisely, that is, to walk in paths of righteousness, in step with divine reality, and to not be distracted and led astray. These are theological issues. They provide a foundation for ethics and inform ethical deliberation, but theological insight exceeds the grasp of reductionist ethical categories of thought. Hence, the value of seeing the issues through the lens of sin and grace.

DOES AI OPEN A NEW DOOR ONTO SIN?

Is there really anything remarkably different about AI as compared to other technologies that increases its propensity for sin? At a very basic level, all technologies are similar in that they can be used for either good or evil. Our contention here in this chapter is this: Even though the fundamental characteristics and risks of technology have always been part and parcel of human culture, there is something new and worthy of fresh consideration in the types of challenges posed by AI.

There is something mesmerizing about the power technology puts in human hands. Until the advent of computers in the mid-twentieth century, this power was essentially physical; technology magnified strength, work, and skills requiring dexterity and speed. In the information age, technology magnified human powers of observation and calculation. Today we are on the cusp of a new era in which AI magnifies mental power. Artificial intelligence can augment, mimic, and even replace human thought. Whether AI can truly be said to match humans in terms of understanding, semantic reasoning, and moral discernment is a question for metaphysics and theological philosophy. The practical reality is that AI has more power over human attention and decision-making than anything in human history. It is incumbent on people of faith, therefore, to seek understanding in the ways that AI might engender channels for sin that other technologies have not. This is the more pointed question that will occupy our attention in the remainder of this chapter.

WHAT IS SIN?

To put it simply, sin is movement away from God. This can take many forms. Sin can be deliberate or unintentional, individual or communal, chaotic or systemic. The Bible shows sin arising in many different forms—disobedience, rebellion, corruption, unrighteousness, pride, folly, and hubris, to name a few. The most fundamental sin in the Old Testament tradition is the wandering astray of Israel, God's people, from covenantal relationship with God. Similarly in the Synoptic Gospels, the fundamental sin is to miss the mark by failing to recognize the promise of God's grace and relationship in the person of Jesus Christ.[4]

The Old Testament uses several different Hebrew words to connote sin, the most frequent being: ḥaṭa (חָטָא), "deviate or miss the mark" (e.g., Exod 20:20; Lev 4:13–14; Hos 13:2); pšaʿ (פָּשַׁע), "rebel, or transgress against God, Torah, covenant, or others" (e.g., 1 Kgs 12:19; Isa 1:2); ʿawōn (עָוֹן), "iniquity, or deliberate wrong doing" (e.g., Gen 44:16; Jer 2:22; Isa 59:2–7; Dan 9:5); rašaʿ a (רשׁע), "to be wicked or to reject God" (e.g., Exod 9:27; 1 Sam

---

4. Biddle, *Missing the Mark*, 44.

24:14; Isa 13:11).[5] The most common New Testament verb is *hamartanō* (ἁμαρτάνω) and its noun cognate, *hamartēma* (ἁμάρτημα). This is the word most often used in the Septuagint to translate *ḥaṭa*, and it carries the core meaning of "to deviate or miss the mark,"[6] miss the target, or take a wrong road.[7] This is the common New Testament term for sin as concrete wrong-doing, moral guilt, conscious opposition to God, and the violation of God's law (John 8:46; Jas 1:15; 1 John 1:8).[8] In Romans 5–8, Paul uses this word to speak of sin as a personal force of evil and wrongdoing (cf. Rom 5:12; 6:12, 14; 7:17, 20; 8:2).[9] Each of these various words from both the Old and New Testament conveys a sense of wrongdoing, so it might seem like common sense to equate sin with moral wrongdoing. This leads to a seriously mistaken understanding of sin, however. Sin and ethics (understood as discerning right vs. wrong action) are not the same thing. Sin is not reducible to a set of ethical principles, the fundamental reason being that ethical principles and moral deliberation do not convey the mind of God.

Cornelius Plantinga reminds us that "sin is a religious concept, not just a moral one."[10] Sin is not an ethical diagnosis, but rather a theological statement. Mark Biddle amplifies this important point: "Sin is not the violation of some moral code, but the inability or unwillingness to recognize the presence of God."[11] As Robert Jenson says, "The only possible definition of sin is that it is what God does not want done."[12] Thus, there exists no free-standing set of biblical rules—neither the Ten Commandments nor the Mosaic law, nor any other discrete biblical injunctions—capable of answering the never-ending stream of ethical questions that arise from the adoption of new technology.

SIN IMPLICIT IN TECHNOLOGICAL CULTURE

To discern the presence and potential for sin, it helps to reflect on the question, "What is happening here that might go against God's desire?" God desires that people live in shalom[13] and righteousness. God desires justice. Sin

---

5. McCall, *Against God and Nature*, 34–37; Milne and Muller, "Sin," 1105.

6. McCall, *Against God and Nature*, 38.

7. Milne and Muller, "Sin," 1105.

8. Kittel et al., *Theological Dictionary of the New Testament*, 48.

9. Kittel et al., *Theological Dictionary of the New Testament*, 48.

10. Plantinga, *Not the Way*, 12.

11. Biddle, *Missing the Mark*, 44.

12. Quoted in McCall, *Against God and Nature*, 341.

13. Shalom is a Hebrew word from the Old Testament that indicates a state of peace,

shows up in the corruption of shalom, which occurs when unrighteousness leads to injustice. These are outwardly visible signs of the effects of sin. Reflecting on the scenario above, we ask if there is any injustice being done to the driver by coercive or unfair treatment. Is shalom being damaged by intrusion of the AI into personal relationships? Is the AI coercive in ways that do not take into consideration the best interests of the people being manipulated?

Technology falls prey to sin when used to fulfill goals that run counter to God's desires. As with other technologies, AIs suffer from the unavoidable presence of sin implicit in the pursuit of goals that suboptimize against the overarching priority of shalom. This problem persists despite even the best intentions of technologists. Good motives are an insufficient shield against the infiltration of sin because the technology itself requires quantifiable objectives, and such constraints are reductionist. The biblical concepts of righteousness, justice, and shalom are irreducible.

Anna Wiener sums up the problem inherent in the goal-seeking technology of platform companies: "The endgame was the same for everyone: growth at any cost. Scale above all. Disrupt, then dominate."[14] Plantinga explains the effect theologically as "the turning of loyalty, energy, and desire away from God and God's project in the world: it is the diversion of construction materials for the city of God to side projects of our own, often accompanied by jerry-built ideologies that seek to justify the diversion."[15]

As mentioned above, the common moral argument in defense of AI-empowered platforms is to say that technology is morally neutral, that is, neither moral nor immoral. It simply exists. Like a hammer, wheel, or gun, the technology is not the source of sin, but rather the person is. At a superficial level, this argument seems logical. Certainly it is correct to say that moral responsibility resides in the person using the tool. However, AI is different than simple tools in that it is automated and is put in control of systems that exercise power on a large scale. This autonomous power comes with moral hazards and the potential to be employed in the outworking of sin. The argument of the moral neutrality of technology is problematic because the creation, development, and usage of technology is bound up with human agents that are sinful, and therefore sin gets embedded in that creation, development, and usage.

---

wholeness, and contentment. It implies a sense of flourishing for all people and the rest of creation, and can be said to be what God intends.

14. Wiener, *Uncanny Valley*, 136.

15. Plantinga, *Not the Way*, 40.

The moral hazards embedded in the autonomous systems controlled by AI are often subtle and easily ignored, especially because the benefits are so clear: success in vaccine development and medical diagnosis, solutions to energy efficiency and traffic jams, improved delivery of social services, and of course cost-saving efficiency in any number of jobs. The valuable benefits of technologies do not however erase the impact of sin. The easiest way to lose sight of the moral and spiritual issues related to AI is to presume that technology is morally neutral and to ignore the influence of sin in our relationship with it.

Injustice and corruption of shalom are visible and tangible outcomes of sin. The deep roots of sin, however, are hidden matters of the heart. The story of Adam and Eve of course serves as the archetype. Their sin originates in the heart and leads to alienation—from God, from each other, and even from the land. Alienation turns out to be the deep-seated, fundamental effect of sin.

ALIENATION

In the scenario depicted above, alienation is a recurring theme. Perhaps in the best case, alienation might be avoided, or at least mitigated, by the goodwill, wisdom, and spiritual awareness of the people in the story. Nonetheless, their engagement with AI puts them in position to be manipulated by systems that do not take their human dignity into consideration. The driver's awareness and behavior present a target of opportunity for the AI that optimizes logistics for the company. Other AIs are aimed at manipulating the passenger's awareness and behavior. The AIs engage with the people as if they were data sets. There is no personal, human interaction or empathy in the system. Grace does not enter into the calculations of the AIs. There is only the mechanization of monetization schemes. Alienation works to the advantage of the AI-based systems. People can be more easily influenced by motivational nudges when they are paying more attention to AI-initiated apps and less attention to God, others, and self. Alienation forms the root of sin. As Donald Bloesch says, sin is "estrangement or alienation from the ground of our being."[16]

This would seem to be the pattern of sin ever since Eve and Adam ate the forbidden fruit. To turn away from God was the first sinful impulse of humanity (Gen 3:8). Paul points to this separation as the root of sin (Rom 1:21–22) and describes both personal and corporate sin in terms of alienation (Eph 2:12, 4:18; Col 1:21). Paul Tillich lends a modern voice to this

16. Bloesch, *Jesus Christ*, 37.

understanding of sin as alienation: "Our basic human condition is a state of estrangement of man and his world from God."[17] For Tillich, alienation is "our act of turning away from participation in the divine Ground from which we come and to which we go [and] the turning towards ourselves . . . making ourselves the center of our world and of ourselves."[18]

The themes of alienation and estrangement are fitting in the context of the relational turn in theology and philosophy during the twentieth century.[19] Trinitarian theology constructs a doctrine of *imago Dei* in terms of the human person's participation in, with, and through the life of the relational God. Karl Barth represents this relational turn in theology, pointing to relationship with God as the source of identity and existence. This relationship is not "merely one of many determinations of our being, derivative and mutable, but the basic determination, original and immutable."[20]

To turn inward on oneself and put the creative self at the center of meaning is an act of alienation, a turning away from divine reality (God) and a turn inward to put oneself at the center as maker of the world and definer of reality.[21] This inward turning movement is spoken of as *homo incurvatus in se*—humanity curved in on itself. Martin Luther built on this idea and developed the theme of *homo incurvatus in se* systematically in his commentary on Romans.[22] Matt Jenson traces this sense sin back to Augustine, who understands it as "the willful re-direction of attention and love from God to the human self apart from God which results in alienation from God and the fracturing of human society."[23]

The link between AI and these sorts of alienation is indirect. The technology itself does not induce alienation; rather, the way that the technology is used is the source of the problem. Alienation becomes an issue when AI is used to isolate and insulate individuals from relationships and from their own moral agency. Reinhold Niebuhr's emphasis on "will to power" as the fundamental source of sin is helpful in tracing the connection between the power of technology and the practical effects of alienation:

17. Tillich, *Systematic Theology*, 2:27.

18. Tillich, *Systematic Theology*, 2:46.

19. Jenson surveys the convergence in philosophy and theology of an ontological view of the human person as being "fundamentally constituted by its relationships." Jenson, *Gravity of Sin*, 1. See also Stiver, *Theology after Ricoeur*, 160.

20. Barth, *Church Dogmatics* III/2, 136.

21. Biddle, *Missing the Mark*, 19.

22. Jenson, *Gravity of Sin*, 6–7.

23. Jenson, *Gravity of Sin*, 7.

> The will to power is the inclination of the human creature to try to subjugate its environment (including other persons) . . . to place itself at the center of its existence and, in so doing, to arrogate to its personal reality the false status of ultimate reality.[24]

Eberhard Jüngel similarly picks up on the theme of alienation, calling sin "the urge towards relationlessness and dissociation."[25] The sinner is so alienated that they become cut off from all relationships, even from God and oneself.[26] For Jüngel, sin is directly linked with the modern psychological ideal of self-realization as the epitome of ego-strength and psychological well-being.[27]

Alienation takes different forms. A person can deliberately turn away from God in an act of defiance, or wander aimlessly away through ignorance or indifference, which is the sin of acedia. In either case, the effect is the same: estrangement increases with distance from God. This is because, in the absence of a healthy relationship with God, the soul, which continues to hunger for connection with transcendence and divinity, will fill the void of its longing by turning inward. Thus, the self becomes the center of all being. Ironically, this form of estrangement develops through a growing separation from God and ends up in the collapse of distinction between God and self-as-god. This is the sin of desiring to be "more than human"—to become equal to God, which in essence merges one's personality into the Godhead without drawing any distinction. This is another aspect of the original sin of desiring the knowledge of good and evil, and thus to be like God (Gen 3:5). Albert Borgmann describes this mechanism of sin as "collapsing dimensions of reality."[28] To collapse the dimension of one's relationship with God, and of participation in the divine purposes God has for the world and for oneself results in a singularity of equivalence between self and God.

Artificial intelligence can enable the process of such a collapse to the extent that it feeds the myth of human capabilities as the ultimate good. As AI becomes better at augmenting human thought, becomes increasingly adept at reading interior moods and discerning how to please, and offers unprecedented control over one's interactions and environment, it has the potential to feed the desire to be "more than human" and to be the master of one's life.

24. Niebuhr, *Moral Man and Immoral Society*, 11–12. For a similar assessment of Niebuhr's theology of sin, see King, "Reinhold Niebuhr's Ethical Dualism."

25. Jüngel, *Justification*, 113.

26. Jüngel, "World as Possibility," 107.

27. Webster, "Justification," 114.

28. Borgmann, "Lure of Technology."

The unprecedented power and potential of AI to augment human reality opens enticing opportunities to take control of reality and life itself. Fanciful as it is, we might even imagine Satan holding up the futuristic prospects of super-AI as a sort of fruit, saying, "eat of this fruit and you can escape your human mortality and live forever." Just as it was with the forbidden fruit in the Garden, this is a blatant lie that elides the fact that AI has nothing to offer when it comes to the living reality of human consciousness, let alone the promise of eternal life.

Preposterous as their ideas might be, some enthusiasts tout AI as a technological route to a godless salvation. Some futurists look forward to the day when AI will surpass humanlike general intelligence and achieve cybernetic immortality. This is the basis for transhumanist theories of evolution, in which intelligent computers supplant the human species.[29] The most "evangelical" transhumanists make the claim that these future intelligent machines will be sophisticated enough that humans will be able to upload their consciousnesses into them.[30] Tom Stonier, for example, predicts, "the cosmic function of Humanity is to act as the evolutionary interface between Life and Intelligence."[31]

This is the epitome of *homo incurvatus in se*. At this point humanity will have so completely curved in on itself that the self will have resurrected itself into eternal life. This represents a singularity in sinfulness. At this point, the self would be the source of eternal life, and at the same time the self would become creator, creation, and redeemer all in one. It is utter idolatry, and (*pace* Barth) utter stupidity.[32] "To replace relationship with God with relationship with our own artifacts, in the form of computers, is the clearest form of idolatry."[33]

To the extent that popular culture leans into this understanding of the prospects unleashed by future developments in AI, idolatry will take root and grow, and the concept of sin will become irrelevant in the face of technological progress. Along the way, this worldview will begin to disparage the meaningfulness of the human body and the finite limitations of human persons. As Noreen Herzfeld points out, this worldview will be appealing to some futurists because it provides "a way to maintain belief in a reductionistic materialism without giving up the hope of immortality."[34]

29. See Moravec, *Mind Children*; Kurzweil, *The Singularity*; Hanson, *Age of Em*.

30. Geraci, *Apocalyptic AI*, 85–87.

31. Stonier, *Beyond Information*, 214.

32. Barth, *Church Dogmatics* IV/2, 412–13.

33. Herzfeld, *In Our Image*, 83.

34. Herzfeld, *In Our Image*, 73.

The concept of cybernetic immortality is based on false assumption that "thoughts, memories, feelings, and actions define the human person."[35]

The limitless potential of AI to mimic human thought and behavior, and to vastly exceed human skills of information processing, may be compared to the limitless height of the Tower of Babel—a story we will examine below. Again, it is important to remember that technology itself is not the problem, but rather the moral and spiritual value that is invested in the outsize goals of human imagination to use technology.

SIN AS A PARASITE

> Sin is a parasite, an uninvited guest that keeps tapping its host for sustenance. Nothing about sin is its own; all its power, persistence, and possibility are stolen goods. Sin is not really an entity but a spoiler of entities.[36]

The scenario described at the beginning of this chapter illustrates how sin can creep in and become a parasitic presence that feeds off the good energy present in the problem-solving prowess of AI. The sinful, parasitic activity that emerges from the AIs in this scenario take the form of manipulation of both the passenger and the driver. AIs manipulate them in ways that serve the economic engines of the corporate entities—the ride-hail company, the social media platforms, and their third-party partners. Sin works parasitically to divert the attention and/or distort the behavior of these persons. The AIs become disembodied agents not treating the persons affected as bearers of the image of God, but rather as objects to be manipulated. Wiener describes the disorienting, disintegrating effect social media programming had on her: "The algorithm told me what my aesthetic was: the same as everyone else I knew. . . . My brain had become a trash vortex."[37] These influences, if unchecked, lead to disintegration of the person. This is a form of alienation because personal relationships with God and with one another have been distorted or overwritten by other demands upon attention. This is a corruption of shalom, as Plantinga says.

These parasitic effects are especially pernicious in that they are prone to arise even in the absence of any identifiable, discrete sinful choice. The parasitic effect is systemic; that is, it arises in social constructs and draws its

---

35. Herzfeld, *In Our Image*, 70.

36. Plantinga, *Not the Way*, 89.

37. Wiener, *Uncanny Valley*, 187–88.

202 Part II: Explorations

energy from the relationships upon which it feeds. The system, as a whole, becomes the host for the parasite.

Again, it is worth pointing out that this evaluation of the influences of sin upon our engagement with AI goes beyond business ethics, stakeholder analysis, utilitarian calculations, or any other philosophical means of weighing costs and benefits in the balance. What we are discussing here has to do with the profound, inherent dignity of human beings and the fulfillment of their dignity by moving in the direction of communion with God and others. To consider the influence of sin upon our AI-mediated interactions and relationships is to open our eyes to the unfortunate, perhaps even unavoidable and unpredictable, ways in which these interactions can go "against God and nature."

One way sin corrupts this inherent goodness in nature is by putting a person in the frame of mind to lose sight of the greater good of holiness, that is, of integral attention to the divine. Sin succeeds by persuading a person to exchange the truth for a lie—the lie in this case being a form of idolatry or false worship, for example, of efficiency, productivity, success, financial gain, or human admiration. McCall identifies this as "the pervasive sense of sin given in Scripture . . . is that it is *opposed to God's good purposes in creation*."[38]

Satan is wily. Sin has no life of its own, but rather it must steal life and energy from that which is good; thus it behaves as a parasite. C. S. Lewis explains, "Goodness is, so to speak, itself: badness is only spoiled goodness. And there must be something good first before it can be spoiled."[39] Similarly, sin could not subsist without distorting reason and persuading human actors to go against their own self-interest and against reason. Luther says in his commentary on Romans 11 that sinners are those who have their eyes "darkened"; they "do not look to grace, which is from above," but rather "their eyes have become blurred, . . . they remain curved in on their own understanding (*curvi in sensum suum*)."[40]

Because sin embarks on an unsustainable course—going against reason as it goes against God and nature—sin is ultimately futile, irrational, and simply "stupid,"[41] to use Barth's term for it. Sin thus needs to rely upon a certain amount of self-deception in order to propagate.[42] Plantinga points this out: "Because it is futile, because it is vain, because it is unrealistic,

38. McCall, *Against God and Nature*, 232.

39. Lewis, *Mere Christianity*, 35.

40. Jenson, *Gravity of Sin*, 72.

41. Barth, *Church Dogmatics* IV/2, 412–13.

42. McCall, *Against God and Nature*, 236.

because it spoils good things, sin is a prime form of folly."[43] Here is another ripe opportunity for sin to grab a foothold in our engagement with AI. People instinctively regard themselves as reasonable and moral actors. It goes against human nature to think of oneself as somehow lacking morality or rational behavior. The same goes for our perception of our involvement with AI. Developers of AI will presume that they are developing something good and providing something beneficial to humanity. Users and customers engaging with AI will naturally presume that they are making rational choices and in control of their actions. This protective instinct regarding one's personal sense of integrity is both good and bad. On the one hand, it can provide confidence to stand up for what is right. On the other hand, it can devolve into a form of self-deception, such as by obscuring the sinful outcomes that may result from the manipulative influences of AI.

Think of the software engineer, for example, who developed the AI for driver management in the scenario above. The driver might presumably have confidence that the AI is merely optimizing business goals and presenting drivers with choices, which they are free to accept or decline in accordance with their free will and best judgment. It seems unfair somehow to find fault with the developer for falling victim to the self-deception of failing to recognize the moral hazards that the AI invites as it learns, acquiring and filtering personal data regarding individual drivers and using that information to manipulate them. Similarly, it seems unfair to find fault with the passenger in our scenario who is oblivious to both the injustices that might befall the driver, as well as the ways in which the social media platform she is using may be manipulating her attention.

Are these large, glaring, capital sins? No, probably not. Nonetheless, these examples show the parasitic effects of sin; it is always at the threshold, awaiting an opening to come in and infect whatever system it can. This is a good lesson to keep in mind, because AI-empowered systems have significant influence on human behavior, decision-making, and relationships, and the very power of AI to make decisions without human oversight means that it is easy to ignore the subtlety with which sin can creep in and infect the network. The "network effect" can magnify the sin before the humans in control notice how large the problem has become. Take, for example, the chatbot experiment that Microsoft had to shut down when it became infected by foul language and racial taunts it picked up from humans on the network.[44] Perhaps the most glaring example of the parasitic effects of sin is the ongoing trend toward divisiveness and conflict fueled by social

43. Plantinga, *Not the Way*, 126.
44. Schwartz, "Microsoft's Racist Chatbot."

network AIs. Facebook and Twitter function as "echo chambers" in this way, as Abhijit Banerjee and Esther Duflo explain:

> Such behavior leads to accidental and probably largely uncon-
> scious segregation. . . . We end up with multiple closed groups
> with contrasting opinions and very little capacity for commu-
> nicating respectfully with each other. Cass Sunstein, a law pro-
> fessor at Harvard and a member of the Obama administration,
> describes these as "echo chambers," where like-minded people
> whip themselves into a frenzy by listening only to each other.
> One result of this is extreme polarization on what should be
> more or less objective facts.[45]

It turns out in the case of these social networks that the AIs can monetize users most efficiently by distracting people from noticing the effects of
sin. The Proverbs are rife with evidence of the clear connection between sin
and the distracted self. Those who delude themselves with folly "set an am-
bush for their own lives" (Prov 1:18), are "held fast in the cords of [their] sin,"
injure themselves (8:36), and so on (cf. 11:5–6; 13:13; 14:32; 28:10; 29:6).

UNINTENTIONAL SIN

As seen in the examples above, sin often arises from unintentional and even
unnoticed choices and behaviors. It may well be true that the most impactful
occasions of sin related to AI may be of this unintentional variety. After all,
there are laws and social mechanisms in place to identify and deal with the
most egregious sins. But unintentional sin can go unnoticed for some time
and do serious damage before the problems are recognized and dealt with.

The Old Testament makes a clear distinction between intentional and
unintentional sin. Leviticus 4 and 5 and Numbers 15 treat unintentional sins
as a separate category of sin and specify different consequences and sacrifices
for atonement of unintentional sins. These passages also make clear that either individuals or an entire community can commit unintentional sins.[46]

Unintentional sin is to be expected in the development and deployment of AI. How many developers and business analysts practice the discipline of worshipful attention to shalom and grace as they plan, design,
and build technology platforms? Some do, of course, and they are salt and

---

45. Banerjee and Duflo, *Good Economics*, 126.
46. McCall, *Against God and Nature*, 248.

light in the industry. They are atypical, however. Wiener describes the normal situation when she tells of her own experience inside a big technology company:

> It was perhaps a symptom of my myopia, my sense of security, that I was not thinking about data collection as one of the moral quandaries of our time. For all the industry's talk about skill, and changing the world, I was not thinking about the broader implications. I was hardly thinking about the world at all.[47]

Like corrosion that slowly and invisibly eats away at the foundation of a house until it collapses, unintentional sin can do significant damage in society and individual lives. This is a problem shared by all humanity. David expresses the dilemma common to human nature, shared by all, when he prays, "Who can discern his errors? Declare me innocent from hidden faults" (Ps 19:12). This prayer reveals the incipient risk of sin that pervades human existence—that even in hindsight, even with a searching heart and a spirit of repentance, we are not able to discern fully the extent of our sins. There will always be unforeseen ramifications resulting from unintentional sins.

Artificial intelligence promises to bring such a wealth of benefits and opportunities to improve life that it can be easy to overlook these unforeseen ramifications. The story of the Tower of Babel helps to illustrate how admirable intentions with respect to new technology can move society in sinful directions.

TOWER OF BABEL

> Now the whole earth had one language and the same words. And as people migrated from the east, they found a plain in the land of Shinar and settled there. And they said to one another, "Come, let us make bricks, and burn them thoroughly." And they had brick for stone, and bitumen for mortar. Then they said, "Come, let us build ourselves a city and a tower with its top in the heavens, and let us make a name for ourselves, lest we be dispersed over the face of the whole earth." And the Lord came down to see the city and the tower, which the children of man had built. And the Lord said, "Behold, they are one people, and they have all one language, and this is only the beginning of what they will do. And nothing that they propose to do will now be impossible for them. Come, let us go down and there confuse

47. Wiener, *Uncanny Valley*, 128.

their language, so that they may not understand one another's speech." So the Lord dispersed them from there over the face of all the earth, and they left off building the city. Therefore its name was called Babel, because there the Lord confused the language of all the earth. And from there the Lord dispersed them over the face of all the earth. (Gen 11:1–9 ESV)

The story is full of mystery and open to interpretation. Technology plays a central role in the events, as represented in brick-making, construction techniques capable of building a tower to the sky, and the complexity of the city itself.[48] It would be a mistake however to read the story as a condemnation of technology. The text makes no particular comment on the morality of technology per se, which is consistent with the tone of Scripture as a whole. References to technology are scattered throughout the Old Testament. The Bible expresses God's judgment upon weapons—"Beat your swords into plowshares" (Joel 3:10; cf. Isa 2:4; Mic 4:3)—but otherwise offers scant moral judgment upon technology.

Sometimes technology is explicitly used for good purposes ordained by God, as with musical instruments for worship (Exod 31:1–11), and tools of bronze and iron for cultivating the land (Gen 4:21–22). Even spears, arrows, and chariots are occasionally called into action in keeping with God's will. Each of these references treats technology as a realistic, even necessary component of human culture, without pronouncing explicit moral judgment.

Thus, it seems technology is not the problem in the story of the Tower of Babel. Rather, it is the more complex and mysterious effects of the state of people's relationship with God and each other that emerges as the crisis. The problem arises from the inclination of people to use their technology in ways that separate them from God and go against God in some indistinct, unspecified manner. Again, alienation is the telltale sign of sin in the story. It is not clear from the text whether the people's sin is intentional or not. That is a question open to interpretation, but it would seem to make no difference with respect to the ramifications of sin and God's action to foil their ambition.

God's severe judgment of the tower's builders rankles. There seems something admirable in their ingenuity and ambition. God's condemnation of their project comes as a surprise, because we have come to regard technology and progress as essential goods. Why does God foil their diligent efforts? These challenging questions serve as warnings to humans in every era to question their motives and seek God's will in the application of technology.

48. Ellul, *Meaning of the City*, 8–13.

Perhaps the tower housed a temple of idolatrous worship, but that is speculative. The story does not mention it. Although the text is silent on the exact nature of the people's sin, it is clear that they have transgressed some God-given limit or limits. The story is a cautionary tale, therefore, for technologists in every age; anytime we embark on a journey of building new societal structures enabled by new technologies applied on a large scale, we should be mindful to hold up the prospects to the divine light of God's will.

So, although technology is implicated in the transgression, the story does not read as an injunction against technology itself. God does not condemn the people for being inventive, or industrious, or imaginative in their technological prowess. Rather, God condemns the desire of the people to "make a name for ourselves" (v. 4). The sin in this case, whether intentional or not, would seem to be willful separation from God. The story catches the people of Babel in the act of either rejecting or ignoring dependence upon God for their identity, security, and livelihood.

Although the story does not mention sin explicitly, sin operates on several levels. First and perhaps most salient is the point that the people desire to attain the power and majesty of God.[49] In the story, the tower with its tops in the heavens represents the overweening pride of this aspiration. This ambition echoes the age-old sin of desiring to be equal to God. Second, the tower itself can be viewed as an object of false worship, since the people will focus all their attention on building it. The very plan to build it requires all language—in other words, all ethnic and cultural diversity—to be subsumed within a single, universal, common language. Third, there is the sin of rebelling against God's divine will. Fourth, there is the sin of broken relationship, because the people do not consider God in their plans. They neither seek after God's will nor ask God's blessing on the endeavor.

The exciting, uncharted territories of AI offer myriad opportunities to construct new "Towers of Babel" and to "make a name for ourselves." One way this shows up is in the vision of many AI-intensive tech companies to "grow to the sky." The network effect says that the value of an information network grows exponentially with the size of the network. This explains why social media platforms, online retail platforms, and other business platforms strive to dominate their market spaces by offering services "for free." The result is a constant and growing pressure to monetize whatever user experience they can through manipulative methods.

It is worth noting that this is not a new problem in political economy. Dominant market power, like any other power, can corrupt. Trust-busting legislation in the United States dates back to the late nineteenth century.

49. Paulus et al., "Framework for Digital Wisdom," 48.

What's new in the case of AI-driven businesses is the scale and scope of information processing power to manipulate behavior, both individual and communal.

The spiritual ramifications of AI today are essentially the same as for the builders of the Tower of Babel—distancing ourselves from God by placing inordinate attention, devotion, and trust in our technology and the work of our hands. Biddle rightly names the problem common to all technological visions:

> Strip away all the technology and gadgetry and one finds that the users are the same human beings who thought to ascend to heaven via a tower made of bricks with pitch for mortar. Christianity does not offer a utopian vision of perfected human society; it issues a call to the kingdom of God.[50]

Bricks and AI are both technologies of construction. The essential difference is that bricks are concrete, visible, and inert, while AI is hidden, intangible, and animated. Artificial intelligence grows with overwhelming complexity to scale new heights of cognition, make discoveries, discern patterns, intervene in personal relationships, and make decisions that are often inexplicable, unpredicted, and unmanaged. All the while, the machinations of AI remain invisible to the people impacted.

Another risk to spiritual health is the illusion that technological progress is capable of perfecting self and society. This faith in progress is "perhaps the most endemic form of rebellion in post-Enlightenment Western culture."[51] The risk of idealism is prevalent in technology companies, and all the more so in those companies working with AI. There is a streak of techno-utopian idealism that pervades the culture of AI development and this idealism is most likely to lead to ethical breakdowns when it ignores the reality of sin.[52] Mark Zuckerberg and Facebook show the problems of idealistic thinking. In testimony before Congress, Zuckerberg assured legislators that AI would solve fake news and other dire problems engendered by the algorithms driving his social media platform. This is a false hope. Artificial intelligence will not cure problems rooted in sin. Recognition of the self-serving idealism that idolizes technological prowess will help protect against unintentional and institutional sins.

The overwhelming power of AI tempts those who wield this power to manipulate and control the world according to their personal desires.

50. Biddle, *Missing the Mark*, 46.
51. Biddle, *Missing the Mark*, 45.
52. See Baker, "Sin and the Hacker Ethic."

Again, this inclination might seem admirable, but only in a superficial way. The root of the problem is alienation as we lose sight of our identity as fallen creatures dependent upon God for life and every blessing.

Perhaps the most egregious sin of alienation that follows from a utopian view of technology would be the outright rejection of God. The Tower of Babel symbolizes the desire of the builders to rise above their dependence on God and become masters of their own destiny. The seemingly unlimited prospects of AI can fuel this desire. This utopian worldview has gained momentum from authors who seize upon the emergent properties of AI as evidence that humankind will soon gain the power to transcend human limitations and claim divinity for itself. Yuval Harari, for example, argues as much in his book *Homo Deus*. Harari sees the eschatological goal of humanity as a technological project in which we will upgrade ourselves into new and improved versions. "Having raised humanity above the beastly level of survival struggles, we will now aim to upgrade humans into gods, and turn *Homo sapiens* into *Homo deus*."[53] The idea that humans could make themselves into gods would be the ultimate fulfillment of the desire of the builders of Babel to "make a name for ourselves." This is the epitome of alienation from God.

Spiritual health demands the rejection of such delusions of grandeur. Therefore confession—that is, acknowledgment of our inability to save ourselves from our sins—is essential for spiritual health. Neither AI nor any other technology will enable humankind to become perfect and redeemed from sin; rather, we rely upon the saving grace of Jesus Christ, and him alone, for that.

We can expect this tension in our relationship with AI to persist for generations to come. For whatever existential or practical question lurks in the heart of human beings, there will be AIs offering to solve them. There will be AIs developed to provide spiritual counseling, to provide emotional companionship, to optimize lifestyle, habits, and interpersonal relationships. There will be AI personal agents to conduct business and intercede in conflicts. There will be AIs deployed to make any and all sorts of decisions, including decisions bearing significant moral freight.

In each case, there is a way to develop and deploy these technologies with wisdom, while staying aware of the dangers of alienating sin. There is another route that ignores or denies sin, and this route leads to death. The challenge set before the faithful, as always, is to choose life (Deut 30:19).

---

53. Harari, *Homo Deus*, 21.

INSTITUTIONAL SIN

The sin of hubris might be most glaringly apparent in egoistic and individualistic efforts to become "more than human," but the most dangerous variety of sin is institutional and systemic. In the scenario above, for example, the AIs not only influence the drivers and riders, but they also have a system-wide impact on traffic in neighborhoods and a host of other outcomes built into the business models of institutional partners of the ride-sharing platform. The sinfulness of these AI-controlled platforms is not premeditated. It comes about through the unmitigated and unsupervised operation of the stakeholding organizations. This is typical of institutional sin; it targets no specific individual, but yet it emerges as small, incremental sins flow undetected through channels of institutional power and gain momentum.

Like tiny weeds pushing their way through cracks in the sidewalk, sin creeps into institutions through the small unnoticed fissures in covenantal relationships. Sin needs very little purchase to start growing because it has a motive force, like an animal lust, in the language of Genesis 4:7. When this lust is given an opening to infiltrate human social relations, as it was with Cain and Abel, "everything is exploitation which has taken on a power of its own."[54] As Plantinga says:

> Sin is not only personal but also interpersonal and even supraprersonal. Sin is more than the sum of what sinners do. Sin acquires the powerful and elusive form of a spirit—the spirit of an age or a company or a nation or political movement. Sin burrows into the bowels of institutions and traditions, making a home there and taking them over.[55]

Not only does sin pervert the function of institutions, but it also corrupts the norms and habits that comprise interpersonal communications and relationships. Institutional sin diverts awareness and intentions away from shalom, in rebellion against "God's design for creation and redemption."[56] The self-propagating mechanisms of organizations make them conduits and distilleries for corruption and wrong-doing. Social scientists recognize this phenomenon even without referencing the theological significance of sin:

> Although the beliefs that undergird the ideologies can be used by an individual in isolation, they become far more potent when institutionalized in the collective—when they are a shared

54. Brueggemann, *Genesis*, 58.
55. Plantinga, *Not the Way*, 75.
56. Plantinga, *Not the Way*, 13.

resource that all can draw on and mutually affirm. . . . When the corruption is ongoing, these idiosyncratic social constructions tend to become woven into a self-sealing belief system that routinely neutralizes the potential stigma of corruption.[57]

Institutional sin corrupts relationships at every level—personal, interpersonal, familial, organizational, and societal. Plantinga describes this damaging effect of sin as the "vandalism of shalom."[58]

Gamification is one mode by which AI can become implicit in systemic sin. Although an AI may be intended to pursue an admirable outcome, if the humans involved are objectified and treated as components to be manipulated, the door is open to injustice and dehumanization. Referring back to our ride-hail example, Uber uses notifications and triggers to influence drivers' decisions to stay on the clock in search of additional fares even when conditions lean in the direction that will suboptimize the driver's pay in order to increase incremental profit. Yes, of course, we can argue that the driver has free will to make a decision in these cases. The point remains however that the AI learns to be deceptively good at timing messages and inducements in ways that do not necessarily work to the driver's advantage.

As another example of institutional sin, consider the way in which AI contributes to political divisiveness, bigotry, and conspiracy theories on social media platforms. Even though no particular individual has intentionally mobilized the platform as an agent to corrupt shalom, that is nonetheless what the system ends up doing. The machine-learning algorithms of various AIs resident on the platform learn to feed parasitically on the emotional energy and fear of individuals, and the harm is magnified by the system. We see the problem vividly in the divisiveness which has been magnified in political campaigns. Divisiveness based in manipulation of people's access to objective information and open-minded analysis is maximized by efforts to promulgate fake news and conspiracy theories. It is well documented that conspiracy theories are the most potent and toxic form of click-bait ever designed as manipulative ploys to grab attention and sway people by using spurious arguments and falsehoods.

Other examples of institutional sin include racial profiling in marketing, social services, health care, and the legal system in general. Injustice results when AI applications are not carefully screened and monitored for harmful bias. Ruha Benjamin has documented many examples of the ways in which racist policies propagate through technology.[59]

57. Ashforth and Anand, "Normalization of Corruption," 16.
58. Plantinga, *Not the Way*, 7.
59. Benjamin, *Race After Technology*.

GRACE

In the foregoing pages, we have surveyed paths by which sin parasitically infects AI and harnesses its power to cause alienation—from others, from nature, from God, and from self. The good news is that sin does not get the last word.

Gerald Manley Hopkins captures the inextricable link between sin, grace, and technology in the closing lines of his poem, "God's Grandeur" (1877):

> And all is seared with trade; bleared, smeared with toil;
> And wears man's smudge and shares man's smell: the soil
> Is bare now, nor can foot feel, being shod.
>
> And for all this, nature is never spent;
> There lives the dearest freshness deep down things;
> And though the last lights off the black West went
> Oh, morning, at the brown brink eastward, springs —
> Because the Holy Ghost over the bent
> World broods with warm breast and with ah! bright wings.[60]

The poem lands on solid theological footing with its closing image of grace: "And for all this, nature is never spent. There lives the dearest freshness deep down things."

The smudge is unavoidable; we fallen humans are dependent upon the grace of God. All have sinned and fallen short of the glory of God (Rom 3:23; cf. Eccl 7:20). Everything we touch, every tool we build, and every economic gain we pursue bears, in some fashion, the stain of sin: "And all is seared with trade; bleared, smeared with toil." As Kathryn Tanner says, our creations are, in and of themselves, penultimate, not ultimate goods. Only God's grace can set things right:

> Everything we do, even in the pursuit of penultimate created goods, is done in the wrong way, because done without one thing necessary for every good in life, a gift of God's own goodness through Word and Spirit.[61]

Therefore, we rely upon God's redeeming grace to embrace our creativity and bless the work of our hands. In faith, we carry on in spite of the inescapable reality of sin. There is no other way for humankind to live, prosper, and fulfill the creation mandate to be fruitful and multiply (Gen

---

60. Hopkins, *Major Works*, 128.
61. Tanner, *Christ the Key*, 63.

1:28). John of Damascus speaks of divine grace as "the care that God takes over existing things."[62] We do not have a God who leaves us alone to fall into temptation and get lost in what the Psalmists calls the "pit of destruction" (Pss 40:2; 55:23; 103:4).

Humans are a technological race, endowed with the gifts and propensity to devise and use technology, and charged from the beginning with stewardship of God's creation. Despite the stain of sin, AI applications show the capacity of technology to leverage human strength and ingenuity to solve problems and contribute to human flourishing. The potential is so far-reaching as to be unimaginable.

The doctrine of common grace applies here: "Nature, cursed as it is by itself, can endure only by the action of common grace."[63] In other words, God's preemptive and continuous grace sustains all nature and life, saving everything from death. God's grace is implicitly present everywhere, all the time. "Having created, God does not abandon that good creation or leave it to itself."[64] Thus, the turning point in Hopkins's poem expresses the doctrine of common grace: "There lives the dearest freshness deep down things." Why? Because God's grace covers everything. Common grace means that in every moment and every breath of life, there is a connection to God's original act of creation, which brought all matter and life into existence. Thus, "in common grace there is never anything new, never anything but what can be explained from the original creation."[65] In faith, we trust the faithful God to be at work in our work.

It is exceedingly important to remember that sin and grace go hand in hand. No doctrine of sin is coherent apart from the doctrine of grace, which supersedes and subsumes the doctrine of sin and places it within the holistic context of God's gracious providence. Remarkably, sin is also part and parcel of the act in which God bestows grace. We may as well say that grace is the condition in which sin inevitably sprouts, growing in the direction of any errant inclination of human souls, which, although rooted in the life-giving soil of God's abundant grace, go awry. As Walter Brueggemann points out, this is evident from the very beginning in Genesis 3: "the grace of God is the very premise for sin."[66] Conversely, we may say that sin is the condition in which grace becomes known as grace. It seems that the human person has no other context in which to understand grace other than sin.

---

62. Quoted in McCall, *Against God and Nature*, 339.

63. Kuyper, "Common Grace," 174.

64. McCall, *Against God and Nature*, 339.

65. Kuyper, "Common Grace," 174.

66. Brueggemann, *Genesis*, 20.

Grace overpowers sin. The good news is that "where sin increased, grace abounded all the more" (Rom 5:20). God has intervened to redeem the whole world (John 1:29; Rom 5:18; 1 John 2:2). The link between sin and grace is grounded in the good news that Jesus Christ came to destroy evil and save us from our sins (Mark 10:45; Rom 4:25; Gal 1:4; 1 John 2:2; 3:8; 4:10). Therefore, theological reflection on sin leads not into despair, but rather into hope, for God has intervened to redeem our lives and save us from sin. It is the covenantal promise of God to be "for us"[67] that makes it possible for a reflection on sin to be an edifying exercise.

As we take courage and find hope in God's covenant, we also take responsibility to play our role in mitigating the implications of sin wherever and however we can, by the grace of God. As the old saw goes, "Pray as if God can do all things, and work as if the outcome is in your hands." The unconditional covenant of grace puts humankind in the role of responding in righteousness to fulfill God's commandments.[68] The final word of grace is not a release from responsibility, but rather an invitation and call to join God in the work of righteousness. In closing, therefore, we offer some thoughts on practicing righteousness in light of what we have learned about the implications of sin in relation to AI.

The first and most obvious activities are prayer and attentiveness. "Pray without ceasing," Paul says (1 Thess 5:17; cf. Rom 12:12 and Eph 6:18). The epilogue of this book offers a litany as a guide to regular, disciplined prayer around the issues pertaining to our engagement with AI. Prayer in essence is a focusing of the mind to pay attention. We should therefore strive to attune our awareness to the potentialities of sin to infect institutions, corrupt shalom, and sow alienation. The mere act of paying attention, of being mindful of the ever-present danger of sin crouching at the threshold (Gen 4:7), enables us to work intentionally to avoid, mitigate, and prevail over sin. This attitude causes our work to be worshipful as we trust in God's grace to prevail.

It is important to remember that AIs are goal-driven, and that the goals programmed into them are invariably suboptimal with respect to human flourishing. There is a built-in tendency toward suboptimization when we allow machine learning programs to run freely without oversight. Like an unbridled horse set loose in the field, it is no longer under the control of the rider. We can fool ourselves into believing that we have established fair-minded, just goals for our AI systems. But without continual reflection and faithful accountability directed toward the higher aims of faith embodied

---

67. Barth, *Church Dogmatics* II/2, 493.

68. Torrance, "On Deriving 'Ought' from 'Is,'" 172.

in acts of *agape* love, we may intentionally or unintentionally collapse the dimension between our self-serving instincts and self-sacrificial concern for others who may experience injustice as a result of our technological systems. Weeding out injustices due to biases related to race, gender, nationality, age, and other personal characteristics will require intentional oversight, aided by awareness of the reality of sin.

Some practical guidelines for wise, faithful engagement with AI come to mind. Devotions and spiritual disciplines are a good start, to help keep our attention focused on making the main thing the main thing: our identity and rootedness in relationship with the triune God of grace. Whatever personal rituals help one spend time with and pay attention to spiritual truth are to be commended. These disciplines help put barriers up against the inroads of sin that we have considered.

As users and consumers of AI-driven products and services, we must evaluate our engagement with AI in terms of its impacts on our relationships and most deeply held moral values. This requires reflective thought. Using the scenario above as an example, the passenger might deliberately disable or turn off notifications for a short period of time, and intentionally engage the driver in conversation. The passenger does well to remain curious about the goals programmed into the ride-share AI, as well as the other AIs engaging her attention. Similarly, the driver does well to reflect on the goals of the driver management AI, and the effects its gamification may have on his relationships at home if he plays along.

Those involved in the development and programming of AI software and platforms have a special responsibility to pay attention to the risks of unintentional and institutional sin. Best practices include ethical audits, making a priority of including diverse voices among developers and managers, and ensuring that humans provide oversight of AI systems to identify moral hazards before they do harm.

Finally, the surest path to wise engagement with AI is to remain vigilant to the corrupting, alienating effects of sin, and to live in the hope that God's grace is decisive. Hope comes from realizing that "something can be done for this malady. Something *has* been done for it."[69] It is because the wrath of God is the "*wrath of the Lamb*, the wrath of redeeming love," as T. F. Torrance reminds, that "the very wrath of God is a sign of hope, not a better destruction."[70] Martin Luther King Jr. describes this truth as "the beauty of the Christian faith, that it says that in the midst of man's tragic predicament,

69. Plantinga, *Not the Way*, xii.
70. Torrance, *Incarnation*, 249.

in the midst of his awful inclination toward sin, God has come into the picture and has done something about it."[71]

BIBLIOGRAPHY

Ashforth, Blake, and Vikas Anand. "The Normalization of Corruption in Organizations." *Research in Organizational Behavior* 25 (2003) 1–52.

Baker, Bruce D. "Sin and the Hacker Ethic: The Tragedy of Techno-Utopian Ideology in Cyberspace Business Cultures." *Journal of Religion and Business Ethics* 4 (2020) 1–28.

Banerjee, Abhijit V., and Esther Duflo. *Good Economics for Hard Times*. New York: PublicAffairs, 2019.

Barth, Karl. *Church Dogmatics, Vol. II: The Doctrine of God, Part 2*. Translated by G. W. Bromiley and T. F. Torrance. London: T. & T. Clark, 2004.

Benjamin, Ruha. *Race after Technology: Abolitionist Tools for the New Jim Code*. Medford, MA: Polity, 2019.

Biddle, Mark. *Missing the Mark: Sin and Its Consequences in Biblical Theology*. Nashville: Abingdon, 2005.

Bloesch, Donald. *Jesus Christ: Savior and Lord*. Downers Grove, IL: IVP Academic, 1997.

Borgmann, Albert. "The Lure of Technology: Understanding and Reclaiming the World." Laing Lectures, October 19–20, 2011.

Brueggemann, Walter. *Genesis*. Louisville, KY: Westminster John Knox, 2010.

Ellul, Jacques. *The Meaning of the City*. Grand Rapids: Eerdmans, 1970.

Geraci, Robert. *Apocalyptic AI: Visions of Heaven in Robotics, Artificial Intelligence, and Virtual Reality*. Oxford: Oxford University Press, 2010.

Hanson, Robin. *The Age of Em: Work, Love, and Life When Robots Rule the Earth*. Oxford: Oxford University Press, 2016.

Harari, Yuval. *Homo Deus: A Brief History of Tomorrow*. New York: Harper/HarperCollins, 2017.

Herzfeld, Noreen. *In Our Image: Artificial Intelligence and the Human Spirit*. Minneapolis: Augsburg Fortress, 2002.

Hopkins, Gerard Manley. *The Major Works*. Oxford: Oxford University Press, 2002.

Jenson, Matt. *The Gravity of Sin: Augustine, Luther and Barth on 'homo incurvatus in Se'*. New York: T. & T. Clark, 2006.

Jenson, Robert W. *Systematic Theology, Volume 2: The Works of God*. Oxford: Oxford University Press, 1999.

Jüngel, Eberhard. *Justification*. Translated by Jeffrey F. Cayzer. Edinburgh: T. & T. Clark, 2001.

Jüngel, Eberhard. "The World as Possibility and Actuality." In *Theological Essays*, edited and translated by J. B. Webster, 95–123. Edinburgh: T. & T. Clark, 1989.

King, Martin Luther, Jr. "Man's Sin and God's Grace." In *The Papers of Martin Luther King Jr., Volume VI: Advocate of the Social Gospel*, edited by Clayborn Carson. Berkeley: University of California Press, 2007. https://kinginstitute.stanford.edu/

---

71. King, "Man's Sin and God's Grace," 387.

publications/papers-martin-luther-king-jr-volume-vi-advocate-social-gospel-september-1948-–-march.

———. "Reinhold Niebuhr's Ethical Dualism." In *The Papers of Martin Luther King, Jr. Volume II: Rediscovering Precious Values, July 1951-November 1955*, edited by Clayborne Carson et al. Berkeley: University of California Press, 1994. https://kinginstitute.stanford.edu/publications/papers-martin-luther-king-jr-volume-ii-rediscovering-precious-values-july-1951-november.

Kolb, Robert. "Martin Luther." In *T&T Clark Companion to the Doctrine of Sin*, edited by Keith L. Johnson and David Lauber, 217–34. New York: Bloomsbury T. & T. Clark, 2016.

Kurzweil, Ray. *The Singularity is Near: When Humans Transcend Biology*. New York: Penguin, 2005.

Kuyper, Abraham. "Common Grace." In *Abraham Kuyper: A Centennial Reader*, edited by James D. Bratt, translated by John Vriend, 165–204. Grand Rapids: Eerdmans, 1998.

Lewis, C. S. *Mere Christianity*. New York: Macmillan, 1943.

Marcus, Gary, and Ernest Daniel. "A.I. Won't Fix Fake News." *New York Times*, October 21, 2018. https://www.nytimes.com/2018/10/20/opinion/sunday/ai-fake-news-disinformation-campaigns.html

McCall, Thomas H. *Against God and Nature: The Doctrine of Sin*. Wheaton, IL: Crossway, 2019.

Niebuhr, Reinhold. *Moral Man and Immoral Society: A Study in Ethics and Politics*. New York: Scribner, 1960.

Paulus, Michael J., Jr., et al. "A Framework for Digital Wisdom." *Christian Scholar's Review* 49 (2019) 43–61.

Plantinga, Cornelius. *Not the Way It's Supposed to Be: A Breviary of Sin*. Grand Rapids: Eerdmans, 1995.

Milne, B. A., and J. Muller. "Sin." In *The New Bible Dictionary*, edited by D. R. W. Wood et al., 1105–8. Downers Grove, IL: InterVarsity, 1996.

Moravec, Hans. *Mind Children: The Future of Robot and Human Intelligence*. Cambridge, MA: Harvard University Press, 1988.

Rosenblat, Alex. *Uberland: How Algorithms Are Rewriting the Rules of Work*. Oakland: University of California Press, 2018.

Schwartz, Oscar. "In 2016 Microsoft's Racist Chatbot Revealed the Dangers of Online Conversation." *IEEE Spectrum*, November 25, 2019. https://spectrum.ieee.org/tech-talk/artificial-intelligence/machine-learning/in-2016-microsofts-racist-chatbot-revealed-the-dangers-of-online-conversation.

Stiver, Dan. *Theology after Ricoeur*. Louisville: Westminster/John Knox, 2001.

Stonier, Tom. *Beyond Information: The Natural History of Intelligence*. London: Springer Verlag, 1992.

Tanner, Kathryn. *Christ the Key*. Cambridge: Cambridge University Press, 2010.

Tillich, Paul. *Systematic Theology*. Chicago: University of Chicago Press, 1951.

Torrance, Alan J. "On Deriving 'Ought' from 'Is': Christology, Covenant and Koinonia." In *The Doctrine of God and Theological Ethics*, 167–90. London: T. & T. Clark, 2006.

Torrance, Thomas F. *Incarnation: The Person and Life of Christ*, edited by Robert T. Walker. Downers Grove, IL: IVP Academic, 2008.

Webster, John. "Justification, Analogy and Action. Passivity and Activity in Jüngel's Anthropology." In *The Possibilities of Theology: Studies in the theology of Eberhard Jüngel in his Sixtieth Year*, edited by J. B. Webster, 106–42. Edinburgh: T. & T. Clark, 1994.

Wiener, Anna. *Uncanny Valley: A Memoir*. New York: Farrar, Strauss and Giroux, 2020.

Zuboff, Shoshana. *The Age of Surveillance Capitalism: The Fight for a Human Future at the New Frontier of Power*. New York: PublicAffairs, 2019.

Epilogue

A Litany for Faithful Engagement with Artificial Intelligence

Bruce D. Baker

A litany is a thoughtfully organized prayer for use in public worship by the church, or as a personal devotional practice by individuals. This seems a fitting way to close our reflection on AI, faith, and the future. Prayer will be essential to our faithful response to the new opportunities and challenges AI brings. Our hope is that this litany will serve as a practical guide to thoughtful invocation of the Holy Spirit in prayers for wisdom and discernment, and in the daily disciplines of spiritual growth.

The litany is structured as a set of short paragraphs followed by short sentences (in bold), to facilitate responsive reading in a worship service. However, this versatile structured prayer is suited for use in both public worship and private prayer, with or without responsive reading. The themes addressed by each paragraph offer a survey of seminal ideas regarding the spiritual dimensions of our engagement with AI. We hope this prayer offering will be edifying and worshipful. Lord God, hear our prayers . . .

A LITANY FOR FAITHFUL ENGAGEMENT WITH AI

Heavenly Father, you have created the heavens and earth, and the fullness thereof. All good gifts come from you. We praise you for the bounty of creation, and for the gifts of energy, imagination, and skill to create technologies and bring them into existence. Open the eyes of our hearts to see how you are at work in us, as we develop, deploy, and use these creative gifts.

Lord, grant us wisdom, grant us courage, and bless the work of our hands.

Lord Jesus, you have invited us into relationship with God the Father and with our sisters and brothers throughout humanity. You have saved us from our sins and invited us into eternal life. Help us to see the effects of our technologies on our neighbors, ourselves, and our relationships. Let us be guided by your commandment to love one another, so that you will be our guide to wise use of AI.

Lord, grant us wisdom, grant us courage, and show us the way of love.

Holy Spirit, you are closer than the air we breathe. You discern our thoughts from far away. You intercede with sighs too deep for words when we do not know how to pray. You illumine our minds with understanding. Give us hope and assure us as we walk by faith that you will guide us in paths of righteousness. Holy Spirit, we need your help in the face of mystery, to see the spiritual impact of our engagement with AI.

Lord, grant us wisdom, grant us courage, and illumine our minds.

Heavenly Father, we lift our eyes to you. You are our help and strength. You lift us up and keep us from stumbling. We will trust you always, in all things. Let us not be distracted from your saving grace by the power of our technology. For you alone are God.

Great is your faithfulness. Your mercies are new every morning.

Lord Jesus, you call us to the ministry of reconciliation. Be at work in us so that the time we spend engaging with AI and other emerging technologies may bear fruit in mending and healing our wounds, our relationships, and the hurts of the world. Forgive us our sins and help us use the creative power of technology to restore and protect nature according to your creation mandate.

Great is your faithfulness. Your mercies are new every morning.

Holy Spirit, be at work in us and in the unforeseeable paths of our engagement with AI. Be at work in the designers and coders, that your purposes may shine in their thinking. Be at work in the lives of those touched by the AI we develop, that your wisdom may guide and protect.

Great is your faithfulness. Your mercies are new every morning.

Lord God, where evil threatens to twist the powers unleashed by our AI-driven machines and platforms, may your strong arm protect those in harm's way. Give us eyes to see through the cloak of injustice and expose the error of our ways. Then guide us in paths of wisdom to heal and restore. Let us direct the power of AI in doing justice, and let your will be done.

Lord, you are our rock and redeemer. We put our trust in you.

Lord Jesus, you are the vine, and we are the branches. Where the glitter of convenience and self-serving desires shine brightly in our AI applications, guard us against temptation. Hold us close and let us find our life and meaning in you. We desire the joy of communing with you. Let us not be fooled into searching anywhere else for the deepest desire of our heart.

Lord, you are our rock and redeemer. We find our life in you.

Holy Spirit, be our wisdom. Breathe life into our hopes that we may bear witness to you in creating and using AI. Give us restraint where needed to avoid destructive influences. Give us energy and strength to walk with you, and channel the power of our minds and our technologies toward righteousness. Give us the mind of Christ in the defining moments of our engagement with AI.

Lord, you are our rock and redeemer. Help us to love as you have loved. Amen.

Index

diagnostic systems, physicians
    accessing, 46
"DICast," predicting the weather, 41
Dickmanns, Ernst, 19
differentiation, necessary for human
    personhood, 123
digital age, 73, 129
digital assistants, interacting with, 4
digital technologies, 170
digital transformation, accelerating, 174
digital wisdom, still catching up with
    AI, 71
digitization of society, church
    communities and, 145
dignity, moving in the direction of
    communion with God, 202
direct-to-consumer products, aiming
    to passively read brain data,
    140
disability, contemporary theologies
    of, 106
disciples, 72, 118
discipleship to Christ, Anabaptists
    informed by, 145
disciplinary approaches, to AI, 22–24
diversity, based on God's grace itself,
    75n13
divided tongues, of fire, 118
divine image, God renewing, 73n10
divine life, irruption into the world, 109
divisiveness, magnified in political
    campaigns, 211
Docetism, 109n29
Dodd, Charles H., 88n53
dominant culture, non-conformity
    to, 145
Domingos, Pedro, 171
dominion, 80, 80n28, 102, 102–3n10
dopamine, 138, 138n29
driverless taxis, 20
drivers (Uber), 191, 192, 197, 215
drug discovery, 45, 47
drug repurposing, artificial intelligence
    and, 47
Du Sautoy, Marcus, 159
dualism, 59–60
Duflo, Esther, 204
dystopia, 177–79, 181

dystopic future, of work, 171–72

Eastern Mennonite University, 143
ecology, of salvation, 83n33
economic models, 147
education, AI and, 11, 152, 153, 154, 166
effective reasoning, focusing on, 160
"election," in the sense of Barth, 83n35
electrical signal, sent through the axon,
    34
Eliot, T. S., 187
ELIZA chatbot, created by Joseph
    Weizenbaum, 19
Princess Elizabeth of Bohemia, 59
Ellul, Jacques, 165
emotion recognition, 42
emotional and cognitive states, subject
    to reinforcement processes, 135
emotional and social content, process
    of forming, 131
empathy, AI lacking, 161
empirical data, 58
end of all things, Jesus's timetable, 89–90
entry-level workers, communication
    skills for, 162
environment, 132, 133
environmental enrichment, altered
    behavioral responses, 133
environmental movement, 147
epistemological community of
    revelation, 77
epistemology
    Christian, 76
    question of, 73
epistles, from Paul and others, 73
"eschatological realism," 176
eschatological role, of AI, 121
eschatology
    asking questions of, 182
    as a Christian theology of hope,
        86–90
    Pentecost text especially relevant
        to, 118–19
    as a resource on the future of work,
        176
    as the study of "last things," 73
    of work, 182–85
eschatos, meaning "last things," 86

Made in United States
Orlando, FL
27 December 2022

27740193R00143